Texas History

Guided Reading
Workbook

Permission is hereby granted to individuals using the corresponding student's textbook or kit as the major vehicle for regular classroom instruction to photocopy entire pages or sheets from this publication in classroom quantities for instructional use and not for resale. Requests for information on other matters regarding duplication of this work should be addressed to Houghton Mifflin Harcourt Publishing Company, Attn: Contracts, Copyrights, and Licensing, 9400 Southpark Center Loop, Orlando, Florida 32819-8647.

Printed in the U.S.A.

ISBN 978-0-544-32665-1

10   0982 20 19 18

4500702518   B C D E F G

Houghton Mifflin Harcourt

Contents

Guided Reading Workbook

How to Use This Book

The *Guided Reading Workbook* was developed to help you get the most from your reading. Using this book will help you master geography content while developing your reading and vocabulary skills. Reviewing the next few pages before getting started will make you aware of the many useful features in this book.

Section summary pages allow you to interact with the content and key terms and places from each section of a chapter. The summaries explain each section of your textbook in a way that is easy to understand.

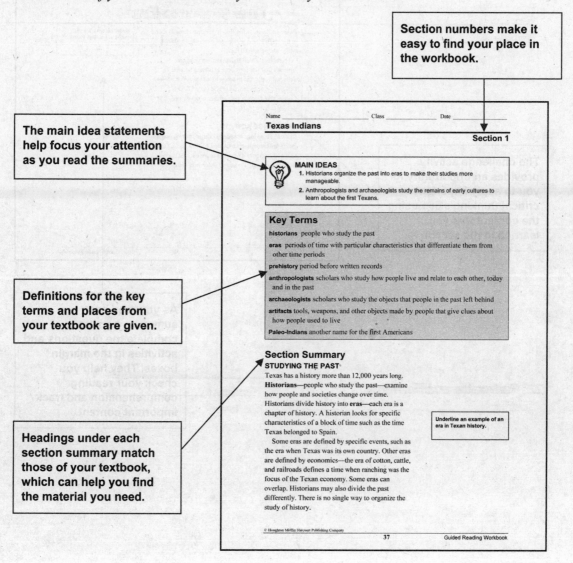

Section numbers make it easy to find your place in the workbook.

The main idea statements help focus your attention as you read the summaries.

Definitions for the key terms and places from your textbook are given.

Headings under each section summary match those of your textbook, which can help you find the material you need.

Name _____ Class _____ Date _____
Texas Indians

Section 1

MAIN IDEAS
1. Historians organize the past into eras to make their studies more manageable.
2. Anthropologists and archaeologists study the remains of early cultures to learn about the first Texans.

Key Terms

historians people who study the past

eras periods of time with particular characteristics that differentiate them from other time periods

prehistory period before written records

anthropologists scholars who study how people live and relate to each other, today and in the past

archaeologists scholars who study the objects that people in the past left behind

artifacts tools, weapons, and other objects made by people that give clues about how people used to live

Paleo-Indians another name for the first Americans

Section Summary
STUDYING THE PAST
Texas has a history more than 12,000 years long. **Historians**—people who study the past—examine how people and societies change over time. Historians divide history into **eras**—each era is a chapter of history. A historian looks for specific characteristics of a block of time such as the time Texas belonged to Spain.

Some eras are defined by specific events, such as the era when Texas was its own country. Other eras are defined by economics—the era of cotton, cattle, and railroads defines a time when ranching was the focus of the Texan economy. Some eras can overlap. Historians may also divide the past differently. There is no single way to organize the study of history.

Underline an example of an era in Texan history.

© Houghton Mifflin Harcourt Publishing Company

37

Guided Reading Workbook

The key terms and places from your textbook are in boldface, allowing you to quickly find and study them.

The challenge activity provides an opportunity for you to apply important critical thinking skills using the content that you learned in the section.

Name _____ Class _____ Date _____
Section 1, *continued*

THE FIRST TEXANS

The earliest Texans lived before the invention of writing. This period before written records is called **prehistory**.

Much of what we know about how early Texans lived is from the work of **anthropologists**—scholars who study how people and societies lived. One type of anthropologist is the **archaeologist** who studies the objects that people in the past left behind. Archaeologists dig through layers of earth and explore oceans to find **artifacts**—tools, weapons, and other objects made by people. Artifacts give clues about how people lived in the past.

In parts of Texas, scholars have found images painted or carved into stone. Some of these images show important events, such as hunts or wars. Some places in Texas are very important for the study of **Paleo-Indians**, or the first Americans. Fossils found in the High Plains region, for example, explain which animals lived there.

Over time, Paleo-Indian culture changed. Animals that the early people hunted became extinct. People had to adapt to new ways of life. Different groups moved in and out of Texas. Groups that lived in the same area developed similar culture traits.

CHALLENGE ACTIVITY
Critical Thinking: Mapping Three sites known for Paleo-Indian artifacts include Lubbock Lake, Gault site, and Buttermilk Creek. Locate each of these sites on a map of Texas and share with the class.

> What do archaeologists study?

> Underline what fossils found in the High Plains tell us.

© Houghton Mifflin Harcourt Publishing Company
38   Guided Reading Workbook

As you read each summary, be sure to complete the questions and activities in the margin boxes. They help you check your reading comprehension and track important content.

*The third page of each section allows you to demonstrate your understanding
of the key terms and places introduced in the section.*

**Some pages have a word
bank. You can use it to help
find answers or complete
writing activities.**

**A variety of activities help
you check your knowledge
of key terms and places.**

**Writing activities require
you to include key words
and places in what you
write. Remember to check
to make sure that you are
using the terms and places
correctly.**

Name _____ Class _____ Date _____
Section 1, *continued*

artifact	era	Paleo-Indian	anthropologist
archaeologist	prehistory	historian	arrowhead

DIRECTIONS Read each sentence below and circle the word from the
pair that best completes each sentence.

1. An (archaeologist / anthropologist) studies the objects that people from the past leave behind.

2. The period before written records is called (prehistory / Paleo-Indian).

3. People who study history are called (anthropologists / historians).

4. An (artifact / arrowhead) is a tool or other object used by people in the past that can give clues as to how those people lived.

5. Texas has a few cultural sites that are valuable for the study of (Paleo-Indians / historians).

DIRECTIONS Write two adjectives or descriptive phrases that describe
each term given.

6. Paleo-Indians _____

7. artifacts _____

8. eras _____

The Geographer's Tools

MAIN IDEAS
1. Geographers study physical and human systems.
2. The six essential elements of geography are a way for geographers to organize their studies.

Key Terms

geography study of the world, its people, and the interaction between them

environment physical surroundings

culture shared beliefs, traits, and values

geographic information systems (GIS) a computer database that stores huge amounts of geographic data

ecosystem an area's plants and animals together with the nonliving parts of their environment

migration the movement of people

urbanization an increase in people living or working in cities

Section Summary

THE WORLD IN SPATIAL TERMS

Geography is the study of the physical and human characteristics of a place or region. Geographers study the relationship between humans and their environment. The term **environment** refers to physical surroundings. A geographer might also study **culture**, which is a learned system of shared beliefs, traits, and values.

Geographers use maps, charts, graphs, photographs, and other tools. Geographers also rely on high-tech tools such as satellites and computer databases. Some computer databases, like geographic information systems (GIS), store huge amounts of information.

PLACES AND REGIONS

Geographers often speak in terms of places and regions. A place has physical and human characteristics. Physical characteristics include animal

List three things geographers might study.
_____
_____
_____

and plant life, water sources, and landforms. Human characteristics include ethnicity, language, political systems, population distribution, and standards of living. A region is an area—large or small—that shares common characteristics. A region can be as large as Texas or as small as a neighborhood.

> **What are some examples of human characteristics?**
> _____
> _____
> _____

PHYSICAL SYSTEMS AND HUMAN SYSTEMS

Geographers study the physical processes and interactions among four physical systems—Earth's atmosphere, land, water, and life. Physical processes shape Earth's physical features. Climate and weather affect human life. An **ecosystem** is all of an area's plants and animals together with the nonliving parts of the environment. A beach, an island, and a pond are examples of ecosystems. Geographers also study human systems such as population distribution and growth. They also study **migration**, the movement of people. **Urbanization,** an increase of people living in cities, is an example of migration.

> **Underline examples of an ecosystem.**

ENVIRONMENT AND SOCIETY

How people interact with the environment is one of the most important topics in geography. People can affect the environment positively and negatively. The environment, in turn, affects humans. Over 60 years ago, Texas naturalist **Roy Bedichek** warned of the dangers of changing the environment.

Many geographers use these six essential elements to guide their studies: the world in spatial terms, places and regions, physical systems, human systems, environment and society, and the uses of geography.

> **List the six essential elements geographers use in their studies.**
> _____
> _____
> _____
> _____
> _____
> _____

CHALLENGE ACTIVITY

Critical Thinking: Classifying How would you classify Texas in spatial terms? (Where is it located in the world?) Explain in a paragraph.

| geography | environment | culture | ecosystem |
| geographic information systems | migration | urbanization | Roy Bedichek |

DIRECTIONS Read each sentence and circle the term in the word pair that best completes each sentence.

1. An (environment/ecosystem) is all of an area's plants and animals together with the nonliving parts of their area.

2. The increase of people moving to cities is called (migration/urbanization).

3. (Geography/Geographic information systems) is the study of the world, its people, and the interactions between them.

4. Geographers also study (environment/culture), a people's shared beliefs, traits, and values.

5. Over 60 years ago, (Roy Bedichek/geographic information systems) warned of the dangers of humans' effect on the environment.

DIRECTIONS Write two adjectives or descriptive phrases that describe each term given.

6. environment _____

7. migration _____

8. geographic information systems _____

The Geographer's Tools

MAIN IDEAS
1. Maps are useful tools for finding the locations of places.
2. The main parts of a map include a title, scale, legend, and compass rose.
3. Geographers create maps for many different purposes.

Key Terms

relative location where a place is in relation to other places

absolute location the exact position of a place on Earth

latitude imaginary lines that run east-west around the globe and measure distance north and south of the equator

longitude imaginary lines that run north-south circling the globe used to measure distance east and west of the prime meridian

equator an imaginary line circling the globe exactly halfway between the North and South Poles

prime meridian an imaginary line that runs around the globe from the North Pole to the South Pole

compass rose a figure on a map that points to north, south, east, and west

scale the relationship between a measurement on the map and the actual distance on Earth's surface

legend the key on a map that explains the meaning of all the map's symbols

reference maps maps used to find locations

thematic maps maps used to show a specific topic, theme, or spatial distribution of an activity

map projections means by which mapmakers create flat representations of Earth's features

Section Summary
MAPS AND MODELS

Maps are important tools for geographers and historians. A map is a graphic representation of a place or an area that illustrates land, seas, and even space. Many people use maps to locate places.

Relative location describes where a place is in

What does a map show?
_____
_____
_____

relation to other places. **Absolute** location is the exact position of a place on Earth.

Latitude and **longitude** can be used to locate an exact spot on Earth. These are imaginary lines that circle the globe. **Latitude** lines run east–west. **Longitude** lines run north–south. Latitude lines measure distance north or south of the equator. The **equator** is an imaginary line circling Earth halfway between the North and the South Poles. Longitude lines measure distance east and west of the **prime meridian**—an imaginary line running around the globe from the North Pole, through Greenwich, England, to the South Pole.

There are several important parts to a map. The title of a map tells you what the map shows. A map's **compass rose** points to north, south, east, and west. A map's **scale** is the relationship between a measurement on the map and the distance on Earth's surface. Perhaps the most useful part of a map is the **legend**. The legend serves as the key to the meanings of the map's symbols.

There are several types of maps. A **reference map** is used to find locations, often of a region's political or physical features. A **thematic map** shows a specific topic, theme, or spatial distribution of an activity such as cattle ranching or rainfall.

Maps are usually flat, but Earth is round. This can make it difficult to create accurate maps. Mapmakers try to create accurate maps by using **map projections.** These allow flat representations of Earth's features.

Where is the equator located?
_____
_____
_____

What is the purpose of map projections?
_____
_____
_____

CHALLENGE ACTIVITY

Critical Thinking: Drawing Inferences List five careers in which using a map is a crucial skill.

DIRECTIONS On the line provided before each statement, write **T** if a statement is true and **F** if a statement is false. If the statement is false, write the term that makes the statement true on the line after the statement.

_____ 1. A description of a place in relation to other places is an <u>absolute location</u>.

_____

_____ 2. <u>Longitude</u> is an imaginary line that runs north–south, circling the globe.

_____

_____ 3. The <u>prime meridian</u> is an imaginary line circling the globe that is halfway between the North and South Poles.

_____

_____ 4. A map's <u>scale</u> is the relationship between a measurement on the map and the actual distance on Earth's surface.

_____

_____ 5. A <u>compass rose</u> explains the meaning of all the symbols on a map.

_____

_____ 6. <u>Thematic maps</u> are used to find locations.

_____

_____ 7. Mapmakers use <u>map projections</u> to create flat representations of Earth's surface.

_____

MAIN IDEAS
1. Bar graphs, line graphs, pie charts, and tables are useful for making comparisons and showing relationships.
2. Time lines, flowcharts, and causation charts are often used by geographers and historians.

Key Terms

statistics information in the form of numbers

bar graph a graph using bars of different lengths to compare information from different places or time periods

line graph a graph that indicates a trend or pattern over time

pie chart a circle graph that shows how parts of a whole are divided

time line a chart that shows a sequence of events

flowchart a chart using boxes, arrows, and images to describe a series of steps

causation chart a chart that uses boxes and arrows to show cause and effect

Section Summary

USING GRAPHS

Geographers and historians often convey information visually. They do so in a variety of ways. Graphs make it easier to compare facts and see the relationship between them. Graphs are also useful for showing **statistics**—information in the form of numbers. A **bar graph** is useful in comparing information about different places or different time periods. A **line graph** indicates a trend, or pattern. Line graphs may show if something is increasing, decreasing, or staying about the same over time.

USING CHARTS, TABLES, AND DATABASES

Pie charts—sometimes called circle graphs—show how the parts of a whole are divided. The pie represents the whole item or total amount. The pie pieces—or segments—represent a percentage of the

What are statistics?
_____
_____
_____

What is a pie chart used for?
_____
_____
_____

whole. Segments are often colored to make them easier to read.

Tables and databases help organize and categorize information. Tables are very useful when information is both statistical and descriptive. Tables use grids with columns and rows of boxes. Each box is called a cell. Labels often appear at the top of each column and at the left of each row.

Charts show the relationship between different subjects. A **time line** shows the sequence of events. Time lines are useful for studying how one event may have led to another. A **flowchart** uses boxes, arrows, and sometimes images to show a series of activities or steps. A **causation chart** focuses on cause and effect. Causation charts may use pictures, diagrams, boxes, arrows, or other visuals to explain cause and effect.

> What elements might you find in a flowchart?
> _____
> _____

CHALLENGE ACTIVITY

Critical Thinking: Making Judgments Imagine you are a geographer studying Texas. Name three topics you might show in a pie chart, a bar graph, and a time line.

statistics	bar chart	line graph	pie chart
time line	flowchart	causation chart	variables

DIRECTIONS Read each sentence and circle the term in the word pair that best completes each sentence.

1. (Statistics/Variables) are information in the form of numbers.

2. A (bar chart/flowchart) is used to show a series of activities of steps in a process.

3. To show a series of events in sequence, geographers use a (line graph/time line).

4. A (causation chart/pie chart) is used to show how the parts of a whole are divided.

5. To show cause and effect, you might use a (line graph/causation chart).

6. A (line graph/time line) is used to show a trend, or pattern.

DIRECTIONS Write the name of the type of chart or graph you would use to show the following.

7. an increase in population _____

8. a sequence of events _____

9. steps in a procedure_____

10. cause and effect _____

A Land Called Texas

MAIN IDEAS
1. Hills, mountains, plains, and plateaus are some of the landforms found in Texas.
2. Texas water resources include rivers, lakes, and aquifers.

Key Terms

plains areas of flat or gently rolling land without changes in elevation

plateaus areas of flat, elevated land that drop sharply on one or more sides

ranges groups of mountains

tributaries small streams or rivers that flow into larger streams or rivers

reservoirs artificial lakes that store water

irrigation system for watering of crops

aquifers formations of natural gravel, rock, and sand that trap rainwater underground

Ogallala Aquifer largest underground water source in Texas and North America

Edwards Aquifer the largest springs in Texas and the water source for San Antonio and the rest of Central Texas

Section Summary

LANDFORMS OF TEXAS

Texas is located in the Northern Hemisphere, which is the northern half of Earth. Texas is also in the Western Hemisphere—the half of the planet west of the prime meridian. Texas is in the southern half of the North American continent, where it borders a large body of water called the Gulf of Mexico. The state is located in the central and southern region of the United States. Texas lies north of Mexico, west of Louisiana, south of Oklahoma, and east of New Mexico. Arkansas borders the northeastern corner of Texas.

The four major landforms of Texas are hills, mountains, plains, and plateaus. **Plains** are areas of

How can Texas be located in both the Northern Hemisphere and the Western Hemisphere?

_____

_____

_____

Underline the major landforms of Texas.

flat or gently rolling land. **Plateaus** are areas of flat, elevated land that drop sharply on one or more sides.

Forests cover East Texas. To the west lie gently rolling prairies. Central Texas has rugged hills, including those in the Hill Country. West of the Hill Country lies the Edwards Plateau. The landscape becomes rocky west of the Edwards Plateau. Several **ranges,** or groups of mountains, rise west of the Pecos River.

THE TEXAS RIVER SYSTEM

On the eastern coast of Texas, the Gulf of Mexico provides a source for fishing and a route for international trade. Several rivers in the northern part of Texas flow into the Mississippi River. A second group of rivers flow directly into the Gulf of Mexico. A third group consists of the Rio Grande and its **tributaries.** A tributary is a small stream or river that flows into a larger stream or river. The Rio Grande forms the border between the United States and Mexico.

> **What boundary does the Rio Grande form?**
> _____
> _____
> _____

TEXAS LAKES AND AQUIFERS

Texas has few natural lakes. However, the state has hundreds of lakes built by people. Texans dam rivers to control floods and create **reservoirs.** Reservoirs are used for drinking water, recreation, and **irrigation,** or the watering of crops. Water is also found in **aquifers.** Aquifers are natural formations of rock and sand that hold rainwater underground. The **Ogallala Aquifer** and the **Edwards Aquifer** are two of the state's aquifers.

> **What is the purpose of a reservoir?**
> _____
> _____
> _____

CHALLENGE ACTIVITY

Critical Thinking: Compare and Contrast Read more about the Ogallala and Edwards Aquifers. Then, write a paragraph in which you compare and contrast them. How do they differ?

plains	plateaus	ranges	tributaries
reservoirs	irrigation	aquifers	Ogallala Aquifer
Edwards Aquifer	Rio Grande	Gulf of Mexico	

DIRECTIONS Look at each set of four vocabulary terms. On the line
provided, write the letter of the term that does not relate to the others.

_____ 1. a. plains   b. plateaus   c. ranges   d. aquifers

_____ 2. a. aquifers   b. reservoirs   c. tributaries   d. plateaus

_____ 3. a. Rio Grande   b. Edwards Aquifer   c. plains   d. Gulf of Mexico

_____ 4. a. irrigation   b. ranges   c. Rio Grande   d. tributaries

DIRECTIONS Write two adjectives or descriptive phrases that describe
the term given.

5. irrigation _____

6. Rio Grande _____

7. Gulf of Mexico _____

8. plateaus _____

A Land Called Texas

MAIN IDEAS

1. The climate and weather of Texas affects life in and the economy of the state.
2. Texas plants and animals are affected by the state's changing landscape and climate.

Key Terms and People

humidity the amount of moisture in the air

drought a long period without rainfall

Lady Bird Johnson wife of U.S. president Lyndon B. Johnson and a founder of the National Wildflower Research Center in Austin

erosion process by which something such as soil is worn away.

habitat environmental home

extinct no longer in existence

Section Summary

WEATHER AND CLIMATE

The climate of Texas is affected by its location. Texas is closer to the equator than the North Pole. As a result, most of Texas experiences hot summers. However, breezes from the Gulf of Mexico help cool the Texas coast, because the temperature of water rises and falls more slowly than that of land. Texans on the Gulf Coast also experience higher **humidity,** the amount of moisture in the air.

The Panhandle is also affected by winds. Winds from the north bring cooler temperatures during winter. Elevation can also affect temperature. The mountains and higher elevations of West Texas tend to have a cooler climate than other parts of the state.

> Why does Texas have hot summers?
> _____
> _____
> _____

RAINFALL IN TEXAS

Climate is also characterized by precipitation, or moisture falling as rain, snow, sleet, hail, or mist.

> Underline the different types of precipitation.

The amount of precipitation increases across Texas
from west to east. When rainfall is much less than
average, Texans experience a drought, which can
cause damage to crops.

SEVERE WEATHER

Texas gets its share of severe weather. Tornadoes
are violent, funnel-shaped storms that develop
inside thunderstorms. Hurricanes are huge storms
that develop offshore. They have high winds, heavy
rains, and huge tidal surges. Texas sometimes gets
hit by blizzards, or large snowstorms.

> **List some kinds of severe weather that Texas experiences.**
> _____
> _____

TEXAS VEGETATION

Many types of plants thrive in Texas. In dry West
Texas the only plants that survive are those that can
live for long periods without water. In South Texas,
which receives more rain than West Texas, grasses,
shrubs, and small trees are common. The eastern
third of Texas receives plenty of rain. Forests and
tall grasses grow there. **Lady Bird Johnson,** the
wife of U.S. president Lyndon B. Johnson, led the
effort to plant wildflowers along the state's roads.
These plants help prevent **erosion,** or soil loss, by
holding soil with their roots.

> **Why are wildflowers on state roads important?**
> _____
> _____
> _____

TEXAS WILDLIFE

The vegetation of Texas provides a **habitat,** or
environmental home, to many animals. The forests
and prairies provide a home to bears, deer, and
other animals. Some Texas species have died out, or
become **extinct.** Texas waters are also full of
wildlife.

CHALLENGE ACTIVITY

Critical Thinking: Cause and Effect Write a
paragraph explaining the various factors that affect
the climate of Texas.

humidity	drought	Lady Bird Johnson
erosion	habitat	extinct

DIRECTIONS Read each sentence and circle the term in the word pair that best completes each sentence.

1. Moisture in the air is called **(humidity/ drought).**

2. An animal species is **(extinct/habitat)** when it dies out.

3. Wildflowers holding onto their roots can prevent soil loss, or **(drought/erosion).**

4. Little or no rainfall can lead to a **(habitat/drought).**

DIRECTIONS Choose five of the words from the word bank. On the lines below, use the words to write a summary of what you have learned in the section.

_____

_____

_____

_____

_____

_____

_____

_____

_____

_____

_____

A Land Called Texas

MAIN IDEAS
1. Texans come from many different countries and have diverse backgrounds.
2. Immigration, a rising birthrate, and a falling death rate have led to the growth of the Texas population.

Key Terms

immigration the movement of people from one country or region to another

demography a branch of geography that studies human populations

growth rate the speed of growth

birthrate the number of births per 1,000 people each year

death rate the number of deaths per 1,000 people each year

age distribution the portion of the population at each age

Section Summary

WHO TEXANS ARE

The first people in Texas were American Indians. After Europeans arrived, the population of American Indians dropped due to warfare and disease. In 2010 about 171,000 American Indians lived in Texas.

> Underline two reasons for the decline in population of American Indians.

Many Texans trace their ancestry to Mexicans who immigrated to Texas in the 1700s and 1800s. At the time Texas was part of the Spanish colony of Mexico. **Immigration** is the movement of people from one country or region to another.

In 2010 the number of Texans who self-identified as white and non-Hispanic made up about 45 percent of the state's population. Some of these people's families arrived as U.S. settlers in the early 1800s. European immigrants also moved to the state.

> Where do most whites and non-Hispanic Texans trace their families from?
> _____
> _____
> _____

Many African Americans were brought to Texas as slaves. In 2010 African Americans made up about 12 percent of the Texas population. In recent years more Asian Americans have made Texas their

Guided Reading Workbook

home. As of 2010, more than 960,000 Asian Americans lived in the state.

WHERE TEXANS HAVE SETTLED

Mexican influences are strong in South Texas, along the Mexico-Texas border. German and Czech influences are evident in Central Texas. Historically, most Texans lived in rural areas. As industries grew, more people moved to cities. In 2010 about 87 percent of Texans lived in cities.

> What are some outside influences evident in Texas today?
> _____
> _____
> _____

THE GROWING POPULATION OF TEXAS

Demography is a branch of geography that studies human populations. When studying a population, demographers look at **growth rate**, the speed of growth; **birthrate**, the number of births per 1,000 people per year; and **death rate**, the number of deaths per 1,000 people per year. In 2010 the Texas birthrate was 15.3 and the death rate was 6.6. More Texans are being born than are dying.

Immigration and migration are also factors that have led to population growth in Texas. **Age distribution**—the portion of the population at each age—changes as Texans live longer and as more Texans are born. Texas has a higher percentage of young people than most states. Women make up a higher percentage of Texans than men. One reason for this is the fact that women live longer.

> List three reasons for population growth in Texas
> 1. _____
> 2. _____
> 3. _____

CHALLENGE ACTIVITY

Critical Thinking: Analyzing Information Choose a region in Texas. Then explain the influences immigrants have had on the area. Think about how immigrants have contributed to the cultural traditions of the area.

| immigration | demography | growth rate |
| birthrate | death rate | age distribution |

DIRECTIONS On the line provided before each statement, write **T** if a statement is true and **F** if a statement is false. If the statement is false, write the term that makes the statement true on the line after the statement.

_____ 1. The movement of people from one country to another is called <u>demography</u>.

_____

_____ 2. An area's <u>birthrate</u> is the number of births per 1,000 people per year.

_____

_____ 3. The portion of the population at each age is called <u>growth rate</u>.

_____

_____ 4. The branch of geography that studies human populations is called <u>age distribution</u>.

_____

DIRECTIONS Choose four words from the word bank. Use them to write an explanation of the study of demography.

_____

_____

_____

_____

_____

_____

_____

_____

MAIN IDEAS
1. Texas has many valuable agricultural and energy resources.
2. Texans use natural resources to build and support a strong economy.

Key Terms and Places

agriculture the growing of crops and raising of livestock

nonrenewable resources resources in limited supply because they cannot be replaced by Earth's natural processes

renewable resources resources, such as trees and wind, that are replaced by Earth's natural processes

Section Summary
AGRICULTURAL RESOURCES

Some Texans make their living from **agriculture,** or growing crops and raising animals. East Texas receives much rainfall and has rich soil. Farmers there grow a wide range of crops.

Many farmers in drier regions of Texas irrigate their crops. South Texas farmers grow crops such as citrus fruits and cotton. Farmers in the Panhandle can grow huge crops of cotton and wheat by drilling and pumping water from the Ogallala Aquifer.

The livestock industry is very important in Texas. The main livestock in Texas include cattle, chickens, horses, pigs, sheep, and turkeys. Cattle ranching is a big business in Texas. In 2011 Texas ranchers had about 13.3 million head of cattle worth over $6 billion.

> What are some crops that Texas farmers grow?
> _____
> _____
> _____

ENERGY RESOURCES

Coal, natural gas, and oil are some of Texas's most valuable natural resources. Energy resources fuel automobiles, heat homes, and power industry. Oil and natural gas production in Texas is worth over $67 billion per year.

> Underline some of Texas's most important natural resources.

Coal, natural gas, and oil are **nonrenewable resources.** This means that they cannot be replaced by Earth's natural processes. Some Texans use **renewable resources,** such as sunshine and wind. These are easily replaced by Earth's natural processes. The variety of resources in Texas has allowed many Texans to build successful businesses. Texans work to balance current economic growth and the needs of the future.

Other resources important to the economy of Texas include sand and gravel used in the construction industry and copper, salt, and sulfur, which are mined.

> **What is the difference between renewable and nonrenewable resources?**
> _____
> _____
> _____

CHALLENGE ACTIVITY
Critical Thinking: Drawing Inferences Imagine you are a cattle rancher arriving in Texas. In what region of Texas will you locate your ranch? Explain why.

| agriculture | nonrenewable resources |
| livestock | renewable resources |

DIRECTIONS Use all of the words in the word bank to write a summary of the section you just read.

_____

_____

_____

_____

_____

_____

_____

_____

_____

_____

_____

_____

_____

_____

_____

_____

_____

_____

_____

_____

The Regions of Texas

MAIN IDEAS
1. Texas is considered the crossroads of natural regions.
2. There are four main natural regions found in Texas.

Key Terms

Sunbelt the southern region of the United States

natural regions areas with common physical environments defined by physical features

Section Summary

COMMON REGIONAL NAMES

Many places are named for some geographic characteristic or feature. For example, the southern region of the United States, which enjoys a warm climate, is often called the **Sunbelt.** Texas is part of the Sunbelt. Northwestern Texas is called the Panhandle because the area's shape looks like the handle of a pan.

Texas is often divided into regions based on their locations—East Texas, West Texas, South Texas, or North Texas. The boundaries of these regions are vague because they are based on perceptions. Other types of perceptual regions are cultural or political regions. For example, the German Hill Country is named for its early German settlers. Political regions (such as cities or counties) are based on political boundaries.

> **What is another name for the region of Northwestern Texas?**
> _____
> _____

NATURAL REGIONS OF TEXAS

Geographers study **natural regions**—areas with a common physical environment defined by physical features. These features include climate types, landforms, plant life, and soil.

Geographers often divide the continental United States into 10 regions. Four of these natural regions are found in Texas, more than in any other state.

> **What are some physical features that define a natural region?**
> _____
> _____
> _____

Guided Reading Workbook

This is why Texas is called the crossroads of natural regions.

The Coastal Plains region is one of the largest natural regions in Texas. It covers the entire coast of Texas and extends a few hundred miles inland. Along the coast, the land is marshy. Inland, the land has both forests and prairies.

The North Central Plains are characterized by rolling prairies. There are abundant resources for ranching and farming. The Great Plains region is known as one of the flattest areas on Earth. In the southern part of the region, the flat grassland becomes more rugged.

The fourth region of Texas is called the Mountains and Basins. This area lies west of the Pecos River in Texas. It is dry and its landscape includes canyons, mountains, landforms, and basins.

Each of the four natural regions of Texas have different climates, landforms, and vegetation. Studying these regions reveals much about life in Texas.

> **List the four natural regions of Texas.**
> _____
> _____
> _____
> _____

CHALLENGE ACTIVITY
Critical Thinking: Mapping Reread the descriptions of each of the four regions of Texas. Locate each of these sites on a map of Texas and share with the class.

| Sunbelt | natural regions | Coastal Plains |
| North Central Plains | Great Plains | Mountains and Basins |

DIRECTIONS Read each sentence and circle the term in the word pair that best completes each sentence.

1. The (North Central Plains/Great Plains) are characterized by gently rolling prairies.

2. The southern United States is sometimes called the (Great Plains/Sunbelt) because of its warm climate.

3. (Coastal Plains/Mountains and Basins) cover the entire coast of Texas and extend inland a few hundred miles.

4. The flattest natural region in Texas is the (Great Plains/Coastal Plains).

DIRECTIONS Write two adjectives or descriptive phrases that describe each term given.

5. natural regions_____

6. Mountains and Basins _____

7. Sunbelt _____

The Regions of Texas

 MAIN IDEAS
1. The five subregions of the Coastal Plains have varied landscapes and economies.
2. Texans in the Coastal Plains have both changed their environment and adapted to it.

Key Terms

subregions divisions of a region

bayous slow-moving, swampy sections of a river or lake

petrochemicals chemicals made from oil and natural gas

Rio Grande valley a rich farming region in the South Texas plains

lignite a type of soft coal

Metroplex a large metropolitan area comprising Dallas and Fort Worth

Section Summary

THE PINEY WOODS

The easternmost **subregion,** or smaller region, of the Coastal Plains is the Piney Woods. Most of the land in the Piney Woods is rolling hills. Gum hickory, oak, and pine trees are important sources of timber. Farming and oil are also important contributors to this subregion's economy. Many people in the Piney Woods live in rural areas or small towns. The Big Thicket National Preserve was established to protect the trees and wildlife in a large portion of the Piney Woods.

> What industries contribute to the economy of the Piney Woods?
> _____
> _____

THE GULF COAST PLAIN

South and west of the Piney Woods lies the Gulf Coast Plain. A chain of barrier islands runs nearly the length of the Texas coast. On the mainland near the coast, there are many **bayous**—slow-moving, swampy sections of a river or lake. The soil and climate of the Gulf Coast Plain are good for farming. The Gulf of Mexico is valuable for fishing and shrimping. Oil is another valuable offshore resource. This is the center of the Texas and U.S. oil-refining industry. The making of **petrochemicals,** chemicals made from oil and natural gas, is another big industry. Many port cities of the Gulf Coast Plain, such as Houston and Corpus Christi, have become increasingly busy as global markets have expanded.

THE SOUTH TEXAS PLAINS

The South Texas Plains subregion lies to the west of the Gulf Coast Plain. Most of this region is flat, although hills are found in the north and west. The climate is drier than the Gulf Coast Plain. The rich farming areas of the **Rio Grande valley** are in this subregion. Citrus fruit and other crops are grown there. Ranches are also common. The subregion's largest city is San Antonio.

> **What crops are grown in the South Texas Plains?**
> _____
> _____

THE POST OAK BELT

The Post Oak Belt lies west of the Piney Woods and Gulf Coast Plain. Parts of the Post Oak Belt are covered in trees such as post oak, elm, palm, and walnut. Cotton, corn, and sorghum are major crops. The regional economy also depends on natural resources such as oil, natural gas, and **lignite,** a type of soft coal. This subregion is largely rural.

THE BLACKLAND PRAIRIE

The Blackland Prairie subregion stretches west alongside the Post Oak Belt. Its wet and mild climate is similar to the Post Oak Belt and it has rich soil. Dallas is its largest city. Together with Fort Worth, Dallas makes up the region called the **Metroplex.**

> **Underline the two cities that make up the Metroplex.**

CHALLENGE ACTIVITY

Critical Thinking: Drawing Inferences Which subregion of the Coastal Plains would you most like to visit? Explain.

subregions	bayous	petrochemicals	Rio Grande Valley
lignite	Metroplex	sorghum	

DIRECTIONS On the line provided before each statement, write **T** if a statement is true and **F** if a statement is false. If the statement is false, write a corrected statement on the line after the false statement.

_____ 1. A soft coal found in the Post Oak Belt is called sorghum.

_____

_____ 2. The Coastal Plains are divided into four subregions.

_____

_____ 3. Bayous are slow-moving sections of rivers or lakes found in the Rio Grande Valley.

_____

_____ 4. Chemicals made from oil and natural gas are called petrochemicals.

_____

_____ 5. The interlinked cities of Dallas and Austin are sometimes called the Metroplex.

_____

_____ 6. The Rio Grande Valley, located in the South Texas Plains, is one of the richest farming areas in the nation.

_____

MAIN IDEAS
1. The Grand Prairie, Cross Timbers, and the Rolling Plains are the subregions found in the North Central Plains.
2. The physical features of the North Central Plains affect industry in the region.

Key Term

transportation center a place where goods arrive to be shipped to other destinations

Section Summary

THE GRAND PRAIRIE

The Central Plains contains three main subregions: the Grand Prairie, the Cross Timbers, and the Rolling Plains. The Grand Prairie's climate is very similar to that of the Blackland Prairie. Covered by grasses, shrubs, and small trees, this subregion is well suited for raising cattle. Its thin soil limits crop production. Much of the Grand Prairie's farming consists of crops grown as animal feed. Fort Worth is the largest city in the Grand Prairie. It plays a vital role in the subregion's economy. Its busy rail yards make Fort Worth a notable **transportation center,** a place where goods arrive to be shipped to other destinations. Most importantly, Fort Worth specializes in manufacturing airplanes, helicopters, and electronics equipment.

> Why is the Grand Prairie not suited for crop production?
> _____
> _____

THE CROSS TIMBERS

The Cross Timbers subregion is made up of two belts of forestland, the Western Cross Timbers and the Eastern Cross Timbers. The Western Cross Timbers lies west of the Grand Prairie, and the Eastern Cross Timbers lies to the east of the Grand Prairie. Much of the forestland was cut down when farmers first moved to the region. Farmers grow crops including peanuts, corn, cotton, and hay.

> Underline the names of the two forestlands that make up the Cross Timbers.

Ranchers raise cattle, horses, and sheep there. The Eastern Cross Timbers cuts the Metroplex in half between Dallas and Fort Worth.

THE ROLLING PLAINS

The Rolling Plains are located in the westernmost part of the Central Plains. Prairie grasses cover most of its hilly terrain. This subregion is well suited for cattle ranching. Steep valleys provide shelter for cattle and the grasslands and rivers provide them with food and water. In the farmland, crops such as cotton, sorghum, and wheat are grown. The Rolling Plains are also a source of oil and natural gas. Abilene and Wichita Falls are its largest cities.

> **What features of the Rolling Plains make it good for cattle ranching?**
> _____
> _____
> _____

CHALLENGE ACTIVITY

Critical Thinking: Compare and Contrast

Compare and contrast the three subregions of the Central Plains. Write a paragraph in which you explain their similarities and differences.

DIRECTIONS Write two or three sentences to describe each phrase given.

1. transportation center _____

_____

_____

2. Grand Prairie _____

_____

_____

3. Cross Timbers _____

_____

_____

4. Rolling Plains _____

_____

Section 4

MAIN IDEAS
1. The Great Plains region is divided into the High Plains and the Edwards Plateau subregions.
2. Texans have modified the region's environment to build and support ranching and oil industries.

Key Terms and Places

Caprock a hard bed of rock below the soil of the High Plains

escarpments cliffs created by erosion

fault a break in Earth's crust

Section Summary

THE HIGH PLAINS

The Texas Great Plains region includes two subregions: the High Plains and the Edwards Plateau. The High Plains subregion covers most of the Texas Panhandle. The land of the High Plains is higher than the Central Plains region. A hard bed of rock known as the Caprock is another noticeable physical feature in the area. Erosion of the rock has created cliffs—called escarpments—along its eastern and western sides. The Red River has cut a deep canyon—Palo Duro Canyon—into the Caprock.

The High Plains receive little rainfall. The rich grasslands also support a large cattle industry. Today much of the grasslands has been turned into farmland. Farmers irrigate their crops with water pumped from the Ogallala Aquifer. Oil and natural gas are important resources found in this subregion.

> How has erosion affected the physical features of the High Plains?
> _____
> _____

THE EDWARDS PLATEAU

The Edwards Plateau subregion lies just south of the High Plains. It is separated from the Gulf Coastal Plain by the Balcones Escarpment. This limestone ridge lies on a **fault,** or break in Earth's crust. This

fault extends up from the southwestern part of
Texas through San Antonio and Austin. The
Edwards Plateau is a high, hilly area. Streams have
cut deep valleys into the limestone plateau.

In most areas, soil erosion has left only a thin
layer of soil above the limestone. Only small
clumps of grass, shrubs, and trees grow in the soil.
Where the soil is deeper, short prairie grasses grow.
Here, ranchers raise cattle. In rockier areas, ranchers
raise sheep and goats.

Despite the rugged landscape of the Edwards
Plateau, Texans have prospered here. The largest
city is Austin, the state capital and home to many
high-tech industries and the University of Texas.
The Llano Basin is in the northeastern area of the
Edwards Plateau. The basin was formed by erosion
from the Colorado River. Hunting and tourism are
the basin's main industries.

> **What type of livestock is raised in the Edwards Plateau region?**
>
> _____
>
> _____

CHALLENGE ACTIVITY

Critical Thinking: Analyzing Make a list of the
different ways erosion has affected the subregion of
the Great Plains.

Guided Reading Workbook

Caprock	escarpments	fault	erosion

DIRECTIONS On the lines below, use all the words in the word bank to write a summary of what you have learned in the section.

_____

_____

_____

_____

_____

_____

_____

_____

_____

_____

_____

_____

_____

_____

_____

_____

_____

_____

_____

_____

Guided Reading Workbook

The Regions of Texas

Section 5

MAIN IDEAS
1. The Mountains and Basins region is characterized by its dramatic landscape and dry desert climate.
2. The natural features of this region affect human activity there.

Key Terms and Places

basins lowlands surrounded by higher land

Guadalupe Peak the highest point in Texas, part of the Guadalupe Mountains

tourism the business of attracting visitors to a region or place

Big Bend National Park a popular tourist area in Texas named after its location in the bend of the Rio Grande

Section Summary

MOUNTAINS AND BASINS

The Mountains and Basis region dominates the landscape of far West Texas. Mountains, plateaus, basins, and canyons form the landscape of the subregion. A **basin** is a lowland surrounded by higher land. With its high mountains and low basins, the area's elevation varies greatly. The highest point in this subregion and in Texas is **Guadalupe Peak,** at 8,749 feet above sea level. The peak is part of the Guadalupe Mountains near the New Mexico border. The Davis Mountains rise in the central area of this region.

The climate of this region is also extreme. Summers are very hot, and winters can be cold. This region is almost always dry. The desert climate allows little plant life. Desert grasses, shrubs, mesquite trees, and cacti grow in the dry, rocky soil.

This region's desert climate has limited farming and ranching. By using irrigation, some farmers have been able to grow alfalfa, cotton, pecans, and vegetables. The dramatic landscape has made **tourism** a large part of the economy. Tourism is the business of attracting visitors to a region.

> What state borders Texas to the west?
> _____

> Underline some examples of desert vegetation.

El Paso is the region's largest city. It sits along the Rio Grande in the westernmost corner of the state. Military bases and trade with Mexico have boosted the city's economy. Interstate 10, a major east-west shipping route, has also increased trade in the region.

What industries have helped the economy of El Paso?
_____
_____

TEXAS NATIONAL PARKS

Many businesses in El Paso offer services to tourists. Alpine and Marfa serve as entrances to **Big Bend National Park.** Named for its location in the bend of the Rio Grande, the park covers around 800,000 acres. Big Bend protects a wide variety of plants and animals. The park has a dramatic landscape of towering peaks and deep river canyons.

Where is Big Bend National Park located?
_____

CHALLENGE ACTIVITY

Critical Thinking: Analyzing In a paragraph, describe the different landforms of the Mountains and Basins region.

Guided Reading Workbook

basins	Guadalupe Peak	tourism
Big Bend National Park	El Paso	plateaus

DIRECTIONS Read each sentence and circle the term in the word pair that best completes each sentence.

1. (Basins/Plateaus) are lowlands surrounded by higher land.

2. The largest city in the Mountains and Basin region is (Guadalupe Peak/El Paso).

3. The business of attracting visitors to a region is called (plateaus/tourism).

4. The highest peak in Texas is (Guadalupe Peak/Big Bend National Park).

DIRECTIONS Write two adjectives or descriptive phrases that describe the term given.

5. El Paso _____

6. Big Bend National Park _____

Texas Indians

MAIN IDEAS
1. Historians organize the past into eras to make their studies more manageable.
2. Anthropologists and archaeologists study the remains of early cultures to learn about the first Texans.

Key Terms

historians people who study the past

eras periods of time with particular characteristics that differentiate them from other time periods

prehistory period before written records

anthropologists scholars who study how people live and relate to each other, today and in the past

archaeologists scholars who study the objects that people in the past left behind

artifacts tools, weapons, and other objects made by people that give clues about how people used to live

Paleo-Indians another name for the first Americans

Section Summary
STUDYING THE PAST

Texas has a history more than 12,000 years long. **Historians**—people who study the past—examine how people and societies change over time. Historians divide history into **eras**—each era is a chapter of history. A historian looks for specific characteristics of a block of time such as the time Texas belonged to Spain.

Some eras are defined by specific events, such as the era when Texas was its own country. Other eras are defined by economics—the era of Cotton, Cattle, and Railroads defines a time when ranching was the focus of the Texan economy. Some eras can overlap. Historians may also divide the past differently. There is no single way to organize the study of history.

> Underline an example of an era in Texan history.

THE FIRST TEXANS

The earliest Texans lived before the invention of writing. This period before written records is called **prehistory**.

Much of what we know about how early Texans lived is from the work of **anthropologists**— scholars who study how people and societies lived. One type of anthropologist is the **archaeologist** who studies the objects that people in the past left behind. Archaeologists dig through layers of earth and explore oceans to find **artifacts**—tools, weapons, and other objects made by people. Artifacts give clues about how people lived in the past.

In parts of Texas, scholars have found images painted or carved into stone. Some of these images show important events, such as hunts or wars. Some places in Texas are very important for the study of **Paleo-Indians,** or the first Americans. Fossils found in the High Plains region, for example, explain which animals lived there.

Over time, Paleo-Indian culture changed. Animals that the early people hunted became extinct. People had to adapt to new ways of life. Different groups moved in and out of Texas. Groups that lived in the same area developed similar culture traits.

What do archaeologists study?
_____
_____
_____

Underline what fossils found in the High Plains tell us.

CHALLENGE ACTIVITY

Critical Thinking: Mapping Three sites known for Paleo-Indian artifacts include Lubbock Lake, Gault site, and Buttermilk Creek. Locate each of these sites on a map of Texas and share with the class.

artifact	era	Paleo-Indian	anthropologist
archaeologist	prehistory	historian	arrowhead

DIRECTIONS Read each sentence below and circle the word from the pair that best completes each sentence.

1. An (archaeologist / anthropologist) studies the objects that people from the past leave behind.

2. The period before written records is called (prehistory / Paleo-Indian).

3. People who study history are called (anthropologists / historians).

4. An (artifact / arrowhead) is a tool or other object used by people in the past that can give clues as to how those people lived.

5. Texas has a few cultural sites that are valuable for the study of (Paleo-Indians / historians).

DIRECTIONS Write two adjectives or descriptive phrases that describe each term given.

6. Paleo-Indians _____

7. artifacts _____

8. eras _____

Texas Indians

MAIN IDEAS
1. The Karawankas, who lived along the Gulf Coast, hunted and gathered plants to survive.
2. The Coahuiltecans lived in dry southern Texas.

Key Terms and People

hunter-gatherers people who hunt wild animals and gather plants for food

nomads people who move from place to place

wigwams portable huts built from poles covered with animal hides and reed mats

mitotes all-night celebrations of the Coahuiltecans

Section Summary

THE KARANKAWAS

Known for their tall height, the Karankawas were **hunter-gatherers**—people who hunt wild animals and gather plants for food. The Karanwankas fished, hunted sea turtles, and collected shellfish. They also gathered eggs and hunted deer and small animals.

> Underline the different foods the Karawankas hunted and gathered.

The Karankawas lived along the Texas coast. They were **nomads,** or people who moved from place to place. Different parts of the Karankawa territory were better suited to life at different times of the year. Each season, the Karankawas relocated to a region that supported them at that particular time of year. During the fall and winter, they lived along the Gulf Coast. During the spring and summer, when bison and deer were more common, the Karankawas moved inland.

> Why did the Karawankas travel from place to place?
> _____
> _____

The Karankawa men hunted and fished with bows and arrows. Women collected plants, cooked food, and took care of the camps. The Karankawas built **wigwams,** or portable huts, from bent poles covered with animal skins and reed mats.

DAILY LIFE OF THE KARANKAWAS

Because of the hot summers and mild winters on the Gulf Coast, Karankawa men wore little, if any, clothing. Women wore skirts made of deerskin or grass. Both men and women painted themselves bright colors. They kept insects away by rubbing alligtor fat and dirt on their skin.

The Europeans who arrived in the 1500s noted that the Karankawas treated their children with kindness. Each Karankawa child had two names, one of which was only known to close family. This secret name was supposed to protect the child.

However, Europeans brought diseases with them which caused the Karankawas to die quickly. In addition, the Karankawas fought with other Indians, the French, the Spanish, and the Americans. By the mid-1800s, the Karankawas were all dead.

> **Why did Europeans think the Karankawas were kind to their children?**
> _____
> _____

THE COAHUILTECANS

Not a single, unified group, the Coahuiltecans included many groups who lived near each other. The Coahuiltecans hunted and gathered food in southern Texas. The dry climate there did not support farming. The Coahuiltecans were nomads who used bows and arrows to hunt. They did not build permanent homes, but made dens from animal skins placed over branches.

At times groups would gather for all-night feasting and dancing at celebrations called **mitotes.** Many Coahuiltecans died from European diseases. Some were attacked by Apache Indians. By 1800 few Coahuiltecans remained. Those who survived joined other Indian groups.

> **What happened to the Coahuiltecans?**
> _____

CHALLENGE ACTIVITY

Critical Thinking: Comparing and Contrasting

How were the Karankawas and the Coahuiltecans alike and different? Write a paragraph comparing the two groups.

DIRECTIONS Read each sentence and fill in the blank with the word
from the pair that best completes each sentence.

1. The Coahuitecans sometimes held all-night dancing celebrations called
   (mitotes/wigwams) _____.

2. People who moved from place to place are called _____.
   (hunter-gatherers/nomads)

3. The Karankawas built _____ (mitotes/wigwams), portable
   huts made from bent poles covered with animal skins and reed mats.

4. People who hunt wild animals and gather plants for food are called
   _____. (hunter-gatherers/nomads)

MAIN IDEAS
1. The Caddos of East Texas were advanced farmers.
2. The Wichitas hunted and farmed to survive.
3. Atapaka settlements developed differently based on their locations.

Key Terms

crop rotation the practice of planting a different crop on a plot of land each year

confederacies associations who work together

allies friends or supporters

matrilineal describing families in which the lineage is traced from the mother's side

Section Summary

THE CADDOS AND FARMING

The Caddos moved into eastern Texas from present-day Arkansas, Louisiana, and Oklahoma more than 1,000 years ago. They became expert farmers, developing agricultural techniques still used today. For example, the Caddos practiced **crop rotation,** planting different crops on a plot each year to prevent wear on the soil. Unlike other Indian groups, the Caddo men helped in the farming. The men cleared the fields and made tools. The women worked in the fields, gathered plants, cooked, and cleaned.

> **What is the purpose of crop rotation?**
> _____
> _____

CADDO SOCIETY

The Caddo population grew large due to their efficient farming systems. The Caddos were one of the more complex societies in Texas. They were politically organized into three **confederacies,** or loose associations that worked together. These groups were the Hasinais, the Kadohadachos, and the Natchitoches. These groups shared a language and were **allies,** or friends who supported one another.

Each confederacy built religious temples and mounds. The Caddos had a **matrilineal** society. This means families were traced through the mother's side. Family names came from the mother, not the father. When couples married, they lived with the woman's family. The head of each household was an older woman who directed the 10 to 20 people who lived there.

> **What are some characteristics of a matrilineal society?**
>
> _____
> _____
> _____

THE WICHITAS

West of the Caddos along the Red River lived the Wichita Indians. The Wichitas moved into north-central Texas in the 1700s. The Wichitas lived and farmed along creeks and rivers. They grew melons, beans, and squash. They used horses to hunt buffalo and deer. Like the Caddos, they lived in permanent villages.

THE ATAKAPAS

The Atakapas lived between the Caddos and the Gulf of Mexico. Atakapa communities developed different ways of life depending on where in this territory they lived. Atakapas who lived inland had good land for farming, and they also hunted wild game. Other Atakapas lived closer to the coast. The Atakapas used wooden traps to fish and canoes to gather shellfish from the sea bottom. European diseases had a terrible effect on the Atakapas, and by the early 1900s there were very few left.

CHALLENGE ACTIVITY

Critical Thinking: Analyzing Information How did the area in which they lived affect the Atakapa communities?

crop rotation	confederacies	matrilineal
allies	Caddos	Wichitas

DIRECTIONS On the line provided before each statement, write **T** if the statement is true and **F** if the statement is false. If the statement is false, write a corrected statement on the line after the false statement.

_____ 1. The Caddos were a large group consisting of several confederacies.

_____

_____ 2. The different confederacies were allies, or enemies of each other.

_____

_____ 3. A society in which families are traced by the father's side is called matrilineal.

_____

_____ 4. The Caddos lived mainly near creeks and rivers.

_____

_____ 5. The practice of planting a different crop on the same plot of land each year is called crop rotation.

_____

> **MAIN IDEAS**
> 1. Some Jumanos were farmers who lived in villages, while others roamed the plains hunting buffalo.
> 2. Disease, drought, and attacks ended Jumano culture.

Key Terms

adobe a kind of clay dried in the sun and used in bricks as a building material

hides animal skins

Section Summary

THE JUMANOS

A group of American Indians called the Jumanos lived in villages along the Rio Grande. They built houses out of **adobe** bricks, which they made by drying clay mud in the sun. Although the region was dry, they grew corn and other crops by planting near the river. When the Rio Grande overflowed, the fields filled with water.

> **How did Jumanos make their homes?**
> _____
> _____

The Jumanos gathered plants and used bows and arrows to hunt buffalo. Some became nomads and moved onto the plains of western and central Texas. They supplied the Jumanos near the Rio Grande with **hides,** or animal skins, and meat.

In total, almost 10,000 people lived in the five Jumano villages north of Big Bend. In some villages, houses were built around a central plaza. About 30 or 40 people lived in each house. Inside the house, the rooms were painted with red, yellow, and white stripes.

The Jumanos who hunted buffalo used bows and arrows. Jumano warriors used shields of buffalo hide along with heavy clubs. Buffalo hides were also used to make clothes and shoes. The Jumanos wore jewelry made from copper, coral, and turquoise. They also tattooed or painted their faces with stripes.

> **Underline the different ways the Jumanos used buffalo hides.**

TROUBLED TIMES FOR THE JUMANOS

When the Spanish arrived in Texas, they traded with the Jumanos. The Jumanos admired the horses the Spanish brought with them. Horses made travel and hunting much easier. However, the Spanish also brought diseases from which the Jumanos had no immunity.

Other problems plagued the Jumanos. Drought in western and central Texas made life difficult. When rivers dried up, crops failed. Much of the grasses on the plains also died, driving the buffalo away.

The Jumanos were also attacked by the Apaches who lived to the north. The Apaches wanted to take the Jumanos' hunting territories and trade. The Jumanos asked the Spaniards for help, but little was done. By the mid-1700s, the Jumanos had lost most of their land to the Apaches.

> **What major events caused problems for the Jumanos?**
> _____
> _____
> _____

CHALLENGE ACTIVITY

Critical Thinking: Analyzing Information In a brief paragraph, explain how the Jumanos' interaction with the Spanish affected them.

hides	buffalo	adobe
drought	trade	Apaches

DIRECTIONS Use all the words in the word bank to write a summary
of what you learned about the Jumanos.

_____

_____

_____

_____

_____

_____

_____

_____

_____

_____

_____

_____

_____

_____

_____

_____

_____

_____

_____

_____

Guided Reading Workbook

Texas Indians

MAIN IDEAS
1. Plains Indians, including the Tonkawas, hunted buffalo.
2. The Apaches, Comanches, and Kiowas were fierce warrior groups in Texas.

Key Terms

tepees movable homes made from animal hides stretched over poles

bands groups of families

Comanchería Spanish name for the plains of northern and western Texas

Section Summary

THE INDIANS OF THE PLAINS

The Great Plains stretch from Canada into southern Texas. Before Europeans arrived, American Indians farmed on the edge of the plains. Once in a while they hunted buffalo on the plains.

When the Spanish arrived with horses, buffalo hunting changed dramatically. By 1700 most southern Plains Indians owned horses. With horses, the Indians could roam and hunt over much larger territories.

Most Plains Indians shared some common cultural characteristics. Most lived in **tepees,** portable houses made from animal houses stretched on poles. They used the buffalo for food and to make tools and clothes. In summer Plains Indians gathered in **bands,** or groups of families, for celebrations.

> How did buffalo hunting change when the Spanish arrived?
>
> _____
>
> _____

THE TONKAWAS

The Tonkawas lived on the north-central plains of Texas and on the Edwards Plateau. They depended on the buffalo for food, clothing, and shelter.

In the 1700s, the Tonkawas were driven from their hunting grounds by the Apaches. Without buffalo for food, the Tonkawas suffered. They had little success farming. By the 1900s the Tonkawas no longer existed as a separate group.

THE APACHES

The Apaches also lived on the Texas Plains. Their original homeland was far away in Canada. Two Apache groups, the Lipans and the Mescaleros, settled in Texas. The Mescaleros in western Texas eventually moved to present-day New Mexico.

The Apaches were organized into bands that traveled, hunted, and fought together. Horseback riding changed their way of life. Skilled riders, the Apaches worked in teams when hunting buffalo. They killed the animals with bows and arrows. Then they collected everything they could off the buffaloes' bodies out on the plains.

> Underline how the Apache killed buffalos.

Some Lipan Apaches farmed, which was unusual for Plains Indians. The Apaches often raided their neighbors. They became feared throughout Texas. The arrival of the more powerful Comanches led to their decline. In addition, many Apaches died from European diseases. By the early 1800s, many Apaches had been driven into Mexico and New Mexico.

> Why might settlers be afraid of the Apaches?

THE COMANCHES AND KIOWAS

The Comanches moved into Texas in the early 1700s. Their skill as buffalo hunters quickly made them rich. They traded goods made from the buffalo with other Native American groups. They soon controlled much of the plains, including northern and western Texas, which the Spanish called the **Comanchería.**

The Kiowas were the last Plains group to arrive in Texas. They moved from the northern plains sometime in the early 1800s. The Kiowas hunted buffalo and gathered berries, fruits, and nuts. They were skilled hunters and became allies of the Comanches.

CHALLENGE ACTIVITY

Critical Thinking: Making Inferences Why was the buffalo so important to many Plains Indians? Explain.

| tepees | bands | Comanchería |

DIRECTIONS Read each sentence and fill in the blank with a word
from the Word Bank.

1. Groups of Plains Indians families, or _____, gathered in
   the summers for celebrations.

2. The Spanish called the territory of the Comanches the
   _____.

3. Many Plains Indians lived in _____, or portable homes.

DIRECTIONS Write two adjectives or descriptive phrases that describe
each group below.

4. Comanches _____

5. Apaches _____

6. Kiowas _____

7. Tonkawas _____

The Age of Contact

Section 1

MAIN IDEAS
1. Explorer Christopher Columbus reached the Americas from Europe in 1492.
2. The Spanish wanted to control America to obtain gold, spread Christianity, and gain glory.

Key Terms and People

Christopher Columbus an Italian sailor whose attempt to find an all-water route to Asia led to the discovery of North America by Europeans

conquistadores Spanish soldier-adventurers in search of gold, glory, and land

Hernán Cortés explorer who founded the first Spanish settlement in North America

Moctezuma II last leader of the Aztec Empire

Section Summary

EUROPEANS REACH THE AMERICAS

In the late 1400s, nations in western Europe raced to find an all-water route to China. The Italian sailor **Christopher Columbus** believed that he could reach Asia by sailing west across the Atlantic Ocean. This was a daring idea at the time. King Ferdinand and Queen Isabella of Spain gave Columbus three ships for his voyage.

In 1492 Columbus reached an island in what is now the Bahamas. Although he was nowhere near Asia, he believed he was in the Indies. He called the people he met there Indians.

> **What did Christopher Columbus believe?**
> _____
> _____

SPANISH CONQUEST IN THE AMERICA

Spain's rulers hoped that the lands of the Americas would add to their empire's wealth and power. Spain also hoped to spread Christianity. To accomplish these goals, Spain sent armies led by **conquistadores**—Spanish soldier-adventurers in search of gold, glory, and land. They soon conquered many of the Caribbean Islands. Then, they turned to the North American mainland.

CORTÉS MARCHES THROUGH MEXICO

In 1519 Hernán Cortés sailed from Spanish Cuba to the coast of what is now Mexico. He founded La Villa Rica de Vera Cruz, the first Spanish settlement on the North American mainland. Cortés soon learned of the powerful and wealthy Aztec Empire, led by **Moctezuma II,** also called Montezuma. An Indian woman named Malintzin helped Cortés gain allies among the people the Aztecs had conquered. Thousands joined Cortés on his march toward the Aztec capital Tenochtitlán.

> Underline another name for Moctezuma II.

CORTÉS CONQUERS THE AZTECS

In 1521 the Spaniards defeated the Aztecs, and much of the Aztec gold and silver was sent to Spain. Cortés built Mexico City on the ruins of the Aztec capital. Many of the Aztecs were killed or enslaved. Along with the Caribbean Islands, Mexico became a common starting point for Spanish exploration of the Americas.

> What happened to the Aztecs?
> _____
> _____

CHALLENGE ACTIVITY

Critical Thinking: Drawing Inferences What similarities do you see between the Aztec Empire and the Spanish in North America?

Guided Reading Workbook

DIRECTIONS On the line provided before each statement, write **T** if the statement is true and **F** if the statement is false. If the statement is false, write a corrected statement on the line after the false statement.

_____ 1. <u>Christopher Columbus</u> was an Italian sailor who tried to find a new route to Asia.

_____

_____ 2. The Spanish explorer-adventurers called <u>conquistadores</u> came to America looking for gold and land.

_____

_____ 3. The Spanish leader, <u>Moctezuma II</u>, wanted to defeat the Aztec Empire.

_____

_____ 4. <u>Hernán Cortés</u> was the leader of the Aztec Empire.

_____

DIRECTIONS Write two adjectives or descriptive phrases that describe each term given.

5. Moctezuma II _____

6. Hernán Cortés _____

The Age of Contact

MAIN IDEAS

1. Pineda mapped the Texas coast in 1519.
2. The Narváez expedition was shipwrecked on the coast of Texas, but few of its members survived.
3. Cabeza de Vaca and Estevanico traveled widely through Texas in search of a way back to Spanish lands.

Key People

Alonso Álvarez de Pineda Spanish explorer who first mapped the Texas Gulf Coast

Pánfilo de Narváez Spanish explorer whose expedition to the Gulf of Mexico was shipwrecked on the Texas coast

Álvar Núñez Cabeza de Vaca Spanish explorer from Narváez's expedition who wrote about his experiences in Texas

Estevanico North African who traveled through Texas with Cabeza de Vaca

Section Summary

THE NARVÁEZ EXPEDITION

In 1519 Spanish explorer **Alonso Álvarez de Pineda** and his crew were the first-known Europeans to see the Texas coast. They mapped the northern Gulf of Mexico. After several months Pineda reached a large river along which were several American Indian villages and many palm trees.

In 1527 **Pánfilo de Narváez** led another voyage to the Gulf of Mexico. The expedition landed in Florida. Narváez led a group of soldiers ashore. When the group returned, they found that their ships had left. Desperate, the Spaniards built small boats and set sail for the Gulf of Mexico. Narváez drowned when his boat washed out to sea, and the two remaining boats wrecked on a Texas island—perhaps Galveston or San Luis.

The Spaniards were stranded, hungry, and almost hopeless, so the Karankawa Indians took the men in

What was Pineda's contribution to the exploration of Texas?
_____
_____

What happened to Narváez?
_____
_____

and shared their supplies. One of the survivors,
Cabeza de Vaca, worked as a servant, trader, and
healer.

THE SPANIARDS' ADVENTURES IN TEXAS

Eventually Cabeza de Vaca was captured by the
Coahuiltecan Indians. In captivity, he met three
other explorers from the Narváez expedition who
had become slaves of the Coahuiltecan Indians.
Among these explorers was a North African named
Estevanico. The four men escaped and set off in
search of Mexico. Estevanico's skill at
communicating with American Indians helped. By
the end of the journey, the men were escorted from
village to village by crowds of American Indians.

In 1536, almost eight years after their shipwreck,
the four lost explorers came across a group of
Spanish soldiers. In 1542 Cabeza de Vaca published
his story as *The Narrative of Álvar Núñez Cabeza
de Vaca.* It was the first European description of the
land and people of North American. In it, Cabeza de
Vaca describes the lives and cultures of the various
American Indian groups he and his companions
met.

How did Estevanico help Cabeza de Vaca?
_____
_____
_____

CHALLENGE ACTIVITY

Critical Thinking: Making Inferences Why was
Cabeza de Vaca's book important?

Guided Reading Workbook

DIRECTIONS For each term below, write a sentence about the
person's or group's influence on the Spaniards' adventures in Texas.

1. Alonso Álvarez de Pineda _____

_____

2. Pánfilo de Narváez _____

_____

3. Álvar Núñez Cabeza de Vaca _____

_____

4. Estevanico _____

_____

5. Karankawas _____

_____

6. Coahuiltecans _____

_____

MAIN IDEAS
1. Fray Marcos and Estevanico believed that they had found the fabled cities of gold called Cíbola.
2. Coronado traveled through Texas and surrounding areas in search of gold and silver.
3. The Moscoso expedition traveled through Texas on its way to Mexico but failed to find riches.

Key Terms and People

viceroy royal governor

Francisco Vásquez de Coronado Spanish conquistador who led expeditions through Texas searching for gold

Moscoso expedition led by Luis de Moscoso Alvarado, this expedition traveled through Florida to East Texas and Mexico City looking for gold

Section Summary

THE SEARCH FOR LOST CITIES OF GOLD

Before returning to Spain, Cabeza de Vaca told officials he heard of cities to the north. He also said that he had seen signs of gold in the mountains. This report excited the **viceroy,** or royal governor, of New Spain. In 1539 he sent a Catholic friar named Fray Marcos de Niza to find these cities.

While exploring what is now Arizona and New Mexico, Fray Marcos heard from an advance group of people wearing gold jewelry. He moved to high ground and thought he saw one of the legendary seven cities of Cíbola from a distance. Satisfied, he returned to Mexico City.

CORONADO'S SEARCH FOR CÍBOLA

Officials organized a large expedition led by **Francisco Vásquez de Coronado** to conquer Cíbola in 1540. After a short battle with Zuni Indians at the site Fray Marcos had reported, they did not find any gold but only Zuni Pueblo

> What did the viceroy have to do with the search for gold?
> _____
> _____

villages, whose adobe brick houses sparkled in the sunlight.

CORONADO HEARS OF QUIVIRA

Coronado continued to explore Texas and what would become the southwestern United States. The Spaniards met an American Indian called the Turk. He told tales of Quivira, a region where the cities were said to be full of gold. Coronado planned an exhibition for the following spring.

CORONADO TRAVELS THROUGH TEXAS

Coronado set out in search of Quivira in 1541. His expedition traveled onto the flatlands of the Texas Panhandle. They saw strange humpbacked "cows," which were really American buffalo. Near what is now Wichita, Kansas, they reached "Quivira" and found only grass huts and corn. Angry at the Turk's deception, Coronado had him killed. Because he had not found any treasure, Spanish officials considered Coronado's expedition a failure.

> **What did Coronado find in Texas?**
> _____

MOSCOSO EXPLORES EAST TEXAS

Meanwhile, another Spanish group was moving toward Texas from Florida. The group eventually reached East Texas and the group's leader, **Luis de Moscoso Alvarado,** later reported seeing a thick, black liquid seeping from the ground. Although he did not know it, Moscoso had seen petroleum, or oil. This would one day become the "black gold" of Texas. But the Moscoso expedition failed to discover actual gold.

CHALLENGE ACTIVITY

Critical Thinking: Making Inferences After Moscoso's report, do you think Spanish officials were eager to send more expeditions to Texas? Why or why not?

| viceroy | Francisco Vásquez de Coronado | Moscoso expedition | Cíbola |
| the Turk | Quivira | Zuni Indians | Fray Marcos de Niza |

DIRECTIONS Read each sentence and circle the term from the word pair that best completes each sentence.

1. The (Turk/viceroy), or royal governor, was excited by reports of gold in Mexico.

2. (Coronado/Fray Marcos) reported seeing a golden city of Cíbola.

3. The sparkling gold he saw was really the adobe houses of the (Moscoso expedition/Zuni Indians).

4. The (Moscoso expedition/Coronado) reported seeing a thick black goo seeping from the ground.

DIRECTIONS Write two adjectives or descriptive phrases that describe each term given.

5. Quivira _____

6. the Turk _____

The Age of Contact

MAIN IDEAS
1. Juan de Oñate founded the colony of New Mexico.
2. Interaction between Europeans and American Indians changed both societies.
3. The Columbian Exchange brought both devastating disease and useful horses to North America.

Key Terms and People

Juan de Oñate a wealthy Spaniard who established the colony of New Mexico

epidemics widespread outbreaks of disease

Columbian Exchange the transfer of plants, animals, and diseases among the Americas and other continents

mustangs the wild offspring of Spanish horses

Section Summary

OÑATE FOUNDS NEW MEXICO

By the late 1500s, settlement in New Spain had been slowly spreading northward. In the 1590s **Juan de Oñate**, a wealthy Spaniard, received permission to settle a colony in present-day New Mexico. He hoped to increase Spain's wealth and to convert the local Pueblo Indians to Christianity.

Oñate and more than 500 colonists built the first Spanish settlement north of what is now Santa Fe, New Mexico. Life was hard, and the settlers found no gold. The lack of treasure in Texas caused the Spanish to lose interest in the region. The New Mexico colony continued to thrive.

> Why did Oñate want to settle and govern a colony?
>
> _____
> _____

THE EFFECTS OF SPANISH EXPLORATION

The Spanish exploration of Texas did not yield gold, but it gave Spain a strong claim to the area. The Spanish learned about the land and people of Texas. In addition, Texas was a buffer between the Spanish settlement to the south and American Indians.

> Underline how the exploration of Texas benefitted the Spanish.

Spanish exploration greatly changed the lives of American Indians in Texas. European explorers spread diseases such as measles and smallpox. **Epidemics,** or widespread outbreaks of disease, killed thousands of American Indians. The spread of diseases was part of the **Columbian Exchange.** This term refers to the transfer of plants, animals, and diseases among the Americas and other continents. The Columbian Exchange is so named because it began with Christopher Columbus's arrival in the Americas in 1492.

> What were some of the negative impacts of Spanish exploration?
> _____
> _____

THE RISE OF A PLAINS HORSE CULTURE

The wild offspring of the horses the Spanish brought to the Americas became known as *mesteños,* or **mustangs.** In the 1600s, American Indians in Texas began obtaining mustangs through trade and raids. On horseback, Indians were more effective hunters and fighters. This development marked a new phase in Spanish-Indian relations and warfare.

THE APACHES DOMINATE THE PLAINS

The Apaches had initially been friendly to the Spanish. After the Spanish began settling among the Pueblos, their relationship with the Apaches changed. The Apaches, who had raided the Pueblos for years, began to view the Spanish as enemies. Apache raiders proved unstoppable despite the Spaniards' superior weapons. Conflict between the Spanish and the Apaches continued for many years.

> In what way did the Apaches relationship with the Spanish change?
> _____
> _____

CHALLENGE ACTIVITY

Critical Thinking: Making Inferences How do you think the Spanish settlers reacted to seeing the Apaches on horseback? Explain.

DIRECTIONS On the line provided before each statement, write **T** if the statement is true and **F** if the statement is false. If the statement is false, write a corrected statement on the line after the false statement.

_____ 1. Juan de Oñate and his colonists settled a Spanish colony later called <u>Quivira.</u>

_____

_____ 2. Widespread outbreaks of disease, known as <u>epidemics</u>, killed thousands of Spanish settlers.

_____

_____ 3. The offspring of the horses the Spanish brought to the Americas were known as <u>mustangs</u>.

_____

_____ 4. The transfer of plants, animals, and disease among the Americas and other continents was known as the <u>Columbian Exchange</u>.

_____

_____ 5. The <u>Apaches</u> had raided Pueblo villages for years.

_____

The Spanish Colonial Period

Section 1

MAIN IDEAS

1. Spanish officials promoted the building of missions, presidios, towns, and ranches in the borderlands.

2. The Spanish established missions along the western Rio Grande during the 1680s.

Key Terms

missions religious communities set up by missionaries

presidios forts

ranchos ranches

revolt revolution

Section Summary

THE MISSION-PRESIDIO SYSTEM

At first, Spain was the only European power active in North America. By the early 1600s, however, other nations had begun founding settlements. The Spanish sent missionaries to the borderlands to establish **missions,** or religious communities. They also sent soldiers to provide protection for their fellow Spaniards.

Spain used missions to convert American Indians to Catholicism. Many American Indians helped build the missions. But many other Indians opposed Spanish attempts to change their ways of life. To protect the missions, the Spanish built **presidios,** or military bases. Civilians often built settlements near missions and presidios. Some of these settlements became small towns. Other Spaniards lived on **ranchos,** or ranches. Some of these ranches became small settlements.

> **What was the purpose of the Spanish missions?**
>
> _____
>
> _____

NEW SETTLEMENTS ALONG THE RIO GRANDE

In the late 1600s the Spanish began building missions just south of the Rio Grande and among the Pueblo Indians in New Mexico. Tensions arose when the Spanish tried to make the Pueblos grow food for them. Also, missionaries tried to stop the Pueblos from practicing their traditional religion. In 1680 a Pueblo spiritual leader named Popé led a **revolt,** or revolution, against the Spanish.

The Pueblo Revolt forced the Spanish settlers out of New Mexico. The Spanish extended the mission system along the Rio Grande to give the settlers a place to live. By 1684 five settlements had been established on the south bank of the Rio Grande. One was Ysleta, a home for Tigua Indians near what is now El Paso. When flooding altered the course of the Rio Grande, Ysleta was left on the north bank. It is considered the oldest Hispanic settlement in Texas.

> **Why did the Pueblo Indians revolt?**
> _____
> _____

CHALLENGE ACTIVITY

Critical Thinking: Analyzing Information How did the Spanish try to establish control of Texas?

Guided Reading Workbook

DIRECTIONS Read each sentence below and circle the word from the pair that best completes each sentence.

1. The (ranchos/missions) were religious communities set up by the Spanish in North America.

2. Some civilians lived in (presidios/ranchos) owned by the missions.

3. To protect their fellow Spaniards, soldiers lived in (ranchos/presidios) near the missions.

4. The Pueblo (Revolt/Ranchos) forced Spanish settlers out of northern New Mexico.

The Spanish Colonial Period

MAIN IDEAS
1. The French under La Salle established a settlement on the Texas coast, but it failed.
2. The French presence in Texas led the Spanish to create new missions in the region.
3. The first Spanish missions in East Texas failed.

Key Terms and People

La Salle expedition an expedition led by a French explorer to establish a colony on the Texas coast

Fort St. Louis a settlement established by La Salle near the Gulf coast of Texas

Alonso de Léon a Spanish governor who led an expedition to drive the French from Texas

Damián Massanet a Franciscan priest who traveled with de Léon on his expedition

San Francisco de los Tejas a mission established in East Texas by de Léon and Massanet

Section Summary

LA SALLE'S EXPEDITION

The Spanish soon learned that the French had entered the Gulf of Mexico—Spanish waters. In 1682 French explorer René-Robert Cavelier, Sieur de La Salle canoed down the Mississippi River to the Gulf of Mexico. He planted a French flag and claimed all the land drained by the Mississippi for France. He named the area Louisiana for his king, Louis XIV.

After securing permission from King Louis, the **La Salle expedition** left France in 1684. They were going to establish a colony near the mouth of the Mississippi. La Salle's group became lost, however, and the ships landed at Matagorda Bay on the Texas coast in 1685.

> What was the purpose of the La Salle expedition?
> _____
> _____

Guided Reading Workbook

FORT ST. LOUIS

La Salle and the other settlers moved inland and built **Fort St. Louis** near Garcitas Creek. As the settlement was being built, La Salle led a small group west toward the Rio Grande. He eventually realized that Fort St. Louis was west of the Mississippi.

Hunger, disease, and attacks by the Karankawa Indians killed many settlers at Fort St. Louis. In early 1687 La Salle and 17 men set out looking for help. Tensions mounted, and La Salle was murdered by one of his own soldiers. Despite the expedition's failure, France now had a claim to Texas and challenged Spain's empire north of the Rio Grande.

> **What happened to the settlers at Fort St. Louis?**
> _____
> _____

THE SPANISH SEARCH FOR LA SALLE

Soon after the founding of Fort St. Louis, the Spanish tried to find and remove the French from Texas. A group led by **Alonso de León**, a Spanish governor, led an expedition in 1689. Franciscan priest **Damián Massanet** traveled with de León. By the time they found Fort St. Louis, it was in ruins. The Spanish also met the Hasinai Indians on their travels. The Spaniards called the Indians *Tejas*, after the Hasinai word for "friend." *Tejas* was the origin of the name *Texas*.

SPANISH MISSIONS IN EAST TEXAS

Father Massanet believed that that the Hasanai wanted a mission nearby. Spanish officials agreed, and they built **San Francisco de los Tejas.** The mission struggled, suffering droughts, floods, and hostile Tejas Indians. In October 1693 the Spanish burned the mission to the ground.

> **Underline what happened to the San Francisco de los Tejas mission.**

CHALLENGE ACTIVITY

Critical Thinking: Comparing and Contrasting

How were the expeditions led by the French and the Spanish similar? What were the goals of each?

La Salle expedition	Fort St. Louis	Alonso de León
Damián Massanet	San Francisco de los Tejas	

DIRECTIONS Use all the words in the word bank to write a summary
of what you learned in this section.

_____

_____

_____

_____

_____

_____

_____

_____

_____

_____

_____

_____

_____

_____

_____

_____

_____

The Spanish Colonial Period

Section 3

MAIN IDEAS
1. In response to a perceived threat from the French, the Spanish resettled in East Texas in the early 1700s.
2. The Spanish built several missions, a presidio, and the region's first civil settlement near what is now San Antonio.

Key Terms and People

Francisco Hidalgo Spanish missionary who was placed in charge of the Nuestro Padre San Francisco de los Tejas mission in East Texas

Louis Juchereau de St. Denis French explorer who worked with the Spanish to establish missions in East Texas

Domingo Ramón Spanish explorer who led the expedition to build new missions in East Texas

Antonio Margil de Jesús the religious leader of several Spanish missions near East Texas

Martín de Alarcón the governor of Texas who built a mission-presidio near the San Antonio River

El Camino Real royal road from the East Texas missions south to Mexico City

Section Summary
BACK TO EAST TEXAS

After the failure of San Francisco de Las Tejas, the Spanish ignored East Texas for more than 20 years. But Father **Francisco Hidalgo**, who had served at San Francisco de los Tejas, wanted to return to East Texas and work with American Indians there.

When Spanish officials refused his requests, Hidalgo asked the French governor of Louisiana for help. In 1713 the governor sent **Louis Juchereau de St. Denis,** an explorer, to find Father Hidalgo. When he arrived at the presidio where Hidalgo lived, St. Denis was arrested and sent to Mexico City to meet the viceroy.

The information St. Denis gave the viceroy convinced the Spanish that France wanted to

> Why did Francisco Hidalgo want to go back to East Texas?
>
> _____
>
> _____
>
> _____

move into Texas. Spanish officials decided to build new missions in East Texas. An expedition led by **Domingo Ramón** and guided by St. Denis arrived in East Texas in 1716. The Spaniards built a mission called Nuestro Padre San Francisco de los Tejas near the site of the original mission. Father Hidalgo was placed in charge. Father **Antonio Margil de Jesús** was the mission's religious leader.

> **Why was it unusual for St. Denis to work with the Spanish expedition?**
> _____
> _____

THE SAN ANTONIO SETTLEMENTS

Spanish officials also decided to build an outpost between the East Texas missions and the Rio Grande. In 1718 **Martín de Alarcón,** the governor of Texas, led Spanish colonists to the San Antonio River. They built the mission San Antonio de Valero and the presidio San Antonio de Béxar. Later they built more missions in the area.

> **Where did Alarcón set up his mission?**
> _____

Many Indian groups, including the Coahuiltecans, lived and worked at the San Antonio missions. More families moved into a town near the San Antonio presidio. Together, the missions, presidio, and town along the San Antonio River came to be known as San Antonio de Béxar, or simply San Antonio.

San Antonio became an important stop on the **El Camino Real,** or royal road. This road led from the East Texas missions south to Mexico City.

CHALLENGE ACTIVITY

Critical Thinking: Making Inferences Why were the settlements in San Antonio established?

DIRECTIONS Write two adjectives or descriptive phrases that describe each term or name given.

1. Francisco Hidalgo _____

2. Louis Juchereau de St. Denis _____

3. Domingo Ramón _____

4. Antonio Margil de Jesús _____

5. Martín de Alarcón _____

6. El Camino Real _____

The Spanish Colonial Period

MAIN IDEAS
1. The Aguayo expedition reopened missions in East Texas.
2. José de Escandón helped settle the Rio Grande valley.
3. Missions in Central Texas were attacked by the Apache.

Key Terms and People

Aguayo expedition group of Spanish settlers led by Marqués de San Miguel de Aguayo who set out to drive the French from East Texas in 1720

Los Adaes presidio founded by Aguayo which later became the capital of Spanish Texas

La Bahía presidio founded by Aguayo in East Texas, later known as Goliad, that became one of the largest Spanish settlements in the area

José de Escandón Spanish military officer who established a large colony on the Gulf coast of Texas and a series of settlements along the Rio Grande

Section Summary
THE AGUAYO EXPEDITION

The conflict between France and Spain in Europe spread to East Texas. The Spanish had pulled out of East Texas. In 1720, Marqués de San Miguel de Aguayo, the governor of Coahuila and Texas, commanded the **Aguayo expedition**. It set out for East Texas to drive the French from the region and rebuild the missions.

In 1721, the few French troops in Texas withdrew to Louisiana. The Spaniards quickly reoccupied the missions that had been abandoned.

By the time Aguayo left East Texas, he had established 10 missions and four presidios. The presidio **Los Adeas** later became the capital of Spanish Texas. The presidio **La Bahia,** later known as Goliad, became one of the largest settlements in Texas. The **Aguayo expédition** strengthened Spanish control of East Texas.

> What was the purpose of the Aguayo expedition?
> _____
> _____

NEW SETTLEMENTS ON THE RIO GRANDE

Spanish officials were still worried about their
territory on the Gulf Coast south of Texas. In 1746,
Spaniard **José de Escandón** established colony in
the region. He moved La Bahía to a new location on
the San Antonio River where it thrived. The
population grew, ranching industry developed, and
relations with the nearby Karawanka Indians
improved.

Escandón also established settlements along the
Rio Grande. He offered free land to colonists. He
founded 24 settlements in 6 years, including
Laredo, which was settled in 1755.

> Underline the number of
> settlements Escandón
> established.

CLASHES ON THE FRONTIER

North of Escandón's settlements, Spanish
missionaries were eager to convert American
Indians to Catholicism. When some chiefs of the
Apaches asked to learn about Spanish life,
missionaries built the mission San Sabá and a
presidio a few miles away.

In 1758, enemies of the Apaches attacked San
Sabá, burning the mission and killing a number of
people. The Spanish tried to counterattack but
failed. The attack at San Sabá was the end of
Spanish attempts to spread to Central Texas. Their
missions and presidios were not able to defend
themselves against American Indian attacks.

> What was the result of the
> attack on San Sabá?
> _____
> _____
> _____

CHALLENGE ACTIVITY

Critical Thinking: Making Inferences What
would the Apaches have wanted to learn from the
Spanish missionaries? Write a brief paragraph
explaining your answer.

| Aguayo expedition | Los Adaes | La Bahía | José de Escandón |

DIRECTIONS On the line provided before each statement, write **T** if a statement is true and **F** if a statement is false. If the statement is false, write a corrected statement on the line after the false statement.

_____ 1. The Aguayo expedition strengthened Spanish control over East Texas.

_____

_____ 2. La Bahía, later known as Laredo, became one of the largest settlements in Texas.

_____

_____ 3. The mission Los Adaes was located in East Texas and later served as the capital of Spanish Texas.

_____

_____ 4. José de Escandón moved Los Adaes to a location on the San Antonio River.

_____

The Spanish Colonial Period

MAIN IDEAS
1. Mission life was structured around prayer and work.
2. The life of a presidio soldier could be harsh.
3. Life in Spanish settlements reflected the influence of Spanish culture, which is still felt in Texas today.

Key Terms

ayuntamiento a governing council used to enforce royal and local laws

alcade a member of the *ayuntamiento* who held both judicial and law enforcement powers

vaqueros cowboys who worked on ranches near the settlements

Section Summary

LIFE IN THE MISSIONS

The Spanish wanted Texas Indians to live in the missions and learn the Spanish way of life. Life in the missions followed a daily pattern of worship and work. Many Indians continued to follow their traditional ways of life. Mission life was often harsh for the Indians who lived there. They were forced to work growing food for themselves and for the Spaniards. They could not leave the missions. Nevertheless, some missions, particularly those at San Antonio, became substantial communities.

> In what ways was mission life hard for the Indians who lived there?
> _____
> _____
> _____

LIFE IN THE PRESIDIOS

Missions were more likely to succeed if they had a presidio nearby. These military outposts had a chapel, barracks for soldiers, storage rooms, and a headquarters building. Soldiers in the presidios guarded the missions and protected the Spaniards' horses. They also helped supervise the American Indians who lived there. Tensions sometimes arose between the missionaries and soldiers about who had the higher authority. The low wages of the soldiers led many of them to fall into debt.

> What were some duties of the soldiers in the presidios?
> _____
> _____
> _____

Guided Reading Workbook

LIFE IN THE SETTLEMENTS

Permanent towns grew from the mission system. Many had defined streets and government buildings. San Antonio was the first town that allowed people to participate in their government. The *ayuntamiento,* or governing council, enforced laws. One member, the **alcalde,** had judicial and legislative powers. However, the viceroy in Mexico City still had the ultimate authority.

The economy was mostly based on farming and ranching. **Vaqueros,** or cowboys, worked on ranches. The Spanish strongly influenced Texas. For example, they introduced cattle ranching to the Americas. Cowboys later used the equipment developed by vaqueros. Spanish art, food, language, and music are alive in Texas today.

> How did the Spanish influence Texas culture?
> _____
> _____

CHALLENGE ACTIVITY

Critical Thinking: Comparing How was life in the presidios similar to life in the missions?

| *ayuntamiento* | alcalde | vaqueros |

DIRECTIONS Read each sentence and fill in the blank with a word from the word bank.

1. _____, or cowboys, worked on ranches near the settlements.

2. In San Antonio, people participated in the government by electing a(n) _____, or governing council.

3. A leader who held both judicial and law enforcement powers was called a(n) _____.

Conflicts of Empire

> **MAIN IDEAS**
> 1. In the 1760s the Spanish abandoned much of Texas.
> 2. New settlements and new policies improved relations with American Indians in the 1770s.

Key Terms and People

cede to give officially

Marqués de Rubí Spanish official sent by the king to report on conditions in New Spain

Tejanos Texas settlers of Spanish descent

Antonio Gil Ybarbo Tejano settler who founded the town of Nacogdoches in east Texas

Section Summary

THE MARQUÉS DE RUBÍ REPORT

In 1754 war had begun in North America between France and Great Britain. This conflict was called the French and Indian War. Spain joined the war in 1762 as allies of the French, but they were defeated by the British.

Under the 1763 Treaty of Paris, France was to **cede,** or officially give up, all of its claims east of the Mississippi River. Spain gave up Florida. Under a separate treaty, Spain gained the French Louisiana territory west of the Mississippi River. France no longer posed a threat to Texas.

In 1766 the king of Spain sent an official named **Marqués de Rubí** to tour and report on Spain's American lands. Most of the presidios needed repairs. Spanish attempts to convert the Apaches had failed.

In 1768 Rubí urged Spain to pull back to the "real" frontier. To protect this frontier, he suggested running a string of forts from lower California to southern Texas. He recommended the following changes:

> Underline the areas France and Spain had to give up.

> Why did Rubí suggest that Spain pull back to the "real" frontier?
>
> _____
> _____

1. Spain should abandon all missions and presidios except La Bahía and San Antonio.

2. San Antonio should replace Los Adaes as the capital of Texas.

3. The Spanish population in East Texas should move to San Antonio.

4. The Spanish should befriend the Comanches.

CHANGES IN TEXAS POLICIES

The government approved Rubí's recommendations. In 1773 officials ordered the Spanish withdrawal from East Texas. The settlers included **Tejanos**—Texas settlers of Spanish descent. Many settlers had to give up their homes and farms.

Once in San Antonio, the newcomers were unhappy. The best farmland was already taken. Many newcomers wanted to go home. Eventually they were allowed to return east as far as the Trinity River. Led by **Antonio Gil Ybarbo,** the group eventually settled in Nacogdoches on the site of an old mission.

Spanish policies toward American Indians changed during the 1770s. The Spanish established peace with several northern Indian groups. Apache attacks in Texas continued, however. In 1790 a combined force of Spaniards, Comanches, Wichitas, and other American Indian allies won a major victory over the Apaches.

> Why were some Tejano settlers unhappy?
>
> _____
>
> _____

CHALLENGE ACTIVITY

Critical Thinking: Analyzing Information What were the main goals of the Rubí report?

DIRECTIONS On the line provided before each statement, write **T** if a statement is true and **F** if a statement is false. If the statement is false, write a corrected statement on the line after the false statement.

_____ 1. Under the Treaty of Paris, Spain was to cede Canada and all its claims east of the Mississippi River to Paris.

_____

_____

_____ 2. The king of Spain sent an official named Marqués de Rubí to tour the presidios of New Spain.

_____

_____

_____ 3. Tejanos were Texas settlers of French descent.

_____

_____

_____ 4. In 1779, Antonio Gil Ybarbo and his followers founded the town of San Antonio.

_____

_____

Conflicts of Empire

 MAIN IDEAS
1. Some Spanish officials saw the growth of the United States as a threat to their land in North America.
2. Disputes arose over the border between Texas and Louisiana.

Key Terms and People

Louisiana Purchase a deal in which France sold Louisiana to the United States for $15 million

Neutral Ground the territory between the Sabine River and the Arroyo Hondo declared by the Spanish and the United States to be neutral

diplomats officials who represent countries in foreign affairs

Adams-Onís Treaty agreement signed by Spain and the United States in 1819 which set the boundary between their territories

Section Summary

THE GROWING U.S. THREAT

In 1775, American Patriots in the thirteen colonies began fighting for independence from Great Britain. Later, Spain joined the fight against the British. In 1783 the United States officially won its independence. Some Spanish officials began to see the growth of the United States as a threat.

U.S. settlers soon moved to lands near the Mississippi River. Without permission, some continued into Louisiana. Spanish officials decided to allow U.S. immigration to boost the population. In 1800 Spain returned Louisiana to France and then France sold it to the United States in 1803 for $15 million. This land deal was known as the **Louisiana Purchase.**

> **Why did Spain allow U.S. immigration into their territory?**
>
> _____
>
> _____

BORDER DISPUTES IN TEXAS

The Spanish were alarmed by the Louisiana Purchase—the United States now bordered New Spain. A dispute arose over the undefined boundaries of Louisiana. In particular, both sides claimed the territory that lay between the Sabine River and the Arroyo Hondo. Spanish and U.S. officials agreed to make the disputed region in East Texas neutral, not belonging to either side. This territory became known as the **Neutral Ground.** Both countries would remain out of the area until **diplomats**—officials who represent countries in foreign affairs—set the official border.

In 1819 Spain and the United States signed the **Adams-Onís Treaty,** setting the boundary between their territories. As part of the terms, the United States gave up all claims to Texas in exchange for the Neutral Ground and Florida.

> **Underline the location of the Neutral Ground.**

> **What was the purpose of the Adams-Onís Treaty?**
> _____
> _____

CHALLENGE ACTIVITY

Critical Thinking: Making Inferences Why did the United States present a threat to Spain's colonies?

| Louisiana Purchase | Neutral Ground | diplomats | Adams-Onís Treaty |

DIRECTIONS Use each of the words in the word bank to write a summary of what you learned in this section.

_____

_____

_____

_____

_____

_____

_____

_____

_____

_____

_____

_____

_____

_____

_____

_____

_____

_____

_____

_____

_____

Conflicts of Empire

MAIN IDEAS
1. The Spanish feared that U.S. agents were active in Texas.
2. Mexico began a fight for independence in 1810.
3. Filibusters and rebels tried to take control of Texas.

Key Terms and People

Philip Nolan a horse trader killed by Spanish soldiers after entering Texas illegally

filibusters military adventurers who tried to stir up rebellion in other countries

Miguel Hidalgo y Costilla a Creole priest from Dolores, Mexico who was a leader in the fight for Mexican independence

José Gutiérrez de Lara co-commander of the Republican Army of the North

Republican Army of the North an army of Mexican and U.S. citizens who fought for independence from Spanish rule

siege a military blockade of a city or fort

Battle of Medina decisive victory of the Spanish led by General Joaquín de Arredondo over the rebels in the Republican Army of the North

James Long a rebel from Mississippi who fought unsuccessfully for Texas independence

Section Summary

THE PHILP NOLAN EXPEDITIONS

Philip Nolan, a U.S. citizen, had begun coming to Texas in 1791 as a mustang trader. Spanish officials grew suspicious of him. In late 1800 Nolan and some 20 men returned to Texas. When Spanish soldiers tried to arrest him, he resisted and was killed. Nolan's actions increased Spanish fears of U.S. expansion.

Spanish officials worried about **filibusters,** or military adventurers, who tried to stir up rebellion. Most filibusters wanted to free Texas from Spain. Some were looking for adventure.

> **Why were Spanish officials worried about filibusters?**
> _____
> _____
> _____
> _____

THE CALL FOR MEXICAN INDEPENDENCE

In Mexico, fights broke out between creoles—people of Spanish descent born in Mexico—and *peninsulares,* people born in Spain. In 1810 **Father Miguel Hidalgo y Costilla** of Dolores, Mexico, called for an end to rule by governing *peninsulares.* He was killed in 1811 by Spanish soldiers. His call helped begin a Mexican movement for independence from Spain.

What did Father Hidalgo y Costilla want?
_____
_____

THE GREEN FLAG OVER TEXAS

When Hidalgo's revolution began, **José Bernardo Gutiérrez de Lara** and a U.S. Army officer, Augustus William Magee, raised an army of volunteers. They named their force the **Republican Army of the North.** Flying a solid green flag, the expedition invaded Texas in 1812 to free it from Spanish control. Spanish army under General Joaquín de Arredondo defeated the Republican Army of the North in August 1813 in the Battle of Medina.

PIRATES AND REBELS ON THE COAST

Filibuster and revolutionary activity continued along the Gulf Coast. Henry Perry gathered a force of about 300 and moved into Texas, establishing a base on Galveston Island. The island was home to pirates and smugglers.

THE LONG EXPEDITIONS

Originally from Mississippi, **James Long** thought that Texas should be part of the United States. He organized an army, and in 1819 he declared Texas independent. Spanish soldiers ran his group out of Texas. Long then sailed a second army to Texas. He was captured and killed while awaiting trial.

CHALLENGE ACTIVITY

Critical Thinking: Evaluating Why did some people want Texas to be independent?

| Philip Nolan | Miguel Hidalgo y Costilla | José Gutiérrez de Lara | siege |
| Republican Army of the North | Battle of Medina | James Long | filibusters |

DIRECTIONS Read each sentence and circle the word from the pair that best completes each sentence.

1. Spanish officials thought that (Philip Nolan/James Long) was acting as a spy.

2. Groups of rebels looking for adventure were called (filibusters/Republican Army of the North).

3. A Mexican priest, (Miguel Hidalgo y Costilla/José Gutiérrez de Lara) called for an end of rule by *peninsulares*.

4. Originally from Mississippi, (James Long/José Gutiérrez de Lara) thought Texas should have become a U.S. territory.

5. The (Republican Army of the North/ Battle of Medina) fought under a green flag.

DIRECTIONS Write two adjectives or descriptive phrases that describe each term given.

6. filibusters _____

7. Battle of Medina _____

8. siege _____

9. José Gutiérrez de Lara _____

10. Miguel Hidalgo y Costilla _____

MAIN IDEAS
1. Mexico won its independence from Spain in 1821.
2. The Mexican War for Independence was very costly for Texas and its people.

Key Terms and People

Agustín de Iturbide a leader of the fight to gain Mexico's independence from Spain

jacales one room huts made of sticks and mud

Section Summary

MEXICO WINS INDEPENDENCE

After the Spanish executed Father Hidalgo, a priest named José Maria Morelos y Pavón took control of the fight for Mexican independence. He won several battles and gained more control of Mexico, but in 1815, he was captured and killed. The struggle for Mexican independence seemed at its end.

In 1820 political changes in Spain weakened the government. A new group rose to power that held views with which the Spanish loyalists did not agree. Many loyalists changed sides and opposed Spain.

Mexican rebels saw their chance. An army led by **Agustín de Iturbide**, a former leader of the Spanish forces, and Vicente Guerrero defeated the Spanish in 1821. Although they had planned to share power, Iturbide pushed Guerrero aside and declared himself Emperor Augustín. His reign did not last long—the Mexican people soon turned against him.

> **What happened after Iturbide and Guerrero defeated the Spanish forces?**
>
> _____
> _____
> _____

THE WAR'S IMPACT ON TEXAS

Years of fighting in Texas and by Texans in Mexico took its toll. Many Tejanos had been killed in the fighting or fled from the violence. Only 3,000 Tejanos remained in Texas by 1821.

> **What happened to the Tejano population in Texas?**
>
> _____

About 1,500 Tejanos lived near San Antonio, the capital. Erasmo Seguín and José Antonio Navarro had both fled to Texas during the Gutiérrez-Magee expedition, but both men returned to San Antonio. Seguín later served as San Antonio's postmaster and in city government.

Another 500 Tejanos lived in Goliad, known then as La Bahía. In what is now southern Texas, several thousand people lived along the Rio Grande. Unlike the people in East Texas, they lived in small settlements and isolated ranches. After the war, the ranching industry quickly recovered.

About 30,000 American Indians also lived in the region. But the war had caused tension between the Indians and the Tejanos. American Indians attacked Texas settlements. Wealthy ranchers built fort-like houses to guard against attacks. Less fortunate Tejanos lived in **jacales,** one-room huts made of sticks and mud.

CHALLENGE ACTIVITY

Critical Thinking: Summarizing In a brief paragraph, summarize the effects of the Mexican War of Independence on Texas.

DIRECTIONS Read each sentence and fill in the blank with the word from the pair that best completes the sentence.

1. A former Spanish loyalist _____ (Father Miguel Hidalgo y Costilla/Agustín de Iturbide) joined forces with the rebels to fight for Mexico's independence.

2. The armies of Iturbide and _____ (Vicente Guerrero/José Gutiérrez de Lara) defeated the Spanish in 1821.

3. _____ (Iturbide/Guerrero) wanted to rule Mexico alone, and declared himself Emperor Agustín.

4. People of Spanish descent living in Texas were called _____ (filibusters/Tejanos).

5. After he returned to San Antonio, _____ (Erasmo Seguín/José Antonio Navarro) became the city's postmaster.

6. In southeast Texas, about 500 Tejanos lived in Goliad, also known as _____ (La Bahía/Nacogdoches).

7. Ranching was a popular industry in the south and west, where several thousand people lived near _____ (San Antonio/the Rio Grande).

8. Wealthy ranchers built their houses to protect from American Indian attacks, but those less fortunate lived in one-room huts called _____ (adobes/jacales).

Texas on the Mexican Frontier

MAIN IDEAS

1. To protect the rest of the country, Mexico encouraged people to move to Texas and other frontier regions.

2. The Spanish, Mexicans, and Anglos who settled in Texas had different purposes and methods in doing so.

Key Terms

frontier a region marking the farthest edge of settlement by a country or a group of people

buffer a zone of protection

Anglos white settlers from the United States

secularize to move from religious to civil control

Section Summary

THE SEARCH FOR MORE TEXANS

The Mexican National period in Texas began in 1821 with Mexican independence. This period lasted until 1836 when the Mexican government established new procedures for Texan affairs.

How long did the Mexican National period last?
_____

Many Mexican officials viewed Texas and other northern frontier territories as necessary to protect the rest of the country. A **frontier** is a region marking the farthest edge of settlement by a country or a group of people. Other Mexican frontier territories included New Mexico, Arizona, and California.

Underline three other Mexican territories.

The territories provided a **buffer,** or zone of protection, between Mexico and its northern neighbors. Mexican officials were afraid of attacks by the United States or American Indians. Any invaders would have to pass through the territories, giving the Mexican army time to respond.

Mexico needed to populate the frontiers. Few people were willing. The frontier seemed like a harsh, distant land.

Why did Mexican officials value the northern territories?
_____
_____
_____

The Mexican government agreed to give land to American farmers if they settled in Texas. Historians call these new, white settlers are called **Anglos.**

DIFFERENT VIEWS OF SETTLEMENT

By the 1830s, three different groups had worked to settle Texas: Spaniards, Mexicans, and Anglos.

The presidios and missions originally built by the Spaniards were in decline by the time Mexico won its independence. The government chose to **secularize** them, or move them from religious to civil control.

The Mexican government depended on settlers in Texas to defend themselves. There were not enough Mexican soldiers to secure the land. Mexico hoped to draw more settlers by offering free or cheap land.

Many Anglos took up the offer. Enticed by free land, they settled in Texas for economic reasons. They established farms and ranches. They did not want to share their culture with Indians. They wanted to drive them away from their settlements completely.

CHALLENGE ACTIVITY

Critical Thinking: Drawing Inferences Imagine you were an Anglo settler in Texas. Why did you settle there? What challenges do you face? Write one paragraph about your situation.

> List the three different groups who had settled Texas.
> _____
> _____
> _____

> What drew Anglo settlers to Texas?
> _____
> _____
> _____

DIRECTIONS On the line provided before each statement, write **T** if a statement is true and **F** if a statement is false. If the statement is false, write a corrected statement on the line after the false statement.

_____ 1. The farthest reaches of a country's settlement are called a buffer.

_____

_____ 2. Mexico wanted to populate the northern territories so they could serve as a frontier between them and their northern neighbors.

_____

_____ 3. The Texas population had been greatly reduced by the struggle for Mexican independence.

_____

_____ 4. Non-Anglo settlers in Texas were called Tejanos.

_____

_____ 5. Presidios were built by the Spaniards to teach Christianity to the American Indians.

_____

_____ 6. The Mexican government decided to secularize the failing missions, moving them from religious to civil control.

_____

Texas on the Mexican Frontier

Section 2

MAIN IDEAS

1. Moses Austin made plans to establish a colony in Texas but died before he could accomplish them.
2. Stephen F. Austin continued his father's plan and brought the first Anglo settlers to Texas.
3. Austin's colony faced many challenges in the first few years of its existence.

Key Terms and People

Moses Austin a businessman who first got permission from Mexico to bring Anglo settlers to Texas

Stephen Austin son of Moses Austin, he established a colony of settlers in Texas and was called the Father of Texas

Baron de Bastrop Dutch businessman who eventually settled in San Antonio

Erasmo Seguín rancher who helped Stephen Austin get land from Mexico

cotton gins devices that separate cotton fibers from seeds

militia an army made up of citizens who serve when necessary

Section Summary

MOSES AUSTIN'S TEXAS DREAM

After losing his fortune in 1819, **Moses Austin** came up with a plan to establish a colony of U.S. families in Texas. By charging them fees, he could regain his fortune. Hopeful, he set out for Texas.

Austin met with Spanish governor Antonio María Martínez in 1820. Distrustful of Americans, Martínez ordered Austin out of the city. However, Austin happened to meet the **Baron de Bastrop,** a Dutch businessman who lived in San Antonio. Bastrop offered to help Austin. Together, Austin and Bastrop convinced the governor to urge his superiors to approve the plan.

His plan in place, Austin returned to Missouri. Before he could act, however, he became ill and died.

What was Moses Austin's Texas dream?
_____
_____
_____
_____
_____

STEPHEN F. AUSTIN TAKES OVER

Stephen F. Austin, the son of Moses, was determined to carry out his father's plan. In August

1821, he was led by **Erasmo Seguín** to Governor Martínez. The governor agreed to help Austin get a new contract to fulfill his father's plans from the Mexican government in Mexico City.

Austin picked a site for his colony near the Brazos and Colorado rivers. The farmland would have a mild climate, fertile soil, water, and timber. He also included land along the Gulf for a port.

Austin planned to give each colonist 640 acres of land. Those who provided valuable items, such as **cotton gins**—devices that separate cotton fibers from seeds—would receive extra land. Settlers would pay Austin a fee for his services.

As Austin advertised his land terms, applications poured in. Austin was very selective in choosing settlers. He believed his colony's success depended on hardworking, law-abiding people. Settlers would also have to become Mexican citizens and convert to Catholicism.

What physical characteristics did the site of Austin's colony offer?
_____
_____

EARLY SETTLEMENT OF AUSTIN'S COLONY

By March 1822, about 150 people had settled along the Brazos and Colorado rivers. Food and supplies were scarce. Because the Spanish government no longer ruled Mexico, Austin needed the support of the new Mexican government. In 1822, Austin headed to Mexico City. The journey was long and dangerous. In January 1823, the Mexican government passed the Imperial Colonization Law. Austin's land grant was secure. As the colony's leader, Austin had to form a **militia,** an army of citizens who would serve when necessary. In April 1823, he headed back to Texas.

Underline why Austin needed to get approval for his colony again.

CHALLENGE ACTIVITY

Critical Thinking: Drawing Inferences How would Mexico benefit from Austin's land grant? Explain in a written paragraph.

Moses Austin	Stephen F. Austin	Baron de Bastrop
Erasmo Seguín	cotton gins	militia

DIRECTIONS Read each sentence and circle the term in the word pair that best completes each sentence.

1. The man also known as the Father of Texas is (Moses Austin/Stephen F. Austin).

2. A successful businessman, (Baron de Bastrop/Moses Austin) helped Stephen F. Austin meet with the governor of Mexico.

3. As leader of the colony, Austin was charged with forming (cotton gins/militias).

4. Together with Baron de Bastrop, (Moses Austin/Erasmo Seguín) met Governor Martínez.

DIRECTIONS Write two adjectives or descriptive phrases that describe the term given.

5. Stephen F. Austin _____

6. Baron de Bastrop _____

7. cotton gins _____

8. militia _____

Texas on the Mexican Frontier

Section 3

 MAIN IDEAS

1. In its first years, Austin's colony faced problems that threatened to drive everyone away.

2. The Old Three Hundred helped make Austin's colony, centered on San Felipe de Austin, a success.

3. After the success of his first colony, Austin established four more colonies in Texas.

Key Terms and People

Old Three Hundred the original 297 families and single men who received land grants in Stephen Austin's first colony

Jane Long widow of filibuster James Long who held her own land grant in Austin's colony

San Felipe de Austin town founded by Austin along the Brazos River that served as the capital of the colony

Little Colony an isolated settlement of Austin's whose main town was Bastrop

Section Summary

EARLY PROBLEMS IN AUSTIN'S COLONY

In August 1823 many of the colonists in Austin's colony were discouraged. The settlers had faced a bad drought that had ruined their crops. They had to eat wild game to survive. In addition, local American Indians had raided the colony.

Why were the settlers discouraged?
_____
_____

To bring order to the colony, Austin established a headquarters near present-day La Grange. He set up a system of government and created rules to guide the colony. He also tried to form peaceful relations with the nearby Texas Indians. Austin's efforts paid off, and people stopped leaving.

THE OLD THREE HUNDRED

By the fall of 1824, Austin had nearly fulfilled his contract with the Mexican government. There were 297 families and single men who had received land in the colony. These settlers became known as the

Underline some characteristics of the Old Three Hundred.

Guided Reading Workbook

Old Three Hundred. Most were from the southern United States. Of the 1,790 colonists living in Austin's colony in 1825, about 440 were enslaved African Americans.

The settlers were fairly well educated and tended to be law-abiding because of Austin's regulations. Among them were women who held land grants on their own. For example, Jane Long, the wife of filibuster James Long, received land in Austin's colony.

SAN FELIPE DE AUSTIN

In 1824 Austin founded **San Felipe de Austin,** better known as San Felipe, in present-day Austin County. San Felipe served as the colony's capital and it grew quickly. Many travelers passed through San Felipe. The town sat on a high bluff, which aided its defense. The river provided a good source of water. By the early 1830s San Felipe was the second largest business center in Texas, after San Antonio.

> Why did San Felipe's location make it a good capital for the colony?
>
> _____
> _____
> _____

AUSTIN'S OTHER COLONIES

With the help of Tejano leaders such as José Miguel de Arciniega, Austin was able to acquire contracts for four more colonies. They each overlapped his first, except for one, known as Austin's **Little Colony** near modern Bastrop. It was in an isolated location north of the Old San Antonio Road and east of the Colorado River. Although Little Colony grew slowly, Austin's other colonization efforts were successful.

CHALLENGE ACTIVITY

Critical Thinking: Analyzing Information What qualities helped make Austin's colonies successful?

| Old Three Hundred | San Felipe de Austin | Little Colony |
| Jane Long | | |

DIRECTIONS On the line provided before each statement, write **T** if a statement is true and **F** if a statement is false. If the statement is false, write a corrected statement on the line after the false statement.

_____ 1. The Little Colony was composed of the original settlers who received land grants from Stephen Austin.

_____

_____ 2. Jane Long was a widow who received a land grant in Austin's colony.

_____

_____ 3. Stephen Austin set up a capital for his colony at the Little Colony.

_____

_____ 4. San Felipe de Austin was located in present-day Austin County along the Brazos River.

_____

DIRECTIONS Write two adjectives or descriptive phrases that describe the term given.

5. Little Colony _____

6. Old Three Hundred _____

Texas on the Mexican Frontier

MAIN IDEAS
1. Under Mexico's Federal Constitution of 1824, Texas was united with the state of Coahuila.
2. New colonization laws in Mexico allowed *empresarios* to receive contracts to bring settlers to Texas.
3. Many Tejanos supported immigration from the United States, though relations became strained.

Key Terms and People

Federal Constitution of 1824 constitution adopted by Mexican assembly establishing a new government

republic a government in which people elect their leaders

Coahuila y Texas new state established in 1824 that included Texas and Coahuila

State Colonization Law of 1825 a law that further opened Texas to settlement and immigration by giving land to new settlers

empresarios businesspeople who promoted settlement in Texas

Green DeWitt a successful *empresario* who settled 400 families along the Guadalupe River

Martín de León Tejano *empresario* who founded a colony of primarily Mexican settlers

Section Summary

A NEW CONSTITUTION FOR MEXICO

After Mexican leader Iturbide lost power, the Mexican people officially adopted a new constitution called the **Federal Constitution of 1824.**

Mexico became a **republic,** a government in which people elect their leaders. There was a national government, headed by a president, and individual state governments. Mexico was reorganized into 19 states and five territories. Texas and Coahuila became the new state of **Coahuila y Texas.**

Many Texans did not like the new state. They thought Coahuila, which had a much bigger population, would overshadow Texas.

> **How did the new constitution change Mexico?**
> _____
> _____
> _____
> _____
> _____

MEXICO'S NEW COLONIZATION LAWS

The National Colonization Law of 1824 allowed each Mexican state to create its own colonization policies, but it established some limits. New U.S. immigrants could not establish colonies near the nation's borders or along the coasts.

The State Colonization Law of 1825 further opened Texas to immigration. Many people became *empresarios*—businesspeople who promoted settlement in Texas. Under the new law, a huge wave of U.S. immigrants came to Texas.

> Underline the purpose of each Colonization Law.

THE *EMPRESARIO* COLONIES

In 1825 **Green DeWitt** received a grant to settle 400 families in Texas. His colony was located along the Guadalupe River. More than 525 people lived in Gonzales, the colony's main town, by 1831.

Martín de León was the only successful *empresario* to found a colony of primarily Mexican settlers. In 1824 he received permission to establish a colony along the lower Guadalupe River.

TEJANO LEADERSHIP

Mexican migration to Texas was limited. Anglo settlers outnumbered Mexican settlers by three to one by 1834. Most Tejanos believed that American settlers would help the Texan economy. Conflicts between Tejanos and their new neighbors sometimes arose. Tejano individuals were still important in state affairs even as more American colonists became involved in Texas politics.

> What did most Tejanos think about American settlers?
>
> _____
>
> _____

CHALLENGE ACTIVITY

Critical Thinking: Cause and Effect What were some effects of Mexico's immigration policy on immigration to Texas?

| Federal Constitution of 1824 | republic | Coahuila y Texas | State Colonization Law of 1825 |
| *empresarios* | Green DeWitt | Martín de León | Coahuila |

DIRECTIONS Read each sentence and circle the term in the word pair that best completes each sentence.

1. With the adoption of the (Federal Constitution of 1824/State Colonization Law of 1825), Mexico became a republic.

2. Texas and Coahuila became the new state of (Coahuila/Coahuila y Texas).

3. The only successful *empresario* to found a colony of primarily Mexican settlers was (Martín de León/Green DeWitt).

4. The (National Constitution of 1824/State Colonization Law of 1825) allowed each Mexican state to create its own colonization policies.

DIRECTIONS Write two adjectives or descriptive phrases that describe the term given.

5. republic _____

6. *empresarios* _____

7. Green DeWitt _____

Life in Mexican Texas

 MAIN IDEAS

1. Brought to Texas for a variety of reasons, immigrants settled in all parts of the state.
2. Rivers and climate helped people choose where to live.

Key Terms

G.T.T. an abbreviation for "Gone to Texas"

squatters people who do not legally own the land on which they live

flatboats cargo boats with flat bottoms used in shallow water

Section Summary

GONE TO TEXAS

Texas grew quickly during the 1820s and 1830s. Some new arrivals came from Europe or from other parts of Mexico. Most settlers were farmers from the southern United States. The promise of cheap land and easy payment terms drew many immigrants. Some U.S. settlers moved to Texas to escape debts. Authorities could not follow criminals into Texas. As a result, drifters and outlaws entered the region.

The allure of Texas became part of popular culture. When someone left town in debt or accused of a crime, people often said they had gone to Texas. Many overdue accounts were marked **G.T.T.** for "Gone to Texas."

> List some reasons settlers were drawn to Texas.
>
> _____
> _____
> _____

THE PEOPLE OF TEXAS

In 1834 nearly three-fourths of the people of Texas—about 15,000—were from the United States. While many came with the help of *empresarios,* a few came on their own. Those who came independently did not bother to obtain land titles. Mexican law made it difficult to acquire land independently so they became **squatters,** people who do not legally own the land on which they live.

The Tejano population in 1834 was about 4,000. Tejanos lived mainly in the San Antonio and Nacogdoches areas. Most European settlers were of British, German, French, or Italian backgrounds. In 1834 some 2,000 enslaved African Americans lived in Texas. They lived mostly in East Texas and along the Gulf Coast. About 150 free African Americans also called Texas home. Several American Indian groups also migrated to Texas during the 1820s and early 1830s.

> **Underline the different immigrant groups that came to Texas.**

GETTING TO TEXAS AND CHOOSING LAND

By 1835 an estimated 1,000 settlers from the United States were entering Texas each month. Many immigrants came in covered wagons pulled by horses, mules, or oxen. Others rode on horseback, walked, or arrived on long, low boats called **flatboats.** Most settlers lived along rivers and streams that provided water for drinking, farming, and transportation. Some settlers chose land that resembled their old homes. Most colonists avoided lands frequented by Comanche and Apache Indians.

> **Why would settlers live in areas similar to those they had lived in before?**
>
> _____
>
> _____
>
> _____

CHALLENGE ACTIVITY

Critical Thinking: Categorizing Make a list of the types of settlers that came to Texas. Then, explain their reasons for moving.

| G.T.T. | squatters | flatboats |

DIRECTIONS Answer each question by writing a sentence that contains at least one term from the word bank.

1. What does the abbreviation *G.T.T.* mean, and how was it used in popular culture?

_____

_____

2. Why would an immigrant become a squatter?

_____

_____

3. What purpose did flatboats serve for people migrating to Texas?

_____

_____

Life in Mexican Texas

MAIN IDEAS
1. Early Texans made homes, clothing, and meals out of the resources around them.
2. Roman Catholicism was the official religion of Mexican Texas, but many settlers wanted to remain Protestant.
3. Education was limited in early Texas.

Key Terms

dogtrot cabin a log cabin which included an open passage separating two rooms

quilting bees social gatherings where women quilted together

buckskin tanned deer hide used as clothing

venison deer meat

Section Summary

FRONTIER HOMES

One of the first tasks for newcomers in Texas was to build a house. Settlers had to use the building materials at hand. To the south and west, many Tejanos lived in flat-roofed adobe or stone houses. *Jacales,* small huts made of sticks and mud, were common as well.

In East Texas, where trees were plentiful, settlers built log cabins. Most log homes were small one- or two-room cabins. A popular design was the **dogtrot cabin,** which included an open passage separating two rooms. Breezes flowed through this passage, cooling the cabin. Settlers usually furnished their homes with items they made themselves. Women often made quilts that were functional and beautiful. Many of these quilts were made during **quilting bees,** which doubled as social occasions.

> Underline the materials settlers used to build houses.

> What feature made dogtrot cabins popular?
> _____
> _____

CLOTHING IN EARLY TEXAS

Settlers also used local materials to make clothes. Leather clothing was common. Many people wore **buckskin,** or tanned deer hide. By the early 1830s,

homespun cotton began replacing buckskin. Hats
protected against the harsh sunlight and provided
extra warmth on cold days.

FRONTIER FOODS

Most settlers had to be self-reliant for food. They
depended on crops, livestock, and wild game. Most
settlers planted corn and vegetables such as
cabbages, peas, sweet potatoes, and turnips. The
most common meats were beef, pork, and **venison,**
or deer meat.

RELIGION IN EARLY TEXAS

Mexico's official religion was Roman Catholicism.
Most of the Tejanos living in Texas were Roman
Catholic. Only Catholicism was legal. Most U.S.
settlers, however, were Protestant and unwilling to
change their beliefs. Publicly, they supported the
Roman Catholic Church, but privately they
worshipped as they pleased. Traveling preachers
and missionaries from the United States held
meetings and gave sermons in Texas.

Why would settlers support the Roman Catholic Church publicly?
_____
_____

EDUCATION ON THE FRONTIER

Few settlements had money to establish schools.
Education in early Texas was limited to teaching in
the home or small private schools. Wealthier settlers
sent their children to schools in the United States.
Schools operated in San Antonio as far back as the
1700s. However, demands of farm life kept many
children working in the fields. Enslaved African
Americans were not allowed to go to school.

CHALLENGE ACTIVITY

Critical Thinking: Drawing Inferences Imagine
you are a settler living in Texas in the early 1830s.
Write a diary entry describing a day in your life.

| dogtrot cabin | quilting bees | venison | buckskin |

DIRECTIONS Use each word in the word bank to write a summary of
what life was like in Texas in the early 1830s.

_____

_____

_____

_____

_____

_____

_____

_____

_____

_____

_____

_____

_____

_____

_____

_____

_____

_____

_____

Life in Mexican Texas

MAIN IDEAS
1. During the Mexican period, Texas had a few large settlements, mostly inhabited by Tejanos.
2. In cities, people took part in business and trade.

Key Terms and People

William Goyens a free African American who became a wealthy business owner in Nacogdoches

barter trade

sawmills mills where wood is cut into usable pieces

exports items to be sold in other places

imports items bought from other places

Section Summary

LIFE IN TEXAS CITIES

Most Texans during the Mexican period lived on isolated farms or in small communities. Larger settlements included San Antonio, Goliad, and Nacogdoches. Each of these towns had more than 1,000 people, mostly Tejanos.

These towns had a government called the *ayuntamiento*, or city council. The councils had to establish police forces, maintain roads, and provide food inspection, sanitation, and health care for their towns. Such services were paid for with taxes collected from the townspeople.

San Antonio was the largest town in Texas. Most residents were farmers or ranchers, but others owned businesses. City living presented problems. Canals that carried water through towns were polluted. Outbreaks of disease were common. Some residents kept garden plots to supplement food available from farms and ranches.

The population of Nacogdoches steadily increased after the Mexican Revolution. By 1835,

> **What was the city council responsible for?**
> _____
> _____

> **Underline some common problems found in towns.**

1,000 people lived there, including Tejanos, Anglo settlers, and enslaved African Americans. Most people lived in log cabins and farmed for a living.

BUSINESS, TRADE, AND TRANSPORTATION

Texas towns were home to crafters and merchants. By offering their services to other towns people, blacksmiths, carpenters, and merchants made their livings in towns. One successful business owner was **William Goyens**, a free African American of Nacogdoches who ran a blacksmith shop. Because few people had money, most business was conducted through **barter,** or trade.

Blacksmiths made items needed by farmers, including plows and tools. Carpenters made wagons. A few Texans ran **sawmills,** where they cut wood into usable pieces.

Poor transportation systems made trade difficult. Roads that linked towns were bumpy and dusty in dry weather and muddy when it rained. Transporting goods by river was not much better. Large boats had difficulties navigating through the shallow rivers.

By the 1830s, Texas was producing about $500,000 worth of **exports,** or items to be sold in other places, per year. These included cattle, corn, cotton, furs, horses, pork, and salt. In return, Texas required many **imports,** or items bought from other regions, including manufactured and luxury products.

How did townspeople make a living?
_____
_____

Why was transportation difficult?
_____
_____

CHALLENGE ACTIVITY

Critical Thinking: Analyzing Information What were the advantages and disadvantages of living in a town in Mexican Texas?

William Goyens	barter	sawmills
exports	imports	

DIRECTIONS On the line provided before each statement, write **T** if a statement is true and **F** if a statement is false. If the statement is false, write a corrected statement on the line after the false statement.

_____ 1. <u>Imports</u> are goods sold to other places.

_____

_____ 2. Because money was scarce, most business was conducted through <u>barter</u>, or trade.

_____

_____ 3. <u>William Goyens</u> was a wealthy business owner from San Antonio.

_____

_____ 4. Some Texans ran <u>sawmills</u>, where they cut wood into usable pieces.

_____

DIRECTIONS Write two adjectives or descriptive phrases that describe the term given.

5. William Goyens _____

6. exports _____

Section 4

MAIN IDEAS
1. Farming and ranching were the main industries in Texas.
2. Conflicts arose over the issue of slavery in Texas.

Key Terms

plantations large farms that specialized in growing one crop

Section Summary

FARMING AND RANCHING

Agriculture dominated the Texas economy during the 1920s and 1930s. Most Texans lived on small family farms. They had to prepare fields, harvest crops, and run the household. Few people lived near stores or had cash. As a result, families had to make many of the items they needed, including tools and clothing.

A few wealthy Texans established **plantations,** large farms that specialized in growing one crop. Many plantations resembled small communities. They had a large house, smaller homes for visitors and a doctor, a dairy, and quarters for slaves. Enslaved African Americans were the main labor force of the plantations, both in the house and in the fields.

Cotton became the main crop grown for profit on both large and small farms. Anglo settlers brought large-scale cotton farming to Texas.

Ranching was more popular among Tejanos. The mild climate, open prairies, and river valleys of Texas provided good pasture for livestock. In a region with a small population, only a few men were needed to tend a lot of animals.

> **Why did families have to make their own tools and clothing?**
> _____
> _____
> _____
> _____

> **In what ways is Texas well suited to ranching?**
> _____
> _____
> _____

THE ISSUE OF SLAVERY IN TEXAS

The introduction of large-scale cotton farming to Texas also led to the expansion of slavery. Cotton farming requires a great deal of labor. In the United States, where most Texas cotton farmers came from, enslaved people performed that labor. When these farmers moved to Texas, they brought their slaves with them.

Some Tejanos, especially in Coahuila, were opposed to slavery. The Mexican government viewed the matter the same way. In 1829 President Vicente Guerrero—himself of African ancestry— outlawed slavery in Mexico. However, officials in Texas warned the government that the ban violated their colonization policies. As a result, slavery remained legal in Texas.

Some Texans feared that the government would one day ban slavery. They worried that the possibility of such a ban might keep new settlers from moving to the area. By 1836, some 5,000 slaves lived in Texas—about 13 percent of the population. As time passed, tensions between Anglos and Mexican officials over slavery and other issues arose.

Why did slavery remain legal in Texas?
_____
_____
_____

CHALLENGE ACTIVITY

Critical Thinking: Analyzing Information Why might a ban on slavery keep new settlers from moving to the area? Explain.

Guided Reading Workbook

DIRECTIONS In the lines below, summarize what you learned about the issue of slavery in Texas in the 1830s. Make sure your response includes a description of Texas plantations.

_____

_____

_____

_____

_____

_____

_____

_____

_____

_____

_____

_____

_____

_____

_____

_____

_____

_____

_____

The Road to Revolution

 MAIN IDEAS

1. The Fredonian Rebellion was an attempt to create an independent republic in East Texas.
2. General Mier y Terán toured Texas and concluded that American influence in the area was too strong.
3. The Law of April 6, 1830, banned American immigration to Texas.

Key Terms

Fredonian Rebellion an attempt by a small group of Anglo settlers near Nacogdoches to declare independence from Mexico

Mier y Terán Report a report written by Mexican General Manuel de Mier y Terán describing the growing American influence in Texas

Law of April 6, 1830 law passed by the Mexican government banning U.S. immigration and prohibiting settlers from bringing more slaves into Texas

customs duties import taxes which raised money for the government

Section Summary

THE FREDONIAN REBELLION

In 1825 Haden Edwards, a businessman from Kentucky, received an *empresario* contract. He had permission to settle families near Nacogdoches. When he arrived, he found that many people had been living on the land for years.

Edwards ordered the settlers to show their titles to the land. Many could not, and Edwards demanded that they pay him for a title or leave. The people protested to Mexican officials, who responded by canceling Edwards's contract.

Edwards and his brother, Benjamin, took action. They gathered a small band of settlers and claimed a part of East Texas as the independent Republic of Fredonia. Most Texans opposed the **Fredonian Rebellion,** which was quickly put down.

> **What did Haden Edwards discover when he arrived in Nacogdoches?**
> _____
> _____

> **Underline where the settlers of the Fredonian Rebellion claimed land.**

Guided Reading Workbook

THE MIER Y TERÁN REPORT

The American interest in rebellion greatly worried the Mexican government. The government sent General Manuel de Mier y Terán to investigate conditions in Texas. The general was asked to determine how many Americans lived in Texas and what their attitudes toward Mexico were.

In the **Mier y Terán Report,** he noted that Mexican influence in Texas decreased as one moved northward and eastward. He recommended that trade between Texas and Mexico be increased in an effort to discourage trade with the United States. He also recommended that more soldiers be sent to Texas and that Mexicans and Europeans be encouraged to settle in Texas.

> List two recommendations in the Mier y Terán Report.
>
> 1. _____
> _____
> 2. _____
> _____

THE LAW OF APRIL 6, 1830

In response, the Mexican government passed the **Law of April 6, 1830.** It banned U.S. immigration to Texas and made it illegal for settlers to bring more slaves into Texas. The law also suspended unfilled *empresario* contracts. The government began to tax all U.S. imports into Texas. These import taxes, or **customs duties,** served two purposes. They raised money for the government and they encouraged internal trade within Mexico. The law angered many Tejanos and U.S. settlers.

> What were the two purposes of customs duties?
>
> _____
> _____
> _____

CHALLENGE ACTIVITY

Critical Thinking: Evaluating How did the Mier y Terán Report lead to the passage of the Law of April 6, 1830?

Guided Reading Workbook

Fredonian Rebellion	Mier y Terán Report
Law of April 6, 1830	customs duties

DIRECTIONS Read each sentence below and circle the term in the word pair that best completes each sentence.

1. The (Fredonian Rebellion/Mier y Terán Report) declared Texas settlers free from Mexican rule.

2. According to the (Law of April 6, 1830/Mier y Terán Report), Mexican influence in Texas decreased as one moved northward and eastward.

3. The (Law of April 6, 1830/customs duties) prohibited U.S. settlers from bringing more slaves to Texas.

4. Because of the (Fredonian Rebellion/customs duties), goods from the United States would now be more expensive than goods from Mexico.

DIRECTIONS Write two adjectives or descriptive phrases that describe each term given.

5. Haden Edwards _____

6. Fredonian Rebellion _____

MAIN IDEAS
1. Tension between officials and Texans at Anahuac led to conflict.
2. The Turtle Bayou Resolutions declared Texas support for the Mexican government.

Key Terms and People

resolutions statements of a group's opinions

Turtle Bayou Resolutions declarations from American settlers that explained their actions at Anahuac and expressed support for the Mexican constitution and for the efforts of General Antonio López de Santa Anna

Antonio López de Santa Anna Mexican general who was trying to overthrow President Anastacio Bustamante

Battle of Velasco military conflict between Mexico and Texas settlers; resulted in a Mexican defeat

Section Summary
TENSION AT ANAHUAC

The Mexican government stationed hundreds of troops in Texas to enforce the Law of April 6, 1830. Before long, conflict developed between the military and some settlers. In the fall of 1830, troops built a fort at the mouth of the Trinity River on Galveston Bay near an important trade route. The settlement became known as Anahuac.

> **Why was the settlement of Anahuac important?**
> _____
> _____

Colonel Juan Davis Bradburn commanded the troops in the fort. Bradburn angered many Texans when he arrested a surveyor who was approving land titles for settlers in the area. Tensions grew when Bradburn arrested more citizens, including William B. Travis and Patrick Jack, two recently arrived settlers.

> **Underline causes of the tensions between Bradburn and some Texans.**

THE TURTLE BAYOU RESOLUTIONS

Soon a force of more than 150 people led by settler John Austin marched toward the fort at Anahuac. After an exchange of gunfire, the attackers

withdrew to Turtle Bayou. There they drew up
several **resolutions,** or statements of a group's
opinions. The **Turtle Bayou Resolutions** declared
that the events at Anahuac were not a rebellion
against Mexico. The settlers also expressed support
for **General Antonio López de Santa Anna.** Santa
Anna was trying to overthrow President Anastacio
Bustamante, who had taken control of the
government of Mexico.

> **What did the Turtle Bayou Resolutions declare?**
> _____
> _____

THE BATTLE OF VELASCO

Soon after these events, a Mexican force arrived in
Nacogdoches. The commander blamed Bradburn
for much of the conflict with the U.S. settlers.
Bradburn soon resigned. Unaware that the conflict
at Anahuac was over, in June of 1832, John
Austin's group began fighting with Mexican troops
at Velasco. The Mexican soldiers ran out of
ammunition and had to surrender. The Texans
continued to Anahuac only to find the conflict there
resolved.

Resistance to central Mexican authority
continued to grow. Most Mexican troops left the
area to take sides in the civil war between Santa
Anna and President Bustamante.

> **Why did Mexican troops leave the area?**
> _____
> _____

CHALLENGE ACTIVITY

Critical Thinking: Drawing Inferences How did
the enforcement of the Law of April 6, 1830, lead to
problems at Anahuac?

resolutions	Turtle Bay Resolutions	Antonio López de Santa Anna	Battle of Velasco
Colonel Juan Davis Bradburn	John Austin	President Anastacio Bustamante	Anahuac

DIRECTIONS Read each sentence and fill in the blank with the term in the word pair that best completes the sentence.

1. The settlement at the mouth of the Trinity River on Galveston Bay was known as

_____ . (Anahuac/Turtle Bay Resolutions)

2. _____ (John Austin/Colonel Juan Davis Bradburn) was the

commander in charge of Anahuac.

3. Texan settlers took sides in the civil war in Mexico by supporting

_____ (President Anastacio Bustamante/General Antonio

López de Santa Anna).

4. During the _____ (Battle of Velasco/Turtle Bay

Resolutions), Mexican soldiers ran out of ammunition and surrendered.

DIRECTIONS Write two adjectives or descriptive phrases that describe the term given.

5. Turtle Bay Resolutions _____

6. Battle of Velasco _____

MAIN IDEAS
1. Texans hoped that a new government in Mexico would lead to changes in Texas.
2. The Conventions of 1832 and 1833 requested changes in immigration policy and statehood for Texas.
3. Stephen F. Austin was arrested while in Mexico to present the Convention of 1833's requests.

Key Terms and People

reforms changes in policy

delegates representatives

Convention of 1832 a meeting of representatives from 16 Texas settlements who sought reforms from Mexican government

William H. Wharton delegate to the Convention of 1832 and president of the Convention of 1833

Convention of 1833 a meeting of 56 delegates from Texas to create petitions to bring to the Mexican government

Section Summary
THE CONVENTION OF 1832

Santa Anna defeated Bustamante's forces in 1832. Texans were excited about the rise of Santa Anna, who had promised to restore the Constitution of 1824. Many settlers hoped that the central government might listen to their concerns.

Texan settlers called a convention to discuss possible **reforms,** or changes in policy. Each district in Texas was asked to send **delegates,** or representatives, to San Felipe on October 1, 1832. Delegates from 16 settlements arrived and began the **Convention of 1832.** They adopted several resolutions. These included a request that legal immigration from the United States be allowed and that Texas become a separate Mexican state. The convention chose delegates **William H. Wharton** and Rafael Manchola to present their resolutions to

> Why were Texans happy about Santa Anna's victory?
> _____
> _____

> Underline the resolutions the Convention requested.

the Mexican government. However, the resolutions were never presented.

THE CONVENTION OF 1833

A group of impatient Texans called for another convention. The **Convention of 1833** met at San Felipe on April 1. The delegates chose William Wharton as president. The delegates adopted many of the same resolutions as the earlier convention. Stephen F. Austin was chosen to present the proposals to Santa Anna. He set out for Mexico City on April 22 to present the proposals to Santa Anna.

> Where did Austin go in 1833 and why?
> _____
> _____

AUSTIN IS ARRESTED

When he arrived, he faced one problem after another. Santa Anna was away. Frustrated, Austin wrote a letter to the government in San Antonio. He advised Texans to meet "for the purpose of organzing a local government for Texas."

Eventually, Santa Anna approved nearly all of the Texans' requests. His work done, Austin left Mexico City. He was arrested on his way back to Texas, however, because Mexican officials had read his letter. They thought Austin had challenged Mexican authority. Austin was taken back to Mexico City and kept in prison for nearly a year.

> Why was Austin arrested?
> _____
> _____
> _____

CHALLENGE ACTIVITY

Critical Thinking: Sequencing Make a time line of events leading up to Austin's arrest.

| reforms | delegates | Convention of 1832 |
| William H. Wharton | Convention of 1833 | |

DIRECTIONS On the line provided before each statement, write **T** if a statement is true and **F** if a statement is false. If the statement is false, write a corrected statement on the line after the false statement.

_____ 1. Texas settlers wanted a list of <u>delegates</u> to present to the Mexican government.

_____

_____ 2. William H. Wharton was elected president of the <u>Convention of 1832</u>.

_____

_____ 3. <u>Delegates</u> from 16 settlements attended the Convention of 1832.

_____

_____ 4. Stephen Austin was to present a list of <u>reforms</u> from the Convention of 1833 to Santa Anna.

_____

DIRECTIONS On the lines below, list similarities and differences between the Convention of 1832 and the Convention of 1833.

_____

_____

_____

_____

_____

_____

_____

_____

The Road to Revolution

MAIN IDEAS
1. Under Santa Anna, the Mexican government began to tighten its control of Texas.
2. Frustrated, some Texans began to call for war.

Key Terms and People

Martín Perfecto de Cos military commander of Texas

faction a group

Section Summary

MEXICO TIGHTENS CONTROL

In 1834 Santa Anna declared that Mexico was not ready to be a republic and began to strengthen the central government's power. This was a violation of his pledge to restore the federal Constitution of 1824, the reason many Texans had supported him.

Santa Anna did honor some requests from the Convention of 1833. He legalized immigration from the United States and removed some customs duties. In January 1835 he sent more troops to Texas.

> Underline the requests that Santa Anna honored.

In the spring of 1835 Captain Antonio Tenorio began collecting customs duties at Anahuac, where taxes had not been collected since 1832. This angered Texans who believed they were paying more than people at other ports. William Travis and several supporters sailed to Anahuac, where they demanded Tenorio's surrender. When he refused, Travis ordered an attack. Tenorio surrendered.

Upon hearing of this, General **Martín Perfecto de Cos,** the military commander of Texas, ordered the arrest of Travis and several others. He also ordered more troops to Texas.

> Why was Travis arrested?
> _____
> _____

DEBATING WAR AND PEACE

General Cos planned to put any prisoners on trial in a military court. This concerned many Texans, who believed that they had the right to trial by jury. The arrival of more troops further upset Texans.

Texans began debating how to respond to the problems with the Mexican government. One **faction,** or group, argued that Texans should remain calm. Another group argued for military action. The Tejanos of Texas had their own debates. Most Tejanos opposed Santa Anna's centralist policies. But some Tejanos were equally frustrated with the Anglos who were less concerned about Mexico and more concerned about furthering their own interests.

While the debates continued, Stephen F. Austin returned from his imprisonment in Mexico City. Although he had gone to Mexico to work for peace, he now urged Texans to prepare for war.

How did General Cos continue to upset Texans?
_____
_____
_____

CHALLENGE ACTIVITY

Critical Thinking: Evaluating Why do you think Austin changed his view on the conflict with the Mexican government?

Guided Reading Workbook

DIRECTIONS On the line provided before each statement, write **T** if a statement is true and **F** if a statement is false. If the statement is false, write a corrected statement on the line after the false statement.

_____ 1. Santa Anna honored some of the requests of the <u>Convention of 1832</u>.

_____

_____ 2. <u>Captain Tenorio</u> began collecting customs duties at Anahuac in 1835.

_____

_____ 3. William Travis demanded the surrender of <u>Santa Anna</u>.

_____

_____ 4. One <u>faction</u> of Texans wanted to keep peaceful relations with the government.

_____

_____ 5. <u>Stephen F. Austin</u> urged Texans to prepare for war.

_____

The Texas Revolution

MAIN IDEAS

1. The Battle of Gonzales and the capture of Goliad were among the opening conflicts in the Texas Revolution.
2. The Texas army laid siege to San Antonio and fought several small battles against Mexican troops.
3. The Texas army drove the Mexican forces out of San Antonio.

Key Terms

Battle of Gonzales a battle between Texas militia and Mexicans; considered the start of the Texas Revolution

Juan Seguín a Tejano hero of the Texas Revolution who led a unit at the Battle of San Jacinto and accepted Mexico's surrender of San Antonio

infantry foot soldiers

cavalry soldiers who fight on horseback

Edward Burleson elected by soldiers as commander of the Texas army, replacing Stephen F. Austin; led the siege on Mexican soldiers known as the Grass Fight

Erastus "Deaf" Smith a scout for the Texas army who reported the rumor of Mexican soldiers carrying silver to pay Mexican troops in San Antonio

Grass Fight an incident in which the Texas army ambushed Mexican soldiers for the silver they were rumored to be carrying but found only grass for horses

Ben Milam a colonel in the Texas army who wanted to lead an attack on San Antonio after hearing that the Mexican army was weak and disorganized

Section Summary

THE CAPTURE OF GONZALES AND GOLIAD

Many Texans were upset with the Mexican government because Antonio López de Santa Anna refused to follow the Constitution of 1824. When a Mexican officer ordered settlers at Gonzales to hand over a cannon, they refused. They waved a flag with the challenge COME AND TAKE IT. On October 2, 1835, Mexican soldiers opened fire as the settlers approached their camp. The fighting was brief and the Mexican troops retreated.

> **What was the cause of the Battle of Gonzales?**
> _____
> _____
> _____

The **Battle of Gonzales** signaled the start of a war.
General Cos ordered more Mexican troops to Texas.
In response, a group of settlers captured the garrison
at Goliad.

THE MARCH ON SAN ANTONIO

The growing Texas force set its sights on San
Antonio and chose Stephen F. Austin as its general.
He increased the number of **cavalry**, rather than
infantry, to compete with the Mexican troops.
More than 100 Tejanos—including **Juan Seguín** —
volunteered for the Texas army.

THE GRASS FIGHT

Austin and his troops attacked San Antonio. The siege
seemed to have little effect. Austin left to travel to the
United States and the soldiers elected **Edward
Burleson** to take command. On November 26, a scout
named **Erastus "Deaf" Smith** reported that Mexican
soldiers carrying silver intended as soldiers' pay were
headed to San Antonio. Hoping to find the silver,
some Texans ambushed the Mexican soldiers. They
found that the Mexicans' pack animals were carrying
grass for feeding horses of the soldiers. This event
became known as the **Grass Fight**.

> Underline the cause for
> the ambush on Mexican
> soldiers headed for San
> Antonio.

> How might the ambush of
> Mexican soldiers still be
> considered a success?
> _____
> _____
> _____

THE CAPTURE OF SAN ANTONIO

Colonel Burleson wanted to attack San Antonio, but
his officers refused. Hearing that the Mexican troops
were worn down, Colonel **Ben Milam** organized an
attack on San Antonio. After fierce fighting, the
Texans forced the Mexican troops to retreat. General
Cos surrendered and led his troops out of Texas.

CHALLENGE ACTIVITY

Critical Thinking: Sequencing Create a time line
of the major events between The Battle of Gonzalez
and the capture of San Antonio.

| Battle of Gonzales | Juan Seguín | Edward Burleson | Grass Fight |
| Erastus "Deaf" Smith | cavalry | infantry | Ben Milam |

DIRECTIONS Read each sentence below and circle the word or phrase that best completes each sentence.

1. The (Battle of Gonzales/Grass Fight) occurred in response to the attempt to reclaim a cannon.

2. The branch of an army that fights on foot is the (cavalry/infantry).

3. (Ben Milam/Erastus "Deaf" Smith) wanted to take advantage of the weak Mexican troops in San Antonio and organized an attack on them.

4. Selected by soldiers, (Juan Seguín /Edward Burleson) replaced Stephen F. Austin as the commander of the Texas army.

5. (Juan Seguín /Ben Milam) joined other Tejanos to volunteer for the Texas army.

DIRECTIONS Write a simple explanation of the following battles.

6. Battle of Gonzalez _____

_____

_____

7. Grass Fight _____

_____

_____

The Texas Revolution

 MAIN IDEAS
1. The Consultation met to debate the future of Texas and to form a provisional government.
2. Conflicts soon arose within the new government.

Key Terms

Consultation a convention of Texans organized to discuss plans for dealing with Mexico and to form a temporary government

Declaration of November 7, 1835 a document claiming that Texans were justified in past fighting with Mexico as a privilege under the Constitution of 1824

provisional temporary

Henry Smith a pro-war delegate elected governor by the temporary government created during the Consultation

Sam Houston a soldier and politician who became the commander-in-chief of the professional army established by the Consultation

Section Summary
DEBATING INDEPENDENCE

In October 1835 Texans gathered for the **Consultation**. The purpose of this convention was to discuss plans for dealing with Mexico. Pro-war delegates wanted Texas to declare independence. Pro-peace delegates wanted to remain loyal to Mexico. The Consultation drafted the **Declaration of November 7, 1835**. In this statement, Texans justified previous fighting with Mexico as defense of their rights under the Constitution of 1824. The delegates pledged their loyalty to Mexico, but they warned that they would create an independent government if Mexico did not restore the Constitution of 1824.

They then created a **provisional** government, electing **Henry Smith** as governor and creating a General Council. The delegates also authorized the creation of a new regular army, independent from

> Which group of delegates, pro-war or pro-peace, was successful in drafting the Declaration of November 7, 1835? How do you know?
>
> _____
> _____
> _____

> What was stated in the Declaration of November 7, 1835?
>
> _____
> _____

the existing volunteer army. They selected **Sam Houston** as commander of the new army.

THE PROVISIONAL GOVERNMENT

Disagreements over strategy soon rose. Some Texans in favor of independence wanted to cross the Rio Grande and attack Matamoros. They hoped to gain the support of federalists in Mexico in the protest against Santa Anna's government. Neither Sam Houston nor Governor Smith favored this plan, due to a lack of resources. After much debate, volunteers marched to Matamoros. However, the effort to take the city failed.

Peace efforts were negotiated with the Cherokees of East Texas, who agreed not to side with Mexico in the revolution. However, the provisional government of Texas did not have clear goals or good leadership. In December the General Council scheduled a new convention for March 1, 1836, to solve the government's problems.

> **From which two groups of people did the provisional government hope to gain support?**
>
> _____
>
> _____
>
> _____

CHALLENGE ACTIVITY

Critical Thinking: Supporting Point of View

Create a poster supporting the point of view of a Texas delegate of the Consultation. Include language to persuade.

DIRECTIONS On the line provided before each statement, write **T** if a statement is true and **F** if a statement is false. If the statement is false, write a corrected statement on the line after the false statement.

_____ 1. Texans held the Consultation to discuss the formation of a government.

_____

_____ 2. The Declaration of November 7, 1835 emphasized the rights of Texans established in the Constitution of 1824.

_____

_____ 3. The plan to attack Matamoros was supported by Sam Houston, Governor Smith, and other Texans in favor of independence from Mexico.

_____

_____ 4. A member of the pro-war group, Henry Smith, was elected governor by the Consultation.

_____

_____ 5. Governor Smith, elected by the Consultation, created a provisional government and a professional army.

_____

_____ 6. The provisional government had clear goals and good leadership.

_____

_____ 7. The Consultation scheduled a convention at a later date to solve the government's problems.

_____

Guided Reading Workbook

MAIN IDEAS

1. In early 1836 Mexican forces marched into Texas, while the Texas army was disorganized.
2. The Texas army chose to make a stand against the Mexican army at the Alamo mission in San Antonio.
3. The defenders of the Alamo gave their lives in a desperate effort to hold back the Mexican army.

Key Terms

Davy Crockett a frontiersman and politician from Tennessee who brought volunteers to Texas and became one of the leaders of the Alamo defenders

José de Urrea a Mexican general who led successful advances against the Texas army in Goliad and overtook the Texans headed to Matamoros

James "Jim" Bowie a volunteer from Louisiana and skilled frontiersman who informed leaders to defend the Alamo and shared command at the battle

William B. Travis a colonel in the Texas army who brought volunteers to assist in San Antonio and became one of the commanders at the Alamo

James Bonham led volunteers from Alabama to join the army and sneaked past Mexican troops in an effort to find aid for the Alamo

casualties people killed, wounded, captured, or missing during battle

Susanna Dickinson an Alamo survivor whose life was spared by Santa Anna

noncombatants people not involved in fighting

Section Summary
THE MEXICAN ARMY ADVANCES

Santa Anna led an army of approximately 6,000 soldiers to San Antonio while another group led by General **José de Urrea** moved toward Goliad. After capturing Goliad, Urrea headed to Matamoros, defeating or capturing many Texans along the way.

Other groups of Texas forces were scattered. Sam Houston worried that the army had limited numbers of soldiers scattered among Matamoros, Goliad, and San Antonio. He sent **James "Jim" Bowie** to San Antonio with 25 men to evaluate the Alamo and its

> What led Sam Houston to send troops to San Antonio?
>
> _____
> _____
> _____

artillery. Bowie reported that the Alamo was too important to be destroyed. **William B. Travis** brought soldiers to San Antonio, while **Davy Crockett** and **James Bonham** led dozens of volunteers to join the troops of Colonel James Neill at the Alamo. When the colonel left to care for an ill family member, Travis and Bowie agreed to share command.

> Underline the names of Texas army commanders in San Antonio.

THE SIEGE BEGINS

Troops at the Alamo built up defenses, but 1,000 soldiers were needed for defense, and the Texans numbered around 150. On February 23, 1836, a lookout spotted the approach of the Mexican army. Santa Anna demanded the Texans' surrender. The defenders of the Alamo refused, and the siege began. Travis wrote a famous letter "To the People of Texas and All Americans in the World" requesting aid in the face of certain death. When Bowie fell ill, Travis took sole command.

> What was the main weakness of the Texas army in San Antonio?
> _____
> _____
> _____

THE FALL OF THE ALAMO

More help was needed. The Texas forces increased to approximately 200 soldiers. Santa Anna's army numbered at least 1,800. The Mexican soldiers attacked on March 6 but were halted by the Texans' resistance. They regrouped and soon overwhelmed the Texans, who suffered many **casualties**. Almost every defender was killed. Many **noncombatants** were spared, including **Susanna Dickinson.** Santa Anna wrongly concluded that the Alamo's fall would convince Texans to surrender.

> How would you describe the military efforts of the Texas army?
> _____
> _____

CHALLENGE ACTIVITY
Critical Thinking: Drawing Inferences and Conclusions Write an interview with a soldier who is preparing for battle at the Alamo. Consider motivation, leadership, and preparations.

| Davy Crockett | José de Urrea | James "Jim" Bowie | William B. Travis |
| James Bonham | casualties | Susanna Dickinson | noncombatants |

DIRECTIONS Read each sentence and circle the term in the word pair that best completes each sentence.

1. (José de Urrea/James "Jim" Bowie) was the victor in the battle at Goliad.

2. Volunteers for the Texas army included (Davy Crockett/William B. Travis).

3. One of the few survivors of the battle at the Alamo was (José de Urrea/Susanna Dickinson).

4. Many (casualties/noncombatants) at the Alamo survived the brutal attack of Santa Anna.

5. Prior to the battle at the Alamo, (James Bonham/James "Jim" Bowie) was sent to evaluate the situation in San Antonio.

6. (William B. Travis/José de Urrea) and Bowie shared command at the Alamo.

7. The Texans suffered many (noncombatants/casualties) in the siege by Santa Anna.

8. Joining with volunteers from Alabama, (James Bonham/William B. Travis) fought with the Texas defenders.

9. Word from (James "Jim" Bowie/Davy Crockett) sparked the decision to send reinforcements to San Antonio.

10. One of the Texan leaders at the Alamo who wrote a letter requesting aid was (William B. Travis/ Davy Crockett).

The Texas Revolution

MAIN IDEAS
1. The Convention of 1836 declared Texas independence.
2. The Constitution of 1836 established the first government for the Republic of Texas.

Key Terms

Convention of 1836 a gathering of Texan delegates who met in Washington-on-the-Brazos and accepted the Texas Declaration of Independence

Lorenzo de Zavala a delegate at the Convention of 1836 who had served in the Mexican Congress and was elected as temporary vice president of Texas

George C. Childress the writer of most of the Texas Declaration of Independence

popular sovereignty the idea that the power to create or change the government comes from the people

bill of rights a statement describing individual rights that the government cannot remove from citizens

petition to make a formal request to the government concerning a particular cause

ad interim temporary

David G. Burnet a delegate at the Convention of 1836 who was selected as the temporary president of Texas

Section Summary

TEXAS DECLARES INDEPENDENCE

Just before the conflict at the Alamo, delegates began to arrive at Washington-on-the-Brazos for the **Convention of 1836.** Many of the delegates had served in the U.S. government. Delegate **Lorenzo de Zavala** had served in the Mexican Congress. The convention acted quickly to declare Texas's independence. On March 2, 1836, the delegates, including two Tejanos and one Mexican, unanimously agreed to accept the Texas Declaration of Independence. Delegate **George C. Childress** wrote most of this formal statement. With the adoption of the Declaration, the Republic of Texas was born.

> Why was the Convention of 1836 held?
>
> _____
> _____
> _____

THE CONSTITUTION OF 1836

Some delegates felt the need to assist at the Alamo, which was still under siege. However, Sam Houston urged them to stay and create a plan for the government of the new republic. The delegates then used the U.S. Constitution as a model for a constitution. The document created a government with three branches, as had the U.S. Constitution. The Republic of Texas was based on the idea of **popular sovereignty.** It included a **bill of rights** for citizens that introduced political, civil, and religious freedoms that the government could not take away.

The constitution also established slavery as a legal institution. Citizenship in Texas for African Americans and American Indians was not allowed without the permission of Congress. Those who wanted to stay had to **petition** the government.

In addition, the delegates set up an **ad interim** government, selecting **David G. Burnet** as president and Lorenzo de Zavala as vice president. In the weeks ahead, this temporary government had to flee several times when the Mexican army got close to where the government was meeting. Because of this constant movement, the temporary government had to leave the future of the Republic in the hands of Sam Houston and the Texas army.

> How were African Americans and American Indians affected by the Constitution of 1836?
>
> _____
>
> _____
>
> _____

CHALLENGE ACTIVITY

Critical Thinking: Compare How was the Texas Constitution similar to the U.S. Constitution? Write a paragraph in which you compare the two documents.

| Convention of 1836 | ad interim | bill of rights | George C. Childress |
| popular sovereignty | Lorenzo de Zavala | David G. Burnet | petition |

DIRECTIONS Read each sentence and fill in the blank with the term in the word pair that best completes the sentence.

1. The Republic of Texas was born during the _____. (ad interim/Convention of 1836)

2. Out of the 59 men who signed the Declaration of Independence, _____ was the only delegate born in Mexico. (George C. Childress/Lorenzo de Zavala)

3. After acceptance of the Texas Declaration of Independence, the Constitution of the Republic of Texas was created, written mostly by _____. (David G. Burnett/George C. Childress)

4. The interim government selected _____ as president until republic-wide elections could be held. (Lorenzo de Zavala/David G. Burnet)

DIRECTIONS Write two adjectives or descriptive phrases that describe the term given.

5. bill of rights _____

6. ad interim _____

7. popular sovereignty _____

8. petition _____

The Texas Revolution

MAIN IDEAS
1. In the Runaway Scrape, Texas fled the Mexican army.
2. A Texan army surrendered at Goliad but was massacred a few days later at Santa Anna's orders.
3. Texas won independence at the Battle of San Jacinto.

Key Terms and People

Runaway Scrape a movement of settlers to avoid advancing Mexican forces

Battle of Refugio a fight in which the Texans were defeated and captured

James Fannin a colonel whose outnumbered forces surrendered to Mexican troops outside of Goliad and were executed

Battle of Coleto a battle near Goliad during which the Texans were severely outnumbered and Colonel Fannin decided to surrender

Goliad Massacre a massacre of more than 400 Texas prisoners

Francita Alavez a Mexican woman who helped Texans escape during the Goliad Massacre, known as the Angel of Goliad

Battle of San Jacinto a surprise attack in which Santa Anna was captured and Texas won its independence

Section Summary
THE RUNAWAY SCRAPE

Sam Houston left Washington-on-the-Brazos for Gonzales, where he learned of the defeat at the Alamo. Word spread that Santa Anna was heading to Gonzales. Scouts were sent to learn where Santa Anna's forces were. The scouts returned with details of the Alamo and with a few survivors. They confirmed that the Mexican army was advancing on them. Houston ordered a retreat of the army and burned the town of Gonzales. Many civilians followed the army. This movement of settlers became known as the **Runaway Scrape**. Conditions were made worse by rains and flooding. Many settlers died from disease during the Runaway Scrape.

How did the Texas army use scouts?
_____
_____
_____

FANNIN'S SURRENDER AT GOLIAD

General Urrea continued up the Texas coast and
defeated the Texans at the **Battle of Refugio**. Urrea
then moved on to Goliad, where Colonel **James
Fannin** was ordered to withdraw troops. Fannin did
not act soon enough, giving Urrea time to advance.
Soon after Fannin left Goliad, he met Urrea's forces
in the **Battle of Coleto.** The Texans were
outnumbered and Fannin surrendered. Urrea's
troops executed more than 400 Texan prisoners.
Francita Alavez, a traveler with the Mexican army,
helped some people escape. However, only a few
prisoners avoided death in the **Goliad Massacre**.

> Why did Sam Houston order the withdrawal of troops in Goliad?
> _____
> _____
> _____

HOUSTON PREPARES THE TROOPS

Sam Houston led the army eastward believing that the
Texas force was too small and untrained to defeat
Santa Anna's. Houston settled his men at a plantation
20 miles north of San Felipe, where he trained and
drilled his troops. They also received two cannons. On
April 12, 1836, Houston's troops marched to
Harrisburg and prepared to meet Santa Anna.

THE BATTLE OF SAN JACINTO

On April 20 the Texans camped in a grove of trees
near a field. The Mexican troops moved to a nearby
position that was vulnerable to the Texans. When the
Mexican army received more troops, Houston decided
to launch a major attack. He assembled soldiers that
afternoon and ordered them to cross the field and surprise
the Mexican troops. The **Battle of San Jacinto** lasted
about 18 minutes. Some 630 Mexican soldiers were killed,
while only nine Texas soldiers were killed or died from
their wounds. Santa Anna was captured the next day. With
this victory, Texas had won its independence from
Mexico.

> What do you think was the biggest factor in the victory at San Jacinto?
> _____
> _____
> _____

CHALLENGE ACTIVITY

Critical Thinking: Cause and Effect Create a
visual showing a series of cause-and-effect
relationships that led to victory at San Jacinto.

Runaway Scrape	Battle of Refugio	James Fannin
Battle of Coleto	Goliad Massacre	Francita Alavez
Battle of San Jacinto		

DIRECTIONS Read each sentence and circle the term in the word pair that best completes each sentence.

1. (Francita Alavez/James Fannin) helped a few Texas prisoners escape execution at the Goliad Massacre.

2. General Santa Anna won the (Battle of San Jacinto/Battle of Refugio) before advancing quickly to seize Texas troops at Goliad.

3. Many Texans died from disease during the (Battle of Coleto /Runaway Scrape).

4. Following their surrender at the (Battle of Coleto/Goliad Massacre) prisoners were executed in Goliad.

DIRECTIONS Choose five of the words from the word bank. On the lines below, use these words to write a summary of what you have learned in this section.

_____

_____

_____

_____

_____

_____

_____

_____

_____

_____

A New Nation

Section 1

MAIN IDEAS
1. Under the Treaties of Velasco, Mexico would recognize Texas independence, but the treaties were not honored.
2. Texas held its first national elections in 1836.

Key Terms and People

Treaties of Velasco two treaties signed in 1836 that were meant to make Mexico agree to recognize that Texas was independent

annexation the formal joining of one political region to another

Mirabeau B. Lamar Texas vice president in 1836 and hero of San Jacinto

Section Summary
THE TREATIES OF VELASCO

Mexican leaders refused to recognize the Texas Revolution's end. However, the captured Antonio López de Santa Anna and Texas ad interim president David G. Burnet signed the two **Treaties of Velasco**. Under the first treaty, the war between Mexico and Texas was officially ended, and Texas was declared independent. The second treaty was secret. It said that Santa Anna would be released. In exchange, Santa Anna agreed to try to persuade Mexican leaders to recognize Texas independence. It also set the Rio Grande as the border between Texas and Mexico.

What did Mexico refuse to recognize?
_____
_____
_____

Texans did not follow through on their part of the treaty. The Texas government chose to send Santa Anna to Washington, DC, rather than back to Mexico. The official purpose of the Washington trip was to negotiate a lasting peace between Texas and Mexico, but nothing came of it. This violated the treaties. At the same time, Mexico refused to recognize the public treaty because Santa Anna had signed it while a prisoner.

How were the Treaties of Velasco violated?
_____
_____

THE ELECTION OF 1836

In 1836, the Republic of Texas formed a new government. Voters elected Sam Houston as president and **Mirabeau B. Lamar** as vice president. They approved the Constitution of 1836, and decided to pursue **annexation** to the United States.

> **What four decisions were made in the election of 1836?**
> _____
> _____
> _____

CHALLENGE ACTIVITY

Critical Thinking: Mapping. Locate the Rio Grande on a map. List the Texas cities that currently border Mexico along the Rio Grande.

| annexation | Mirabeau B. Lamar | Treaties of Velasco |

DIRECTIONS On the lines below, use all the words in the Word Bank
to write a summary of what you have learned in the section.

_____

_____

_____

_____

_____

_____

_____

_____

_____

_____

_____

_____

_____

_____

_____

_____

_____

_____

_____

_____

A New Nation

 MAIN IDEAS

1. As president, Sam Houston created a cabinet to help him resolve issues facing the Republic.

2. Problems with military discipline, debt, and public land faced the first Houston administration.

3. President Houston wanted to protect the rights of American Indians in Texas.

Key Terms

cabinet trusted advisers who help the president

Texas Rangers a defense force that tried to keep peace along the frontier; established on November 24, 1835

Texas Navy official navy of the Republic of Texas created to protect and defend the coastline of Texas

expenditures spending

revenue income

ratify approve

Chief Bowles a Cherokee leader

Section Summary

HOUSTON'S ADMINISTRATION

Sam Houston became president of the Republic of Texas on October 22, 1836. Houston's presidential goals were to establish peace with American Indians, to stay on guard against Mexico, and to see Texas annexed to the United States. Houston appointed trusted advisers to his **cabinet**. Soon after, a court system was established.

> **What were Sam Houston's goals as president?**
> _____
> _____
> _____

DEFINING TEXAS

The Republic of Texas needed to establish clear land boundaries and a permanent capital. The Texas Congress claimed the Rio Grande as the southern and western boundary of Texas, but Mexico and many Texans did not recognize this boundary. In late 1836, Congress chose Houston as the new

> **What was the boundary that the Texas Congress claimed divided Texas and Mexico?**
> _____
> _____

capital. In 1837, the United States recognized Texas
as an independent nation.

HOUSTON AND ARMY UNREST

Unrest and risky behavior in the Republic of Texas
army forced Sam Houston to place most of the
troops on leave. Houston relied instead on militia
companies and the **Texas Rangers** for defense. The
Texas Navy also had some difficulties. Navy ships
were lost and destroyed, and Houston's
administration was unable to pay for repairs.

> **Why did Houston place
> most of his army troops on
> leave?**
> _____
> _____
> _____

ECONOMIC POLICIES

The Republic of Texas suffered serious economic
problems. Its **expenditures** far exceeded its
revenue. Debt rose and expenses increased. The
United States had a financial crisis in 1837.
Business slowed down between Texas and the
United States and goods were scarce.

> **What effect did the U.S.
> financial crisis have on the
> Republic of Texas?**
> _____
> _____
> _____

LAND POLICY UNDER HOUSTON

Officials hoped to help the economy by increasing
settlement and charging tax on the land to bring in
revenue. Texas gave land to settlers and contracts to
agents to settle immigrants in Texas.

HOUSTON'S AMERICAN INDIAN POLICY

Houston and Congress developed an American
Indian policy to reduce conflict and to protect
settlers. The policy established a line of forts along
the frontier and encouraged trade with American
Indians. Houston believed that Indians and settlers
could live in peace, but most Texans disagreed.
Chief Bowles, a Cherokee leader, tried to help
Houston's administration establish peaceful
relations with the Plains Indians.

CHALLENGE ACTIVITY

Critical Thinking: Drawing Inferences How did
increasing settlement in Texas affect the economy?
Explain.

cabinet	Texas Rangers	Texas Navy	expenditures
revenue	ratify	Chief Bowles	

DIRECTIONS On the line provided before each statement, write **T** if a statement is true and **F** if a statement is false. If the statement is false, write a corrected statement on the line after the false statement.

_____ 1. Money that is spent is <u>revenue</u>.

_____

_____ 2. <u>Chief Bowles</u> was a leader of the Cherokees and an ally of Sam Houston.

_____

_____ 3. A <u>cabinet</u> is a group of trusted advisors that supports the president.

_____

_____ 4. The <u>Texas Navy</u> is a defense force that kept peace along the frontier.

_____

_____ 5. When a government takes in money, the amount of money collected is called <u>expenditures</u>.

_____

_____ 6. To <u>ratify</u> something is to disapprove of something.

_____

_____ 7. The <u>Texas Rangers</u> protected and defended the coastline of Texas.

_____

A New Nation

MAIN IDEAS

1. As president, Mirabeau Lamar tried to create a public education system in Texas.
2. Lamar's administration faced great financial challenges.
3. Under Lamar, Texas adopted a harsh policy toward American Indians.

Key Terms and People

charter a document granting permission to operate

Edwin Waller a judge who arrived in Austin to lay out streets and begin building government offices

capitol a building in which government officials meet

homestead law a law that protected a family's home and up to 50 acres of land from being sold to pay off debt

redbacks new paper money certificates that were issued by the Republic

Battle of the Neches a battle between Texans and Cherokees that took place near the Neches River after the Cherokees refused to leave Texas when Lamar ordered them to

Council House Fight a fight between Texans and Comanches that broke out at the Council House in San Antonio after an agreement to return captured Texans was not fulfilled

Battle of Plum Creek a Texas battle of revenge against Comanches by volunteers, soldiers, and Texas Rangers

Section Summary

LAMAR IN OFFICE

In 1838 Texans elected Mirabeau B. Lamar as president. Lamar believed that Texas needed a good education system. Congress passed education acts in 1839 and in 1840. These acts set aside land in each county to support public schools. The government also set aside land for the future establishment of two public universities. Rutersville College was the first college to receive a **charter**.

> **Name the first school to receive a charter.**
>
> _____
>
> _____

A NEW CAPITAL

In 1839 a group appointed by Congress chose Waterloo as the the new state capital. The government renamed this town Austin in honor of Stephen F. Austin. Judge **Edwin Waller** planned streets and built government offices in Austin. A temporary **capitol,** or a building in which government officials meet, was soon completed.

> Who was the capital named after?
> _____
> _____

LAND AND ECONOMIC POLICIES

Congress passed a **homestead law,** which protected a family's home from seizure for debts. The Republic's financial problems worsened. The value of currency fell and the Republic responded by giving out new paper money, called **redbacks.**

LAMAR'S AMERICAN INDIAN POLICY

Texas soldiers attempted to remove the Cherokees, killing more than 100 Cherokees in the **Battle of the Neches.** After a series of conflicts with the army, the Comanches agreed to peace talks, but fighting soon broke out. In the **Council House Fight,** more than 35 Comanches were killed. Comanches struck at several Texas settlements, killing more than 20 settlers. A force of volunteers, regular soldiers, and Texas Rangers searched for those involved in the raid. During the **Battle of Plum Creek** more than 130 Comanches were killed. One Texan was killed, and seven were wounded.

> Underline the names of the battles that took place under Lamar's leadership. Explain why they took place.
> _____
> _____
> _____
> _____

THE RESULTS OF LAMAR'S POLICIES

Following additional conflicts, the Comanches moved farther north out of range of Texas forces. Lamar's American Indian policy was very expensive. During his term, the Republic's debt rose from $3.3 million to more than $8 million.

CHALLENGE ACTIVITY

Critical Thinking: Compare and Contrast Write a paragraph in which you compare and contrast the American Indian policies of Lamar and Houston.

charter	Edwin Waller	capitol	homestead law
redbacks	Battle of Neches	Council House Fight	Battle of Plum Creek

DIRECTIONS Read each sentence and circle the term in the word pair that best completes each sentence.

1. (Edwin Waller/Homestead law) helped plan the building of government offices in Austin.

2. The battle where Texas volunteers, soldiers, and Rangers took revenge on Comanche Indians was the (Battle of Plum Creek/Council House Fight).

3. (Redbacks/Charters) were documents granting schools permission to operate.

4. The (Battle of Neches/capitol) is a building were government officials meet.

5. (Redbacks/Charters) were money certificates issued by the Republic.

6. The (homestead law/Edwin Waller) protected families' homes and land from being sold to pay off debt.

7. The battle caused by the belief that an agreement to return captured Texans was not fulfilled is called the (Battle of Plum Creek/ Council House Fight).

8. The (Battle of Neches/capitol) took place after Lamar ordered the Cherokee Indians to leave Texas, and they refused.

MAIN IDEAS
1. During his second term, Sam Houston tried to reduce the national debt and make peace with Indians.
2. The Regulator-Moderator War was a feud in East Texas.

Key Terms

balanced budget a budget in which spending does not exceed revenue

Treaty of Tehuacana Creek an agreement between Houston and Chief Buffalo Hump of the Penateka Comanches to establish peace and trade

Regulator-Moderator War a feud that began in East Texas in 1840 between Alfred George and Joseph Goodbread over fake land certificates

Section Summary
HOUSTON RETURNS TO OFFICE

In 1841, Texans once again elected Sam Houston as president. Houston hoped to achieve a **balanced budget** by cutting government jobs and salaries, but the Republic's debt continued to rise. Houston had new paper money printed, but the value of this new money quickly fell. Houston established more frontier trading posts to encourage trade with American Indians, and signed peace treaties with various groups. In March 1843 nine Indian groups met with Texas officials at Tehuacana Creek. They agreed to stop fighting. In October 1844 Houston and Chief Buffalo Hump of the Penateka Comanches met and signed the **Treaty of Tehuacana Creek**.

> **What did Houston do to balance the budget? Was he successful? Explain.**
>
> _____
> _____
> _____
> _____

THE REGULATOR-MODERATOR WAR

While relations with Texas Indians were improving, violence broke out among settlers in East Texas. This region bordered the old Neutral Ground, where many bandits and outlaws had moved. In 1840 a feud began between Alfred George and Joseph G. Goodbread over fake land certificates. Two

factions—called the Regulators and the
Moderators—formed around these men. Fighting
broke out and soon escalated beyond local officials'
control. In August 1844 President Houston sent
soldiers to stop the **Regulator-Moderator War**.

CHALLENGE ACTIVITY

Critical Thinking: Sequencing Describe what
Houston did to restore peace and trading between
Texas and Texas Indians.

> **What were the Regulators and Moderators fighting about?**
>
> _____
>
> _____
>
> _____

| balanced budget | Treaty of Tehuacana Creek | Regulator-Moderator War |

DIRECTIONS On the lines below, use all the words in the word bank to write a summary of what you have learned in the section.

_____

_____

_____

_____

_____

_____

_____

_____

_____

_____

_____

_____

_____

_____

_____

_____

_____

_____

Life in the Republic

MAIN IDEAS
1. Immigration caused the population of the Republic of Texas to swell.
2. Most African Americans in the Republic were slaves, but even free African Americans faced challenges.
3. Tejanos and American Indians in the Republic experienced widespread discrimination.

Key Terms

Greenbury Logan former slave who fought in the Revolution and later petitioned Congress for permission to stay in Texas

Ashworth Act bill passed by Congress that allowed the Ashworths and all free African Americans who were in Texas at the time of the Texas Declaration of Independence to stay

Córdova Rebellion uprising led by Tejano Vincente Córdova to fight for Tejano rights

José Antonio Navarro Tejano leader who signed the Texas Declaration of Independence and served in the Texas Congress

Section Summary

A GROWING POPULATION

To encourage immigration, the Republic of Texas extended land grants to more individuals. From 1836 to 1847, the population increased by nearly 100,000. Most immigrants were from the southern United States.

> **Why were immigrants drawn to Texas?**
> _____

AFRICAN AMERICANS

Many slaveholders were attracted to Texas because slavery was legal. The number of slaves in Texas rose from 5,000 in 1836 to at least 30,000 by 1845. Life for slaves was hard. Slaves had no legal right to private property, to marriage, or to having a family. Almost every slave lived under threat of physical punishment.

In 1840 Congress outlawed the immigration of free African Americans to Texas. Even veterans like **Greenbury Logan,** a former slave, risked being

> **Why were slaveholders attracted to Texas?**
> _____

forced to leave. He petitioned the Texas Congress for permission to stay.

In November 1840, three petitions were presented to Congress on behalf of the Ashworth family. In response, Congress passed the **Ashworth Act,** which allowed the Ashworths and all free African Americans who were in Texas at the time of the Texas Declaration of Independence to stay.

The free African Americans who stayed still faced prejudice and persecution. As a result, many chose to leave. By 1850 fewer than 400 free African Americans lived in Texas.

> Underline what the Ashworth Act allowed.

TEJANOS IN THE REPUBLIC

Tejanos often faced hostility from new U.S. immigrants. These settlers thought of Tejanos as Mexican and thought of Mexico as an enemy. In 1838 a group of Tejanos in Nacogdoches, led by Vicente Córdova, took up arms in the **Córdova Rebellion.** President Houston ordered the rebels to return home, but they declared they would fight for their rights. Córdova fled to Mexico and 33 Tejanos were arrested and tried for treason.

José Antonio Navarro, a signer of the Texas Declaration of Independence, served in the Republic's Congress. Tejanos maintained their traditions, to which they added traditions of other groups, creating a unique Texas-Mexican culture.

TEXAS INDIANS

Because bands of independent American Indians were constantly on the move, it was difficult to estimate how many Indians lived in the Texas Republic. Few Texans were interested in living peacefully with the Indians. As a result, the Indians faced discrimination.

> Why is it difficult to know how many American Indians lived in the Texas Republic?
>
> _____

CHALLENGE ACTIVITY

Critical Thinking: Identifying What problems did many minorities face in the new Republic of Texas?

| Greenbury Logan | Ashworth Act | Córdova Rebellion | José Antonio Navarro |

DIRECTIONS Read each sentence and circle the term in the word pair that best completes each sentence.

1. A free African American named (Córdova/Greenbury Logan) had fought in the Revolution.

2. Because of the (Ashworth Act/Córdova Rebellion), free African Americans who were in Texas at the time of the Texas Declaration of Independence were allowed to stay.

3. The (Ashworth Act/Córdova Rebellion) was started by Tejanos who wanted to stand up for their rights.

4. (José Antonio Navarro/Vicente Córdova) started the Córdova Rebellion.

DIRECTIONS Write two adjectives or descriptive phrases that describe each term given.

5. Greenbury Logan _____

6. José Antonio Navarro _____

Life in the Republic

 MAIN IDEAS

1. In the 1840s people moved to Texas from Germany, France, Ireland, and other parts of Europe.
2. The legacy of immigrants can still be seen in the names, architecture, foods, and arts of the places they settled.

Key People

Prince Carl of Solms-Braunfels a German immigrant who acquired lands in the Hill Country and established a port for incoming settlers

John O. Meusebach formerly Baron Otfried Hans Freiherr von Meusebach, the successor to Prince Carl

Section Summary

GERMANS SETTLE IN CENTRAL TEXAS

During the 1830s and 1840s, Germans were the largest European group to immigrate to Texas. A group of Germans formed the German Emigration Company, or Adelsverein. Its members hoped to profit by encouraging Germans to settle in Texas. After acquiring land in the Hill Country, the company sent **Prince Carl of Solms-Braunfels** to Texas in 1844.

Prince Carl established a port—later known as Indianola—for incoming settlers. In 1845 the prince established New Braunfels. When Prince Carl returned home months later, Baron Otfried Hans Freiherr von Meusebach replaced him. In Texas, the baron changed his name to **John O. Meusebach** and continued the company's work. By 1847 the German Emigration Company had sent more than 7,000 immigrants to Texas. Some stayed in towns while others moved into the Hill Country. Today many Hill Country towns reflect German traditions in their architecture, churches, food, and language.

> **What was the mission of the German Emigration Company?**
>
> _____
>
> _____

> **Who replaced Prince Carl?**
>
> _____

OTHER EUROPEAN IMMIGRANTS

In 1840 Texas and France signed a treaty that encouraged French immigration. A few years later, Henri Castro brought one of the first groups of French settlers to Texas. Castro founded the town of Castroville in 1844. The cultural traditions of these French immigrants can still be seen in the architecture, churches, and customs of Castroville and nearby towns.

During the 1820s several Irishmen had received *empresario* contracts. Many Irish immigrants fought for Texas during the Revolution. Irish settlers continued to come to Texas after the Revolution, seeking economic opportunity. By 1850 there were more than 1,400 Irish settlers throughout Texas.

Some Polish and Czech immigrants came to Texas, settling in South and Central Texas. Polish and Czech immigration later increased as difficult economic and political conditions pushed many from their homelands. Like other immigrants, they left their mark on the areas in which they lived.

Underline where the cultural traditions of French immigrants can still be found.

Why were many Polish and Czech immigrants pushed from their homelands? _____ _____

CHALLENGE ACTIVITY

Critical Thinking: Drawing Inferences Why did many Europeans come to the Republic?

DIRECTIONS On the line provided before each statement, write **T** if a statement is true and **F** if a statement is false. If the statement is false, write a corrected statement on the line after the false statement.

_____ 1. Prince Carl of Solms-Braunfels continued the work done by John O. Meusebach.

_____

_____ 2. John O. Meusebach was a prince sent to Texas by a group of German businesspeople to form the German Emigration Company.

_____

_____ 3. Prince Carl of Solms-Braunfels established a port for incoming settlers called Indianola.

_____

_____ 4. Baron Otfried Hans Freiherr von Meusebach changed his name to John O. Meusebach when he arrived in Texas.

_____

Life in the Republic

MAIN IDEAS
1. Most people in the Republic of Texas lived on farms or ranches, though some lived in towns.
2. Games, literature, and art provided leisure activities.
3. Churches and schools were social centers.

Key Terms and People

land speculators people who buy large amounts of land in hopes of selling it for great profits

denominations religious groups with similar beliefs

circuit riders traveling preachers

academies schools that offer classes at the high school level

Théodore Gentilz French painter and surveyor who is known for his scenes of Texas life

Section Summary
FARMING, TOWNS, AND TRANSPORTATION

Most Texans were farmers and ranchers. Their farms varied in size, but most were small family farms. Farmers cleared acres of land to build homesteads, plant crops, and create pastures for grazing animals. Texas farmers mostly grew food for their own needs, but they often produced small cash crops.

Most cattle ranchers raised animals for their own use or to sell. Ranchers supplied townspeople and farmers with food, hides, and other materials. A few ranchers drove their cattle to New Orleans to sell them in markets there.

Most of the jobs in the Republic's small towns related to agriculture. Doctors, shopkeepers, blacksmiths, and bankers operated in the largest towns. **Land speculators** were people who bought large amounts of land in hopes of making profits. They would sell small lots of the land at higher prices to new settlers. Sometimes they could not attract enough settlers to buy their land.

> How did most people in Texas make a living?
>
> _____
> _____

Travel between towns was difficult. Texas roads were poor, particularly in bad weather. Texans used rivers for transporting goods and people. By the 1840s steamboats shipped products from Texas farms and brought in goods for settlers. The lack of a good transportation system slowed the growth of business and towns.

Why were steamboats used to transport goods?
_____
_____

LEISURE, LITERATURE, AND ART

Texans enjoyed a number of leisure activities. Some combined socializing and work, such as building houses for newcomers. Some Texans enjoyed literature and art, although both were scarce on the Texas frontier. Most books published in the Republic dealt with its history or travel. Artists also lived in Texas. For example, French painter and surveyor **Théodore Gentilz** came to Texas with Henri Castro. Gentilz is known for his scenes of Texas life.

CHURCHES AND SCHOOLS

With Roman Catholicism no longer the official state religion, many Protestant **denominations**—organized religious groups with similar beliefs—built churches. The Methodist Church was the largest denomination in the Republic. Jews from central and eastern Europe lived across Texas. Churches and temples served as the religious and social centers of most communities. **Circuit riders,** or traveling preachers, served regions on the frontier. Churches also ran schools. Although President Lamar wanted Texas to establish a system of public education, funds were scarce. Several towns established private **academies**—schools that offered classes at the high school level.

Underline the name of the largest denomination in Texas.

CHALLENGE ACTIVITY

Critical Thinking: Analyzing Information Why were churches important to communities during the years of the Republic?

land speculators	denominations	circuit riders	academies
Théodore Gentilz	Methodists		

DIRECTIONS Read each sentence and circle the term from the word pair that best completes each sentence.

1. People who bought large amounts of land to sell as smaller plots with higher prices were called (circuit riders/land speculators).

2. Schools that offered classes at the high school level were called (academies/denominations).

3. Painters such as (Théodore Gentilz/Methodists) were usually new immigrants.

4. (Circuit riders/Methodists) traveled to serve regions on the frontier.

DIRECTIONS Write two adjectives or descriptive phrases that describe each term given.

5. denominations_____

6. circuit riders _____

7. academies _____

8. land speculators_____

Texas Faces Foreign Challenges

MAIN IDEAS

1. The Republic of Texas sought foreign recognition in part to ease the threat of war with Mexico.

2. Many Texans favored joining the United States.

3. Several countries recognized Texas independence.

Key Terms

foreign relations dealings with other countries

diplomatic recognition the acknowledgment by one government that another government exists

Section Summary

THE QUEST FOR TEXAS STATEHOOD

One of the Republic's greatest challenges in **foreign relations**—official dealings with other countries— was its relationship with Mexico. Mexico did not accept Texas independence. Texas was therefore eager to have other nations recognize, or officially accept, its status as an independent country. This would lessen the chance of another war with Mexico, and it would also encourage immigration to Texas. Recognition would also lead to increased foreign trade and loans. Some Texans hoped that recognition from the United States might pave the way for annexation of Texas. But U.S. officials were hesitant to recognize Texas.

Leaders, including Sam Houston, wanted more than just **diplomatic recognition.** They hoped Texas could join the United States as a new state. Diplomatic recognition is the acknowledgement by one government that another government exists.

But U.S. officials were hesitant to recognize Texas. In 1836 a U.S. agent wrote that the Republic had too much debt, too small a population, and too powerful an enemy—Mexico.

> Why was it important that Mexico recognize Texas as an independent country?
>
> _____
> _____
> _____

Slavery was another obstacle to annexation. In the United States, northerners who were opposed to slavery argued against statehood for Texas, refusing to add another state that allowed slavery.

FOREIGN RECOGNITION

In his last official act as president, Andrew Jackson appointed a minister, Alcée Louis La Branche, to Texas in 1837. The Republic sent Memucan Hunt as its first official representative to Washington.

However, U.S. recognition did not lead to annexation. Texas leaders withdrew their request for annexation. In 1837 Houston sent James Pinckney Henderson to Europe to try to gain recognition for Texas. Because of concerns about U.S. expansion, many European nations wanted Texas to stay independent.

In September 1839 France became the first European nation to recognize Texas. Recognition from Great Britain, Belgium, and the Netherlands followed. Mexico continued to refuse to recognize Texas.

> Why did many European nations want Texas to remain independent?
>
> _____
>
> _____
>
> _____

CHALLENGE ACTIVITY

Critical Thinking: Evaluating What were the main factors that stood between Texas and foreign recognition?

DIRECTIONS Read each sentence below and circle the term from the word pair that best completes each sentence.

1. The Republic's relationship with Mexico was a key issue in its early (foreign relations/diplomatic recognition).

2. The Republic's leaders were hoping for (foreign relations/diplomatic recognition) by the United States and other countries.

DIRECTIONS Write two adjectives or descriptive phrases that describe each term given.

3. foreign relations _____

4. diplomatic recognition _____

Texas Faces Foreign Challenges

Section 2

MAIN IDEAS

1. President Lamar hoped to add Santa Fe to Texas.
2. The Mexican army raided several targets in Texas.
3. Mexico finally recognized the Texas Republic in 1845.

Key Terms and People

Santa Fe expedition an expedition launched by President Lamar to create a trade route between Texas and Santa Fe

Edwin W Moore Texas Navy officer sent by Lamar to the Yucatán coast to help rebels

Mary Maverick San Antonio resident whose diary is a source of information about Texas life

Jack Coffee Hays volunteer Texas Ranger who forced General Woll to retreat to Mexico

Archives War conflict that arose when Austin residents opposed the transfer of government archives to Washington-on-the-Brazos in 1842

Mier expedition invasion of Mier, Mexico led by Colonel William S. Fisher

Section Summary

THE SANTA FE EXPEDITION

President Lamar wanted to secure the land east of the Rio Grande and gain access to the trade moving along the Santa Fe Trail. In June 1841 Lamar launched the **Santa Fe expedition**—an expedition of about 320 people to Santa Fe to take control of the region. When the Texans reached New Mexico, they were captured by Mexican troops and marched 1,200 miles to Mexico City, where they were imprisoned. The expedition was a failure and set the stage for years of conflict between Texas and Mexico.

> **What was the purpose of the Santa Fe expedition?**
>
> _____
> _____
> _____

THE TEXAS NAVY

In spite of the expedition's failure, Lamar continued his campaign against Mexico. He sent the Texas Navy, under **Edwin W. Moore,** to the Yucatán coast to help rebels who were fighting against the Mexican government. The rebels paid Texas $8,000 a month for the use of the navy. When Sam Houston began his second term as president in 1841, he ordered the navy to return home.

THE ARCHIVES WAR

In September 1842, General Adrián Woll and 1,400 soldiers captured San Antonio. Resident **Mary Maverick** described the morning invasion in her diary, a major source of information about Texas life at the time. Ranger **Jack Coffee Hays** and his volunteer force met Woll and forced him to retreat. Fearing an attack on Austin, President Houston ordered the government archives to be moved to Washington-on-the-Brazos. Afraid their city would no longer be the capital, Austin residents opposed the move. They fired at officials who were loading documents onto wagons. This conflict—the **Archives War**—ended with the documents back in Austin.

> Why were Austin citizens upset at Houston's orders to move the archives?
>
> _____
>
> _____
>
> _____

THE MIER EXPEDITION

In November President Houston ordered General Alexander Somervell to the Rio Grande to recapture prisoners taken by General Woll. When Somervell reached the Rio Grande, he realized that he did not have enough supplies or troops. He ordered his troops home, but about 300 of them disobeyed orders. Led by Colonel William S. Fisher and known as the **Mier expedition,** the Texans entered the Mexican town of Mier and demanded supplies. Confronted by Mexican soldiers, the Texans surrendered.

Peace was slowly restored between Texas and Mexico. In 1845 a British diplomat presented a document to Mexican officials. If the Mexican government formally acknowledged the Republic of Texas, Texas would not join the United States. By the time Mexico agreed to recognize Texas independence, however, it was too late. The Texans had decided in favor of annexation.

CHALLENGE ACTIVITY

Critical Thinking: Evaluating What factors eventually led to Mexico recognizing Texas independence?

| Santa Fe expedition | Edwin W. Moore | Mary Maverick |
| Jack Coffee Hays | Archives war | Mier expedition |

DIRECTIONS On the line provided before each statement, write **T** if a statement is true and **F** if a statement is false. If the statement is false, rewrite the sentence to make a true statement.

_____ 1. Led by Colonel William S. Fisher, the Mier expedition led to a defeat for Texas at the hands of the Mexican troops.

_____

_____ 2. Jack Coffee Hays led the Texas Navy in 1841.

_____

_____ 3. Mary Maverick's diary described life in Austin in the 1800s.

_____

_____ 4. The Santa Fe expedition was a success.

_____

_____ 5. The Archives War was a conflict that took place in Austin in 1842.

_____

_____ 6. Edwin W. Moore defeated General Woll in 1842.

_____

MAIN IDEAS

1. Anson Jones was elected president of the Republic of Texas in 1844.
2. During Jones's presidency, Texans increased their calls for annexation with the United States.

Key Person

Anson Jones the fourth and last president of the Republic of Texas

Section Summary

PRESIDENT ANSON JONES

In the election of 1844, the Republic was divided. Newspapers printed harsh criticisms of the candidates for president, Vice President Edward Burleson and **Anson Jones.** Jones had served as secretary of state under Houston. Because of their shared views, Jones received Houston's support in the election. Mirabeau B. Lamar supported Burleson.

Jones easily defeated Burleson in the election. As president, Jones inherited the Republic's economic problems. He tried to control the debt by limiting government spending. He also continued to work for peace with Texas Indians, a policy that was also aimed at reducing spending. As annexation seemed more likely, the value of Texas currency began to climb. By 1845 the value of Texas currency in many parts of the Republic had become equal to that of U.S. currency.

| Underline the names of the two presidential candidates. |

| How did Jones try to control the debt? |
| _____ |
| _____ |
| _____ |

TEXANS DEBATE ANNEXATION

Although economic problems were a major concern, President Jones worried more about the prospects of annexation. At first, Jones kept silent on the issue. Many Texans urged Jones to take action on the issue. Jones wanted Texans to have the option of becoming part of the United States or of maintaining independence. Independence

| What did Jones want for Texas? |
| _____ |
| _____ |
| _____ |

depended on peaceful relations with Mexico, so he tried to obtain Mexico's recognition.

Few Texans were interested in negotiating with Mexico. As the demand for a convention to decide the issue of annexation grew stronger, word arrived that Mexico might soon recognize Texas. Texans debated whether their country should stay independent or continue to seek annexation.

CHALLENGE ACTIVITY
Critical Thinking: Evaluating Why did President Jones want to wait on the issue of annexation?

DIRECTIONS On the line provided before each statement, write **T** if a statement is true and **F** if a statement is false. If the statement is false, write a corrected statement on the line after the false statement.

_____ 1. Anson Jones won the presidential election in 1844.

_____

_____ 2. Anson Jones received Houston's support in the election.

_____

_____ 3. Jones wanted Texas to have the option of being independent.

_____

_____ 4. Texans wanted Jones to be decisive on the issue of annexation.

_____

Texas Joins the United States

MAIN IDEAS
1. Support for annexation in the United States was divided over the issue of slavery.
2. Texas became a state in 1845.

Key Terms and People

manifest destiny belief that the United States was meant to expand all the way across North America to the Pacific, including Texas

Jane McManus Cazneau journalist who helped sway opinion in the North in favor of annexation

political parties groups who help elect officials and influence government policies

joint resolution formal expression of intent

Convention of 1845 convention called by President Anson Jones to consider annexation

Texas Admission Act the act by which Texas became the 28th state in 1845

Section Summary
THE TREATY TO ANNEX TEXAS

Texans and people in the United States continued to debate annexation. Americans were divided on the issue largely along regional lines. The North had developed an economy based on commerce and manufacturing. The South relied on agriculture and slave labor. Many northerners opposed slavery and did not want Texas to be admitted to the Union as a slave state. Doing so would tip the balance of power in Congress toward the South. Most southerners wanted Texas to join the Union. U.S. President John Tyler, a southerner, favored annexation. In 1844, Tyler sent an annexation treaty to the U.S. Senate for approval. The Senate rejected it.

At the time many U.S. settlers were moving westward. Many Americans believed that their country was meant to expand across North America. This belief became known as **manifest destiny**.

> Why did many northerners not want Texas to be admitted to the Union?
>
> _____
> _____
> _____
> _____

Newspaper columnist **Jane McManus Cazneau** helped turn northern opinion in favor of annexation.

THE ANNEXATION RESOLUTION

The annexation treaty and manifest destiny became important issues in the U.S. presidential election of 1844. The **political parties** differed on these issues. Political parties are groups who help elect officials and influence government policies. The Democratic Party nominated, or chose, as its candidate James K. Polk. Polk favored annexation. His opponent was Whig Party candidate Henry Clay, who at first opposed annexation. Polk won the election. President Tyler considered Polk's victory a sign of the public's approval of annexation. Tyler therefore requested that both houses of Congress pass a **joint resolution**, or formal expression of intent, for annexation. In February 1845 the U.S. Congress passed the joint resolution to annex Texas.

> Who were the two main political parties in the 1844 election?
>
> _____
>
> _____
>
> _____

TEXAS ENTERS THE UNITED STATES

To be admitted as a state, Texas had to approve annexation and then write a new constitution. The new state could keep its public lands, but some would have to be sold to pay the public debt. Texas president Anson Jones called for a convention to consider annexation. The delegates to the **Convention of 1845** quickly approved annexation. They then worked on a new constitution. On October 13, Texas voters approved annexation and the new constitution. On December 29, 1845, President Polk signed the **Texas Admission Act**, making Texas the 28th state.

> What did Texas have to do to be admitted as a new state?
>
> _____
>
> _____
>
> _____

CHALLENGE ACTIVITY

Critical Thinking: Sequencing Make a time line of events leading up to the **Texas Admission Act** of 1845.

| manifest destiny | Jane McManus Cazneau | political parties |
| joint resolution | Convention of 1845 | Texas Admission Act |

DIRECTIONS Use each of the words in the word bank to write a summary of what you learned in this section.

_____

_____

_____

_____

_____

_____

_____

_____

_____

_____

_____

_____

_____

_____

_____

_____

_____

Section 2

MAIN IDEAS
1. The Convention of 1845 created a new state constitution for Texas.
2. The state constitution set up a new government and established protections for citizens and the government.

Key Terms and People

James Pinckney Henderson first governor of the state of Texas

Thomas J. Rusk president of the Convention of 1845

biennial every two years

corporations companies that sell shares of ownership to investors to raise money

Section Summary

THE CONVENTION OF 1845

On February 19, 1846, President Anson Jones formally turned the Texas government over to **James Pinckney Henderson**, the state's first governor. When the Convention of 1845 had begun, delegates chose **Thomas J. Rusk** as convention president. The only Tejano delegate, José Antonio Navarro, was also the only native Texan at the convention. The delegates used the constitutions of the United States, the Republic of Texas, and the state of Louisiana as models.

> **Which constitutions were used as models for Texas?**
> _____
> _____
> _____
> _____

THE CONSTITUTION OF 1845

The constitution divided the Texas government into three branches. The governor headed the executive branch and served a two-year term. The legislative branch consisted of a senate and a house of representatives. The state legislature met in **biennial** sessions, once every two years. The judicial branch consisted of the Supreme Court and the district courts. Not everyone could vote. Only white and Tejano men 21 years of age or older were allowed to cast ballots. The new state constitution continued to protect slavery. It also protected

> **What three branches was the Texas government divided into by the constitution?**
> _____
> _____
> _____
> _____

homesteads, or families' homes and lands up to 200 acres each, from creditors. It also banned banks because most Texans distrusted them.

Corporations, or companies that sell shares of ownership to investors to raise money, needed the legislature's permission to operate in Texas.

THE FIRST STATE ELECTION

The first state election was held on December 15, 1845. **James Pinckney Henderson** won the governor's race. State officials took office on February 19, 1846. The daily operations of government were transferred from the Republic to the state. The state legislature chose Sam Houston and **Thomas J. Rusk** to represent Texas in the U.S. Senate

CHALLENGE ACTIVITY

Critical Thinking: Summarizing Draw a diagram to represent the three branches of the Texas constitution established in 1845.

| James Pinckney Henderson | biennial |
| Thomas J. Rusk | corporations |

DIRECTIONS On the line provided before each statement, write **T** if a statement is true and **F** if a statement is false. If the statement is false, write a corrected statement on the line after the false statement.

_____ 1. James Pinckney Henderson was the last President of the Texas Republic.

_____

_____ 2. Thomas J. Rusk was chosen to represent Texas in the U.S. Senate.

_____

_____ 3. The executive branch met on a biennial basis.

_____

_____ 4. Corporations were banned by the Texas Constitution of 1845.

_____

DIRECTIONS Write two adjectives or descriptive phrases that describe the term given.

5. The Convention of 1845 _____

6. The judicial branch _____

Texas Joins the United States

MAIN IDEAS
1. Political parties became active in Texas for the first time after annexation.
2. Texas used its public lands to pay off its remaining debt, to promote education, and to improve life.

Key Terms and People

Democratic Party especially popular in Texas, this political party generally represented the views of farmers and small business owners

Republican Party political party that believed that slavery should be banned in all states and territories of the United States

Know-Nothing Party political party whose members supported slavery and wanted to keep immigrants and Catholics out of government

Elisha M. Pease elected Governor in 1853

Section Summary

POLITICAL PARTIES

In the late 1840s Texans started to join political parties that had been organized in the United States. The **Democratic Party** generally represented the views of farmers and small business owners. The party was very strong in Texas and the South. Some Texans supported the Whig Party, the other major U.S. political party. Whigs supported banking and large business interests. In the mid-1850s the Whig Party collapsed when its members became divided over the slavery issue. Many Whigs joined the **Republican Party**. Republicans believed that slavery should not be allowed anywhere in the United States. In the mid-1850s the American Party—commonly called the **Know-Nothing Party**— briefly appeared. This party supported slavery and wanted to keep immigrants and Catholics out of government. Most Texans did not support the Know-Nothing Party.

> **Which party did most Texans support?**
>
> _____
> _____
> _____
> _____

EARLY GOVERNORS OF TEXAS

James Pinckney Henderson served one term in office, and he did not seek re-election. Texas voters chose George T. Wood as their new governor. Wood lost the next election to Peter Hansborough Bell. Like Wood, Bell worked to establish the extent of the state's territory. He resigned to take a seat in the U.S. Congress, and Lieutenant Governor J.W. Henderson became governor for the remaining 28 days of his term. **Elisha M. Pease** was the next governor. Pease was a popular governor who supported education and other reforms. He won a second term in 1855. In 1857 Sam Houston and Hardin Runnels ran for governor. Houston lost in a bitter campaign. However, he defeated Runnels in the 1859 race.

> How many terms did Pease serve as governor?
> _____

DEBTS AND LAND ISSUES

The governors, like the presidents of the Republic, had to deal with the public debt and create a land policy. In 1845 the Republic of Texas owed some $10 million. The annexation resolution made the state responsible for paying this debt by selling public lands. But there were few buyers, and the debt continued to rise. The federal government and Texas developed a plan to eliminate the debt. Texas gave up its claim to 67 million acres of land in present-day Colorado, Kansas, New Mexico, Oklahoma, and Wyoming. In return, the federal government gave Texas money to help pay the debt. The debt was paid off by 1855. The state gave much of its remaining public land to settlers. The state also set aside land for public schools and universities.

> How did Texas pay off its public debt?
> _____
> _____
> _____
> _____

CHALLENGE ACTIVITY

Critical Thinking: Sequencing Name in order the governors of Texas during the 1840s and 1850s.

Guided Reading Workbook

DIRECTIONS Read each sentence below and circle the word from the pair that best completes each sentence.

1. The (Democratic Party/Republican Party) was especially popular in Texas.

2. The (Democratic Party/Know-Nothing Party) supported slavery.

3. The (Republican Party/Know-Nothing Party) believed slavery should be banned.

DIRECTIONS Write two adjectives or descriptive phrases that describe each term or person.

4. Elisha M. Pease _____

5. Know-Nothing Party _____

Western Expansion and Conflict

Section 1

MAIN IDEAS
1. The United States and Mexico went to war over issues involving Texas and California.
2. Many Texans took part in the U.S.–Mexican War.
3. The United States defeated Mexico in 1847.

Key Terms and People

Zachary Taylor sent in 1845 to Texas to protect the state from Mexican attack

John S. "Rip" Ford Ranger recognized for bravery in the war

offensive a major troop advance

Winfield Scott commander of the U.S. army that captured the Mexican port of Veracruz in 1847

Section Summary

FIGHTING BREAKS OUT

The U.S.-Mexican War occurred because many Mexicans feared that the annexation of Texas was just a first step toward the annexation of Mexico. The war is sometimes called the Mexican-American War or the Mexican War.

Another reason for the war involved a dispute over the boundary between Mexico and Texas. Mexico claimed that the Nueces River marked the boundary. The United States supported the Texas claim that the Rio Grande was the boundary. In addition, many U.S. citizens wanted to be paid for damage done to their businesses and property in Mexico. U.S. leaders were angry because Mexico had ordered U.S. settlers to leave the Mexican territory of California.

President James K. Polk sent General **Zachary Taylor** and thousands of soldiers to protect Texas. On April 25, 1846, a force of 1,600 Mexican cavalry attacked more than 60 U.S. soldiers across the Rio Grande. Most of the U.S. troops were

> List two reasons war broke out between the United States and Mexico.
>
> _____
> _____
> _____

captured, and 11 were killed. Congress declared war
on Mexico on May 13, 1846.

TEXANS IN THE WAR

Thousands of volunteers rushed to join the army
when war was declared. Many welcomed a chance
to fight, and get revenge for suffering experienced
during the Revolution. Among them, several Texas
Rangers served as army scouts. **John S. "Rip"
Ford**, John Coffee Hays, and Ben McCulloch were
recognized for their leadership and bravery during
the war. Some Rangers' actions caused problems
when they refused to follow orders. Many Mexicans
feared the Rangers calling them "devils."

> Underline a reason Texans
> volunteered.

A U.S. VICTORY

After winning a few major battles in Texas, Taylor
began an **offensive**. He defeated a Mexican army at
Monterrey and pushed farther into Mexico,
defeating an even larger Mexican army at Buena
Vista. Taylor became a hero but was replaced as
commander by General **Winfield Scott.** In 1847
General Winfield Scott and some 9,000 troops
landed on the Mexican coast near Veracruz. From
there they moved inland and captured Mexico City
by mid-September. Most fighting ended on
September 14, 1847, when U.S. troops raised the
American flag over the National Palace in Mexico
City. Some 116,000 U.S. soldiers had served in the
war. Most of those who died lost their lives to
disease rather than to battle. More than 60 Texans
died in battle, and more than 270 Texans died from
disease or accidents. Many lives were lost and much
property was destroyed in Mexico.

> What killed most soldiers
> in the U.S-Mexican war?
> _____

CHALLENGE ACTIVITY

Critical Thinking: Analyzing What do you think
was the definitive battle of the U.S.-Mexican War
and why?

Zachary Taylor	John S. "Rip" Ford
offensive	Winfield Scott

DIRECTIONS Use each of the words in the word bank to write a summary of the U.S.-Mexican War .

_____

_____

_____

_____

_____

_____

_____

_____

_____

_____

_____

_____

_____

_____

_____

_____

_____

_____

_____

_____

_____

_____

Western Expansion and Conflict

MAIN IDEAS

1. The United States gained new territory after the Mexican War, leading to debates about slavery.

2. Many Tejanos faced discrimination as a result of the Mexican War.

3. The population of Texas grew in the 1840s and 1850s, largely through immigration.

Key Terms and People

Treaty of Guadalupe Hidalgo treaty signed in 1848 officially ending the Mexican War

Mexican Cession some 529,000 miles ceded by Mexico to the United States

Compromise of 1850 a plan to settle border conflict whereby Texas was paid $10 million to give up its claim to land in present-day New Mexico

Section Summary

THE TREATY OF GUADALUPE HIDALGO

On February 2, 1848, U.S. diplomat Nicholas Trist and Mexican officials signed the **Treaty of Guadalupe Hidalgo**, officially ending the Mexican War. Mexico recognized the annexation of Texas, with the Rio Grande as the state's border. The United States agreed to cover the $3.25 million in claims that its citizens had against the Mexican government. Mexico ceded some 529,000 square miles of its northern territory to the United States for $15 million. Mexicans living in this region, known as the **Mexican Cession**, were to be granted all the rights of U.S. citizenship.

The U.S. Congress was divided over the issue of slavery in the new territories. Pro-slavery legislators wanted slavery to be allowed in the new territories, while antislavery legislators wanted to ban it. The **Compromise of 1850**, a plan by Senator Henry Clay, was an attempt to settle the dispute. The compromise included a $10 million payment to Texas by the U.S. government for the state to give up its claim to land in present-day New

> **What did Mexico gain from the Treaty of Guadalupe Hidalgo?**
>
> _____
> _____
> _____

Mexico. Texas voters approved the plan. The state government needed the money to pay its debt. The U.S. government then established the present-day border between Texas and New Mexico.

TEJANOS AND THE WAR

Since the Texas Revolution, many Tejanos had been treated with suspicion and distrust by other Texans. Their loyalty was called in question. The **Treaty of Guadalupe Hidalgo** guaranteed that Tejanos would receive equal protection under the law. Many Tejanos, however, experienced discrimination. Some were forced to leave under threats of violence. Despite this, many remained in Texas, some becoming political leaders.

NEW MIGRATION TO TEXAS

In 1850 the Texas population was 212,592. By 1860 it had risen to 604,215. The African American population rose also, from more than 58,000 in 1850 to 183,000 in 1860. Fewer than 800 free African Americans lived in Texas. The Texas population also included more than 12,000 Tejanos, most of whom lived in the southern region of the state. Many Europeans also came to Texas at this time. Immigrants arrived from Ireland, Germany, France, Poland, and Czechoslovakia. Jewish immigrants settled in Galveston, Houston, and San Antonio. Norway, Italy, the Netherlands, and Belgium were also represented

List three European countries from which immigrants came to Texas.
_____
_____
_____

CHALLENGE ACTIVITY

Critical Thinking: Summarizing Summarize the main events following the Treaty of Guadalupe Hidalgo.

DIRECTIONS Read each sentence and fill in the blank with the word
from the pair that best completes the sentence.

1. The Mexican War officially ended with the _____. (Treaty
   of Guadalupe Hidalgo /Mexican Cession)

2. The _____ (Treaty of Guadalupe Hidalgo /Compromise of
   1850) included a $10 million payment to Texas to give up land claims.

3. Under the _____ (Treaty of Guadalupe Hidalgo /
   Compromise of 1850), Mexico ceded 529,000 square miles of additional
   territory.

4. Mexico recognized the U.S. annexation of Texas in the
   _____ (Treaty of Guadalupe Hidalgo /Compromise
   of 1850).

DIRECTIONS On the lines below, write a description of the Mexican
Cession.

_____

_____

_____

_____

_____

_____

_____

_____

Western Expansion and Conflict

Section 3

MAIN IDEAS
1. The Texas Rangers protected Texans on the frontier.
2. Conflict between frontier settlers and American Indians led to the creation of reservations.
3. Texas Indians were forced to leave the state.

Key Terms and People

reservations limited areas of land reserved for American Indians.

Robert S. Neighbors Federal Indian agent who helped the Indians with their move to Indian Territory

Section Summary

CONFLICTS ON THE FRONTIER

The movement of settlers onto the lands of American Indians created conflicts. The Texas Rangers, who had horses and the new Colt six-shooter, were effective at frontier warfare. The federal government agreed to pay the Rangers to guard the frontier. Rangers patrolled the frontier throughout the 1850s and fought several battles with the Comanches.

> **What were the Rangers paid to do?**
> _____
> _____
> _____

ESTABLISHING FRONTIER FORTS

The federal government built forts to protect settlers and travel routes. By 1849 a line of forts stretched from the Rio Grande to the Trinity River. When settlers moved west of the original line of forts, the army abandoned those forts and built new ones farther west. The army built yet another line of forts across West Texas during the 1850s. The forts were too far apart to protect settlers or prevent them from moving west, however.

> **Why did the forts fail? Give two reasons.**
> _____
> _____

THE RESERVATION POLICY

Due to the continuing conflicts, the United States government decided to move the Texas Indians onto reservations—limited areas of land reserved for American Indians. In 1854 the U.S. Army opened the Brazos Indian Reservation just south of Fort Belknap. About 2,000 American Indians settled there. These Indians used part of their land for farming. They received supplies and cattle from the federal government. A Comanche Indian Reservation was created some 40 miles away. About 450 Penateka Comanches settled there. Government agents taught the Comanches how to farm, but the Comanches had little success. A drought complicated matters. A planned reservation for the Lipan Apaches failed because the Apaches refused to move onto the land.

> Underline two reasons reservations failed.

THE REMOVAL OF TEXAS INDIANS

The creation of reservations did not end conflicts. By the late 1850s, some Texans were calling for an end to the system. They wanted American Indians totally removed from the state. By 1859 the Texas Indians living on the Brazos and Comanche Indian Reservations had been removed to Indian Territory in what is now Oklahoma. Federal Indian agent **Robert S. Neighbors** helped the Indians with their difficult move. The Alabama-Coushattas were allowed to stay in Texas. During the Runaway Scrape, the Alabama-Coushattas had aided settlers fleeing east. In 1854 Texas granted the Alabama-Coushattas 1,280 acres of land in Polk County. Today the Alabama-Coushatta Reservation, the Tigua Reservation near El Paso, and the Kickapoo Reservation near Eagle Pass are the only Indian reservations in Texas.

CHALLENGE ACTIVITY

Critical Thinking: Summarizing Summarize the main reasons the reservations were created.

DIRECTIONS On the line provided before each statement, write **T** if a statement is true and **F** if a statement is false. If the statement is false, write a corrected statement on the line after the false statement.

_____ 1. The federal government agreed to pay Rangers to guard the frontier from attack.

_____

_____ 2. Forts were a success in preventing conflicts between Texans and American Indians.

_____

_____ 3. The Comanches learned to farm their reservation successfully.

_____

_____ 4. The Apaches refused to move onto a reservation.

_____

_____ 5. Texans called for the removal of American Indians from the state.

_____

_____ 6. No reservations remain in Texas today.

_____

MAIN IDEAS
1. Most Texans in the early statehood period made their livings in agriculture or related fields.
2. Merchants and professionals could be found in towns.

Key Terms

cotton belt the southern region of the United States known for cotton production

planters large-scale farmers

Richard King a successful rancher and founder of the King Ranch in South Texas

Aaron Ashworth a free African American owner of a large ranch in southeastern Texas

Cristóbal Benavides a successful sheep and cattle rancher from Laredo

gristmills machines that grind grain into meal or flour

tanneries places where animal hides are prepared

Section Summary

FARMERS AND PLANTERS

In 1850, 95 percent of Texans lived in rural areas, and most worked on farms or ranches. The number of farms more than doubled between 1850 and 1860. Some were small family farms, while others were large plantations.

Many farmers grew a cash crop such as cotton to sell for a profit. By the 1850s Texas was an important part of the **cotton belt,** the southern region that grew most of the country's cotton. The demand for—and price of—cotton rose as textile factories bought up cotton. Most Texas cotton was grown on plantations in East and Central Texas or along the Gulf coast. Growing cotton required many hours of labor. About one in every 4 families in Texas owned slaves for labor. A few wealthy **planters**, or large-scale farmers, held up to 100 slaves. In 1860 about 2,000 planters in Texas controlled the state's economy and government.

What is a cash crop?

_____

_____

RANCHERS

After cotton, cattle were the state's second largest export. Ranching increased more than 400 percent from 1850 to 1860. Cattle provided food, hides, and tallow—animal fat used to make soap and candles. Most cattle were sold locally, but some were driven to out-of-state markets.

One successful rancher, **Richard King,** founded the King Ranch on thousands of acres of land in South Texas. **Aaron Ashworth,** a free African American, owned a large ranch in southeastern Texas. In the Laredo region, **Cristóbal Benevides** ran a huge cattle and sheep ranch.

TRADES, PROFESSIONS, AND INDUSTRY

In towns, businesses focused on agricultural services. By 1860 San Antonio had replaced Galveston as the state's largest town. Even in towns, most people were somehow involved in agriculture. Merchants provided farmers with goods. Blacksmiths, carpenters, masons, and wagon makers made products farmers needed.

Industry was only a small part of the Texas economy. Most towns had **gristmills**— machines for grinding grain into meal or flour. Cotton gins were also common as were **tanneries**—places where animal hides were prepared

CHALLENGE ACTIVITY

Critical Thinking: Identifying Cause and Effect

What was the basis of the Texas economy, and how did that affect Texas industry?

> Underline some uses of cattle.

cotton belt	planters	Richard King	Aaron Ashworth
tanneries	gristmills	Cristóbal Benavides	

DIRECTIONS Read each sentence below and circle the word from the pair that best completes each sentence.

1. In Texas towns, (gristmills/tanneries) were places where animal hides were prepared.

2. (Richard King/Aaron Ashworth) ran one of the biggest ranches in South Texas.

3. A free African American, (Aaron Ashworth/Cristóbal Benavides), owned a large ranch in southeastern Texas.

4. Large-scale farmers, also called (planters/gristmills), had a lot of power in the Texas economy and government.

DIRECTIONS Write two adjectives or descriptive phrases that describe each name or term given.

5. Cristóbal Benavides _____

6. cotton belt _____

Life in a Frontier State

MAIN IDEAS
1. Poor roads and shallow rivers made travel and transportation of goods in Texas difficult.
2. Stagecoaches, steamboats, and railroads each offered advantages and disadvantages as means of travel.

Key Terms and People

oxcarts large, slow two-wheeled carts with solid wheels

steamboats boats whose power came from burning wood or coal

Harrisburg Railroad the first railroad line in Texas

Section Summary

STAGECOACH AND FREIGHT LINES

Transportation in Texas was often slow. Most roads turned to mud during wet weather. Stagecoaches carried passengers and mail between towns, including Houston, Austin, San Antonio, and Indianola. Stagecoach travel was dangerous. Passengers often found themselves repairing broken wheels, fighting bandits, or pushing the coach through streams.

In 1858 the Butterfield Overland Mail Company began service in Texas. The line ran from St. Louis, through Texas, and on to San Francisco. Stagecoaches were not large enough to move heavy freight such as food products, dry goods, and the farm supplies Texans needed. To transport such goods, Texans used freight wagons— heavy wagons with iron axles and large wheels pulled by horses, mules, or oxen.

In San Antonio and South Texas, much freight was carried on **oxcarts**—large, slow, two-wheeled carts with solid wheels. Mexican Americans played an important role in overland freight in this area, working for less than other freighters.

> What were some of the difficulties of transportation in Texas?
>
> _____
>
> _____
>
> _____

STEAMBOATS

Texans also used rivers for transport.
Steamboats—which got power from burning wood
or coal—could travel along many of the lower parts
of the state's rivers. Houston became a
transportation center and the state's third largest
city. Steamboats carried goods, particularly cotton,
from Houston to Galveston and then onto New
Orleans.

What advantages did steamboats offer?
_____
_____

RAILROADS

Railroads could carry heavy loads even in bad
weather, but were expensive to build. In 1851 the
Buffalo Bayou, Brazos, and Colorado Railway
began construction on the first Texas railroad line,
commonly called the **Harrisburg Railroad.** Other
railroads built lines in the Houston area during the
1950s. Lines connected Victoria with Port Lavaca,
and Marshall with Caddo Lake. The state gave
grants of land to companies to encourage railroad
construction. Even so, by 1860 fewer than 500
miles of lines existed in Texas.

CHALLENGE ACTIVITY

Critical Thinking: Analyzing Information How
did weather affect transportation in Texas?

Guided Reading Workbook

DIRECTIONS On the line provided before each statement, write **T** if a statement is true and **F** if a statement is false. If the statement is false, write a corrected statement on the line after the false statement.

_____ 1. <u>Oxcarts</u> were heavy wagons with iron axles and large wheels pulled by teams of oxen, horses, or mules.

_____

_____ 2. <u>Steamboats</u> were boats powered by burning coal or wood.

_____

_____ 3. The <u>Harrisburg Railroad</u> was the first railroad line in Texas.

_____

DIRECTIONS Write two adjectives or descriptive phrases that describe each term given.

4. oxcarts _____

5. steamboats _____

6. Harrisburg Railroad _____

Life in a Frontier State

MAIN IDEAS
1. Frontier Texans depended on schools and church for education, spiritual guidance, and social events.
2. Newspapers spread word of local events and issues.
3. Many Texans were active in the arts.

Key Terms and People

telegraphs devices that sent coded signals along wires to communicate over vast distances

Gail Borden Jr. founder of the *Telegraph and Texas Register*, the newspaper with the largest circulation in Texas

Hermann Lungkwitz landscape painter from Germany who moved to Texas

Section Summary

FRONTIER SCHOOLS AND CHURCHES

The state legislature set aside $2 million for schools in 1854. Towns like San Antonio and some German communities built schools. Log-cabin schools were common in rural areas. As time passed, more students took time off from farm work to attend school.

Churches also built schools. Churches provided spiritual and moral guidance that brought a social aspect to the often isolated lives of rural Texans. The most common churches in Texas were Protestant denominations. Many Tejanos and European immigrants remained Catholic. Some churches printed newspapers to communicate with members.

> Why were churches important on the frontier?
> _____
> _____

NEWSPAPERS

For a frontier region, Texas had a large number of newspapers. The *Telegraph and Texas Register* was first published in 1835 by **Gail Borden Jr.** and two other men. It had the largest circulation in Texas. Newspapers carried more national and world news in the 1850s after **telegraphs** were introduced. The telegraph allowed people to communicate across vast distances by sending coded signals over wires. In 1854 a telegraph line connected Galveston, Houston, and Marshall.

LITERATURE AND ART

Between 1850 and 1860 the number of libraries in the state rose from 12 to 132. Some libraries were opened by churches. Swante Palm, a Swedish settler in Austin, owned a large number of books. He later gave his book collection to the University of Texas. Most families had a Bible or a McGuffey's *Reader* to teach their children to read. The first published histories of Texas also appeared in the 1840s and 1850s. Artists were captivated by Texas. **Hermann Lungkwitz** was a respected landscape artist in the 1850s who was trained in Germany. The artists illustrated the people and places of Texas.

> Underline the titles of books that most families owned.
>
> _____
>
> _____

CHALLENGE ACTIVITY

Critical Thinking: Identifying Cause and Effect

How did the telegraph change newspapers in Texas?

Guided Reading Workbook

telegraphs	Gail Borden Jr.	Hermann Lungkwitz

DIRECTIONS On the line provided before each statement, write **T** if a statement is true and **F** if a statement is false. If the statement is false, write a corrected statement on the line after the false statement.

_____ 1. <u>Hermann Lungkwitz</u> was a famous portrait painter born in Germany.

_____

_____ 2. The <u>telegraph</u> helped people communicate over vast distances.

_____

_____ 3. <u>Gail Borden Jr.</u> founded the *Austin State Gazette*.

_____

Life on the Texas Frontier

MAIN IDEAS
1. Slaves performed many jobs on plantations.
2. Some Texans argued against slavery.

Key Terms

spirituals religious folk songs

abolition the end of slavery

Section Summary

SLAVE LABOR

Most Texas slaves worked on farms. They built and repaired fences, dug and cleaned out ditches, cooked, cleaned, and sewed. Work began at daybreak with little time to rest. Planters expected slaves to pick many pounds of cotton every day.

By 1850 slaves made up almost 20 percent of the population of Austin, Galveston, and Houston. Slaves who lived in towns did a variety of jobs. Men worked as carpenters or blacksmiths; women were cooks, babysitters, or housekeepers. Some slaveholders hired out slaves for work. A few were allowed to keep part of their wages and buy their freedom.

> Underline the types of jobs slaves were expected to perform on farms.

SLAVE CULTURE

Slaves worked at least six days a week. Many had Sundays off. Their diets and shelter were often poor. During their rare leisure moments, slaves spent evenings with families and friends. On Saturday nights, they might attend dances or family gatherings.

Music and religion were important in slave communities. Slaves sang while working, and often played instruments such as fiddles or banjos when not working. **Spirituals**—religious folk songs—

were sung in African American churches, carrying
message of hope and faith.

SLAVE ESCAPES AND REBELLIONS

Some of those enslaved in Texas were willing to
risk their lives to escape slavery by fleeing to
Mexico where slavery was illegal. But slaveholders
severely punished runaway slaves who they caught.
Many slaves who considered running away also did
not want to leave family members behind. Thus
most slaves did not try to escape.

Some white Texans feared slave rebellions. Few
such rebellions actually occurred, however. A slave
uprising was planned in 1856 in Colorado County.
Before it could take place, slaveholders learned of
the plan. They hanged several slaves. In 1860
rumors spread that a North Texas fire was part of a
slave plot. Many African American and white
Texans were executed for the supposed plot.

The Texas legislature, which planters dominated,
passed pro-slavery laws. Some Texans supported
abolition, or an end to slavery. Some opposed
slavery for moral or religious reasons, believing that
it was wrong for one person to own another. Others
objected for political reasons, arguing that slavery
went against the ideals of democracy and freedom.
Abolitionist Melinda Rankin was forced to leave
Texas. Abolitionists in Texas kept their opinions to
themselves.

> What might prevent an
> enslaved person from
> running away?
> _____
> _____
> _____

CHALLENGE ACTIVITY

Making Inferences Why were slaveholders
opposed to abolition?

abolitionist	spirituals

DIRECTIONS On the line provided before each statement, write **T** if a statement is true and **F** if a statement is false. If the statement is false, write a corrected statement on the line after the false statement.

_____ 1. Slaves often sang <u>spirituals</u>, or religious songs, while they worked.

_____

_____ 2. Many slaveholders were in favor of <u>abolition</u>.

_____

DIRECTIONS Answer each question below using a word from the word bank in your response.

3. Why were spirituals popular among enslaved people?

_____

_____

4. What were some reasons people supported abolition?

_____

_____

Texas and the Civil War

MAIN IDEAS
1. The United States divided along sectional lines because of regional economic differences.
2. Many Texans supported secession because of states' rights.

Key Terms

states' rights rights held by states that place limits on the implied powers of the federal government over state governments

Kansas-Nebraska act an act passed by Congress in 1854 allowing the Kansas and Nebraska Territories to decide whether to be free or slave states

Dred Scott **decision** ruling by U.S. Supreme Court that declared that African Americans were not citizens and that Congress could not ban slavery in any federal territory

secede formally withdraw

Unionists people who wanted to stay in the Union

Confederate States of America government formed by the states seceding from the Union, also called the Confederacy

sovereignty supremacy in power

Section Summary

GROWING NATIONAL DIVISIONS

The issue of slavery divided the United States along sectional, or regional, lines. Some southerners argued that they had the right to ignore federal laws. Under this **states' rights** argument, state power was greater than federal power.

> **Underline the meaning of the states' rights argument.**

The 1854 **Kansas-Nebraska Act** allowed two territories to decide whether to be free or slave states. This act angered many northerners. In the 1857 *Dred Scott* **decision,** the Supreme Court ruled that African Americans were not citizens and Congress could not ban slavery in any federal territory. The ruling shocked many northerners.

> **What was the reaction of northerners to the *Dred Scott* decision?**
>
> _____
> _____

Tensions increased in 1859 when John Brown led a raid on a federal armory in Harpers Ferry,

Virginia, to start a slave revolt. He and his followers were hanged for treason.

TEXAS JOINS THE CONFEDERACY

In 1860 Republican Abraham Lincoln won the presidential election. Many southerners feared that he would support abolition. After the election, South Carolina and several other southern states voted to **secede,** or formally withdraw, from the Union. Many Texan leaders wanted the state to secede. This angered many **Unionists**—people who wanted to stay in the Union and work out the issue of slavery. Governor Sam Houston tried to delay the efforts of Texans who wanted to secede.

> **How did southerners react to the election of Lincoln?**
> _____
> _____
> _____

THE CONFEDERACY

Despite Houston's opposition, a secession convention met on January 28, 1861. The next month Texans voted to secede. Texas and the other southern states soon formed the **Confederate States of America,** also called the Confederacy. The Confederate constitution emphasized the **sovereignty,** or supremacy, of the states and the right of people to hold slaves. Governor Houston was removed from office when he refused to take an oath to the new state constitution.

> **What was another name for the Confederate States of America?**
> _____

CHALLENGE ACTIVITY

Critical Thinking: Drawing Inferences Why do you think Houston refused to take an oath to the Confederacy?

states' rights	Kansas-Nebraska Act	*Dred Scott* decision	secede
Unionists	Confederate States of America	sovereignty	

DIRECTIONS On the line provided before each statement, write **T** if a statement is true and **F** if a statement is false. If the statement is false, write a corrected statement on the line after the false statement.

_____ 1. The <u>Kansas-Nebraska Act</u> declared that African Americans were not citizens.

_____

_____ 2. <u>Unionists</u> were opposed to states that wanted to secede from the Union.

_____

_____ 3. The <u>Confederate States of America</u> was composed of Texas and the southern states.

_____

_____ 4. According to the argument for <u>states' rights,</u> federal power was greater than state power.

_____

_____ 5. The <u>*Dred Scott*</u> decision ruled that Congress could not ban slavery in any federal territory.

_____

_____ 6. As part of the constitution, the Confederacy established the <u>sovereignty</u> or supremacy of the states.

_____

Guided Reading Workbook

MAIN IDEAS

1. Texans responded swiftly to the Confederate call to arms to join the Civil War.

2. Texas prepared for the war by establishing new industries.

3. The South's experienced military leaders were an important resource during the first half of the war.

Key Terms and People

regiments military units made up of a number of battalions, or groups of troops

Albert Sidney Johnston the second-highest-ranking officer in the Confederate army until his death in battle

Thomas Green a key Confederate officer who rose to the rank of brigadier general

cotton diplomacy tactic used by southern leaders to secure foreign support during the Civil War by withholding cotton shipments to other nations until they offered aid

ironclads ships used during the Civil War that were heavily armored with iron plates

Section Summary

A CALL TO ARMS

The Civil War began in April 1861 when Confederate forces attacked Fort Sumter, a federal fort at Charleston, South Carolina. Thousands of Texans volunteered to fight. Texans usually joined **regiments**—units of around 1,000 soldiers—from their hometowns or counties. Texan **Albert Sidney Johnston** was the second-highest-ranking officer in the Confederate army. Texan **Thomas Green** was another key Confederate soldier who rose to the rank of brigadier general.

> **What event started the Civil War?**
>
> _____
>
> _____

TEXAS READIES FOR WAR

Many of the Texas troops were ill-equipped, reporting with a variety of weapons, uniforms, and supplies. Texans established industries to help supply the troops. The state's resources of cattle, cotton, and food crops also helped the Confederacy.

RESOURCES AND STRATEGIES

The North had a larger population and more railroads to move troops and supplies. The South had experienced military leaders and soldiers. Southern leaders tried to establish foreign support through **cotton diplomacy**—cotton shipments to British textile mills, hoping to convince Britain to offer help. This strategy failed, however, because Britain's storehouses were fully stocked before the war.

The North faced the difficult task of having to conquer large amounts of enemy territory. Union forces planned to take control of the Mississippi River and cut the Confederacy in two. The Union used naval blockades to prevent the Confederacy from importing war supplies. Also, the Union planned to capture Richmond, Virginia, capital of the Confederacy. These strategies established three theaters, or regions, of the war.

> **What advantages did the North have over the South?**
> _____
> _____
> _____
> _____

THE MAJOR BATTLES OF THE CIVIL WAR

The major battles of the war took place east of the Mississippi. Union and Confederate forces clashed at Bull Run, Antietam, and other sites. In the summer of 1863 Confederate general Robert E. Lee's forces lost a major battle at Gettysburg, Pennsylvania.

Meanwhile, Union troops under the command of General Ulysses S. Grant began the six-week Siege of Vicksburg, Mississippi, supported by a fleet of **ironclads**—ships heavily fortified with armored plates. When the town surrendered on July 4, 1863, the Confederacy was split in two. It became very difficult to get supplies from Arkansas, Louisiana, and Texas to the battlegrounds in the East.

> **Underline where most of the battles took place.**

CHALLENGE ACTIVITY

Critical Thinking: Cause and Effect Why was the Battle of Vicksburg considered a turning point in the war?

regiments	Albert Sidney Johnston	Thomas Green
cotton diplomacy	ironclads	

DIRECTIONS Read each sentence and circle the term in the word pair
that best completes each sentence.

1. A soldier who rose to the rank of brigadier general in the Confederate army was
(Albert Sidney Johnston/Thomas Green).

2. A group of (regiments/ironclads) supported Grant in the Battle of Vicksburg.

DIRECTIONS Write two adjectives or descriptive phrases that describe
the term given.

3. regiments _____

4. cotton diplomacy _____

5. ironclads _____

Texas and the Civil War

MAIN IDEAS
1. By fighting in and around Texas, the Confederacy hoped to avoid Union occupancy.
2. Geographic features affected the outcome of the military campaigns fought in the region.

Key Terms and People

Henry H. Sibley Confederate general who led three Texas regiments in an unsuccessful attempt to seize the Southwest for the Confederacy

Battle of Glorieta Pass decisive battle in New Mexico in which Union troops forced Sibley's retreat

cottonclads boats lined with cotton bales and converted to gunboats during the Civil War

Richard Dowling Confederate lieutenant who protected Fort Griffin and halted the Union attack on Galveston

Davis Guards a Confederate all-Irish unit led by Lieutenant Dowling and charged with protecting Sabine Pass

Battle of Galveston 1863 battle led by General Magruder in which Confederate troops restored their control over Galveston

Battle of Sabine Pass battle won by Dowling and the Davis Guards, restoring southern confidence

Santos Benavides highest-ranking Mexican American in the Confederate army, who stopped the Union attack on Laredo

Red River Campaign series of battles led by General Taylor along the Red River in Louisiana, ending in victory for the Confederate troops

Section Summary

THE NEW MEXICO CAMPAIGN

Shortly after the war began, Texas forces led by Colonel John R. Baylor marched into New Mexico Territory. In the fall of 1861, **General Henry H. Sibley** took three Texas regiments and marched to seize the Southwest. After some initial success, Sibley's force was defeated in the **Battle of Glorieta Pass** in March of 1862.

> Who won the Battle of Glorieta Pass?
> _____

Guided Reading Workbook

BATTLE OF GALVESTON

A Union fleet captured the key port of Galveston in October. Confederate general John H. Magruder had his men make **cottonclads** by converting two steamboats to gunboats and lining the sides with cotton bales for protection. His plan worked and he recaptured the town in early 1863.

BATTLE OF SABINE PASS

Union forces attacked Sabine Pass in the fall of 1863. They planned to march from there to attack Galveston from land. Confederate lieutenant **Richard Dowling** and about 45 Irish soldiers known as the **Davis Guards** stopped the Union forces. The **Battle of Sabine Pass** helped restore southern confidence.

Why was the Battle of Sabine Pass important?
_____
_____

THE COAST AND SOUTH TEXAS

Soon after the Battle of Sabine Pass, Union forces captured Brownsville. However, a Union attack on Laredo failed. Texas troops led by Colonel **Santos Benavides,** the highest-ranking Mexican American to serve in the Confederate army, turned back the attack. After Union forces were called away from Brownsville, Confederate troops quickly recaptured the city.

What did Santos Benavides accomplish?
_____
_____

THE RED RIVER CAMPAIGN

Union leaders wanted to invade northeastern Texas from Louisiana along the Red River. In April 1864 Confederate soldiers defeated Union forces in a stunning victory called the **Red River Campaign** at Sabine Crossroads near Mansfield, Louisiana.

CHALLENGE ACTIVITY

Critical Thinking: Sequencing Make a time line of battles and their outcomes for these years of the Civil War.

| Henry H. Sibley | Battle of Glorieta Pass | Red River Campaign | Richard Dowling |
| Davis Guards | Battle of Galveston | Battle of Sabine Pass | Santos Benavides |

DIRECTIONS Read each sentence and circle the term in the word pair that best completes each sentence.

1. (Henry H. Sibley/Richard Dowling) led the campaign to capture the New Mexico territory for the Confederacy.

2. At the (Battle of Glorieta Pass/Battle of Galveston), the Confederacy lost their campaign.

3. A Confederate leader named (Santos Benavides/Richard Dowling) led the Battle of Sabine Pass.

4. The Davis Guards operated under the leadership of (Richard Dowling/Henry H. Sibley).

5. The (Red River Campaign/Battle of Glorieta Pass) was another decisive victory for the Confederacy.

DIRECTIONS Write two adjectives or descriptive phrases that describe the term given.

6. Henry H. Sibley _____

7. Battle of Galveston _____

8. Red River Campaign _____

MAIN IDEAS
1. Texans endured many hardships during the Civil War.
2. Unionists lost some of their rights during the war.

Key Terms and People

draft requirement of military service

Francis Lubbock governor of Texas who entered the Confederate army after his term ended

martial law rule by armed forces

Section Summary

THE WARTIME ECONOMY AND THE DRAFT

Few Civil War battles were fought in Texas, but Texans still experienced many hardships. Goods became scarce and expensive. To feed the army, farmers grew less cotton and more corn and wheat. Crop production increased as slaveholders in other states sent slaves to Texas to prevent their being freed by Union forces. Women and children ran farms and plantations. They also worked in small factories and organized groups to support the war effort by making uniforms, badges, and other supplies.

> **What role did women play in the war effort in Texas?**
> _____
> _____
> _____

All political officeholders supported the Confederacy. **Francis R. Lubbock,** who had been elected governor in 1862, worked to improve the military's capabilities. After his term ended, he joined the Confederate army as a lieutenant colonel.

Although thousands of men had volunteered at the beginning of the war, they were not enough soldiers to meet the army's needs. In April 1862 the Confederate Congress passed a **draft,** or requirement of military service. All white males between the ages of 18 and 35 had to serve in the army. However, there were loopholes in the law. People with certain key jobs were exempt. Men could also buy their way

> **Why did the Confederate Congress pass a draft?**
> _____
> _____

out of service or provide a substitute. Some southerners complained that the conflict was a "rich man's war, poor man's fight." Even with a draft, the Confederacy struggled throughout the war to put enough soldiers in the field.

UNIONISTS IN TEXAS

The Confederate draft sparked fierce opposition from some Unionists. Although many had joined the southern war effort, some refused to take sides. Many German Americans and Mexican Americans remained neutral. After the draft was passed, however, Texans had to choose sides. Some Unionists fled Texas to avoid the draft.

Confederate officials regarded many Texas Unionists as potentially dangerous traitors. Officials placed some areas with a large Unionist population under **martial law,** or rule by armed forces. Unionists in the Hill Country and in North Texas were violently attacked. Some 40 suspected Unionists were hanged in Gainesville.

> Underline how some Unionists felt about the draft.

CHALLENGE ACTIVITY

Critical Thinking: Summarizing What happened to some Unionists in Texas during the war?

Guided Reading Workbook

draft	Francis H. Lubbock	martial law

DIRECTIONS On the lines below, use all the words in the word bank to write a summary of what you have learned in the section.

_____

_____

_____

_____

_____

_____

_____

_____

_____

_____

_____

_____

_____

_____

_____

_____

_____

_____

_____

_____

Texas and the Civil War

Section 5

MAIN IDEAS
1. Decisive victories in 1863, 1864, and 1865 ended the Civil War.
2. The Texas economy was badly damaged by the Civil War.

Key Terms

March to the Sea Union General Sherman's march to Savannah in which his army burned much Confederate property

Emancipation Proclamation order issued by President Lincoln that freed slaves in the areas rebelling against the United States

Section Summary
THE WAR DRAWS TO A CLOSE

After the Battle of Gettysburg and the fall of Vicksburg in July 1863, Union forces moved steadily into the South. President Lincoln ordered General Ulysses S. Grant to take command in the eastern theater. He moved his army to eastern Virginia and engaged General Lee's troops in a series of battles. Lee's army was greatly outnumbered and was eventually defeated by the Union. Grant continued his drive toward Richmond.

Union general William Tecumseh Sherman led a devastating sweep across the lower South. As he marched through Georgia to Savannah, his army destroyed crops, livestock, railroads—any resources that could help the South. Sherman's **March to the Sea** ended when he reached Savannah in December 1864. Meanwhile, Grant was pursuing Lee. On April 9, 1865, Lee surrendered at Appomattox Courthouse, Virginia.

BATTLE AT PALMITO RANCH

Despite Lee's surrender, many soldiers stayed at their posts. On May 12, Union troops moved inland to occupy Brownsville. The next day—more than a month after General Lee's surrender—Union and

> Who was the commander of the Union army in the eastern theater?
>
> _____

> Why do you think Sherman's forces destroyed property on their way to Savannah?
>
> _____
>
> _____

Guided Reading Workbook

Confederate forces clashed at Palmito Ranch near Brownsville. Led by Colonel John S. Ford, the Confederate troops defeated the Union forces and captured more than 100 prisoners. The Confederate troops won the last land battle of the Civil War, but the South had already lost the war.

CONSEQUENCES OF WAR

About 620,000 Americans lost their lives in the Civil War, making it the deadliest conflict in U.S. history. Some 90,000 Texans served during the war, and thousands were killed or wounded. Although Texas suffered few battles, the war left the state's economy in shambles. The cotton trade had nearly stopped. When Governor Murrah and other officials fled to Mexico at the end of the war, the state's government collapsed. No one seemed to know who was in charge. It took some time before Union forces could move in and restore order.

Enslaved Texans saw the war as a struggle for freedom. In 1863 President Lincoln had issued the Emancipation Proclamation. This stated that slaves were free in those areas rebelling against the United States. But the 250,000 freed slaves in Texas were uncertain what would happen next.

> Underline some of the consequences of the war in Texas.

CHALLENGE ACTIVITY

Critical Thinking: Making Inference Why do you think some Texas soldiers continued to fight even after Lee surrendered?

DIRECTIONS Read each sentence and circle the term in the word pair that best completes each sentence.

1. (General Murrah/Abraham Lincoln) signed the Emancipation Proclamation in 1864.

2. The leader of the Union troops in the eastern theater was (Ulysses S. Grant/Robert E. Lee).

3. (Wiliam Tecumseh Sherman/Ulysses S. Grant) led the March of the Sea towards Savannah, Georgia.

4. At the Battle of Palmito, (Confederate/Union) troops were victorious.

DIRECTIONS Write two adjectives or descriptive phrases that describe the term given.

5. Emancipation Proclamation _____

6. March to the Sea _____

Guided Reading Workbook

Reconstruction

MAIN IDEAS
1. After Emancipation, many former slaves left the plantations to look for family or find work.
2. In order to rejoin the Union, Texas had to write a new constitution, abolish slavery, and declare secession illegal.
3. The lives of freedpeople in Texas remained restricted under the Black Codes.

Key Terms

Juneteenth holiday celebrating or commemorating a proclamation freeing Texas slaves, issued on June 19, 1865

freedpeople former slaves

Reconstruction a period in which the U.S. government began the process of reuniting the nation and rebuilding the southern states

Thirteenth Amendment added to the U.S. Constitution to abolish slavery

Freedmen's Bureau government agency that provided help and legal aid to freedpeople

suffrage voting rights

Black Codes Texas laws that denied African Americans' civil rights

civil rights individual rights guaranteed to people by the U.S. Constitution

Section Summary

EMANCIPATION

At the end of the Civil War, U.S. troops took control of Texas. When Union general Gordon Granger landed at Galveston in 1865, he issued a proclamation freeing Texas slaves. That day is celebrated as **Juneteenth.** Former slaves now had the freedom to travel. Texas roads were filled with **freedpeople** who searched for family members, paying jobs, and military protection.

> Who controlled Texas following the Civil War?
> _____
> _____
> _____

THE FREEDMEN'S BUREAU

The U.S. government began **Reconstruction.** In February 1865 Congress proposed the **Thirteenth Amendment,** which ended slavery. Next, it created the **Freedmen's Bureau** to provide help and legal aid to freedpeople. By 1870 more than 9,000 African

Americans were enrolled in 150 schools, resulting in an increase in literacy among African Americans.

PRESIDENT JOHNSON'S PLAN

Andrew Johnson became president after Abraham Lincoln was assassinated. Under Johnson's plan for Reconstruction, for Texas to rejoin the Union, a temporary government had to be created along with a constitution that declared secession illegal and abolished slavery. Texas also needed representation in the U.S. Congress.

Johnson appointed Unionist Andrew J. Hamilton as temporary governor of Texas. In an election to select delegates to the constitutional convention, African Americans were not given the right to vote.

At the Texas constitutional convention in 1866, delegates failed to give African Americans equal rights. Black Texans could not testify in court cases involving white Texans, they could not hold office, and they were not granted **suffrage.** Texas voters approved the new constitution. James W. Throckmorton became governor. When former secessionists won control of the new legislature, it refused to ratify the Thirteenth Amendment.

> List three civil rights that the constitutional convention failed to give African Americans in 1866.
>
> 1. _____
>
> 2. _____
>
> 3. _____

THE BLACK CODES

The Texas legislature passed the **Black Codes** that denied African Americans' **civil rights.** These Codes restricted the movement and work of many African Americans and allowed employers to benefit from unfair labor contracts. Threats and violence against African Americans were common and justice through the courts was difficult.

> Why do you think Black Codes were passed?
>
> _____
>
> _____
>
> _____

CHALLENGE ACTIVITY

Critical Thinking: Analyzing Information Explain differences between the rights of African Americans under the U.S. Constitution and the new Texas constitution of 1866.

Guided Reading Workbook

Juneteenth	freedpeople	Reconstruction
Thirteenth Amendment	Freedmen's Bureau	suffrage
Black Codes	civil rights	

DIRECTIONS On the line provided before each statement, write **T** if a statement is true and **F** if a statement is false. If the statement is false, write the corrected statement on the line after the false statement.

_____ 1. As soon as news of a proclamation freeing slaves spread, freedpeople filled the streets of Texas in celebration.

_____

_____ 2. A department of government was created during Reconstruction to support the rights of Texan freedpeople.

_____

_____ 3. Suffrage was granted to all Texans during the constitutional convention in 1866.

_____

_____ 4. The U.S. government passed Black Codes that denied the civil rights of African Americans.

_____

_____ 5. A proclamation made soon after the Civil War is celebrated as Juneteenth.

_____

_____ 6. To help freedpeople with employment contracts, the U.S. government created the Freedmen's Bureau.

_____

_____ 7. Before a state could rejoin the Union, it had to create an approved constitution that ratified the Thirteenth Amendment.

_____

Reconstruction

MAIN IDEAS
1. Congress took control of Reconstruction because freedpeople were being denied their rights.
2. Texas and other southern states wrote new constitutions in order to gain readmission to the Union.

Key Terms and People

Radical Republicans members of the Republican Party committed to the equal treatment and enfranchisement of freedpeople

Civil Rights Act of 1866 act that gave citizenship and basic rights to African Americans

Fourteenth Amendment amendment to guarantee citizenship and equal rights to African Americans passed in 1869

Reconstruction Acts 1867 act marking the beginning of Congressional Reconstruction, which divided the south into five military districts, with each under the command of an army officer

impeach to bring charges of wrongdoing against a public official

Edmund J. Davis Radical Republican who defeated Andrew J. Hamilton for the office of Texas governor

George T. Ruby African American delegate and leader of the Union League in Texas

Union League during Reconstruction, an organization that urged African Americans to support the Republican Party

Fifteenth Amendment amendment that gave suffrage to African American men

Section Summary

RADICAL REPUBLICANS REACT

Radical Republicans believed that loyal southern state governments could be created only with the participation of Unionists and African Americans. They passed the **Civil Rights Act of 1866,** which gave citizenship to African Americans and guaranteed them basic rights. That summer, Republicans proposed the **Fourteenth Amendment** to guarantee citizenship and equal rights to all African American men. Most southern states, including Texas, refused to ratify this amendment.

> Underline what Radical Republicans believed about southern state governments.

THE RECONSTRUCTION ACTS

In March 1867, Congress passed **Reconstruction Acts** which marked the beginning of Congressional Reconstruction. Southern state governments were again declared provisional, and the South was divided into five military districts. President Johnson tried to block Congressional Reconstruction, prompting his impeachment. To **impeach** is to bring charges of wrongdoing against a public offical. Johnson avoided being removed from office by one vote.

THE TEXAS REPUBLICAN PARTY

Republicans split into two factions. One group hoped to put Radical Republicans, including African Americans, in control of the state government. **Edmund J. Davis** and **George T. Ruby** led this faction. Ruby was an African-American delegate and a leader of the **Union League,** a political organization that urged African Americans to support the Republican Party. The second group favored few changes.

THE CONSTITUTION OF 1869

Texas voters approved the new constitution. Davis won the governor's race, which gave equal rights to African Americans. The **Fifteenth Amendment** gave suffrage to African-American men. In March 1870 President Ulysses S. Grant signed an act of Congress admitting Texas senators and representatives. The next month, control of Texas returned to the state government.

CHALLENGE ACTIVITY

Critical Thinking: Comparing and Contrasting

How did the rights of African Americans differ under the Texas constitutions of 1866 and 1869?

Radical Republicans	Civil Rights Act of 1866	Fourteenth Amendment	Reconstruction Acts
Fifteenth Amendment	Edmund J. Davis	George T. Ruby	Union League

DIRECTIONS On the line provided before each statement, write **T** if a statement is true and **F** if a statement is false. If the statement is false, rewrite the sentence to make a true statement.

_____ 1. Radical Republicans believed that southern state governments needed the participation of Unionists and African Americans to be loyal.

_____

_____ 2. Reconstruction Acts were vetoed by President Johnson.

_____

_____ 3. The Fourteenth Amendment gave suffrage to African American men.

_____

_____ 4. Edmund J. Davis led the Union League in Texas.

_____

_____ 5. The Fifteenth Amendment guaranteed citizenship and basic civil rights to African Americans.

_____

_____ 6. Texas voters elected Edmund J. Davis governor of Texas.

_____

Reconstruction

Section 3

MAIN IDEAS
1. The Davis administration improved education and transportation in Texas but increased the state debt.
2. Reconstruction ended in Texas in 1874 when Republicans lost political power.

Key Terms and People

Ku Klux Klan a secret society that threatened and murdered African Americans to prevent them from expressing their political views

bonds notes that represent money owed by a government to private citizens

scalawags name given to southerners who supported Reconstruction for personal economic gain

carpetbaggers northerners who moved to the South after the Civil War; so called because they often carried all they owned in bags made of carpet

Richard Coke Democratic candidate who became governor of Texas in 1873

Section Summary
THE DAVIS ADMINISTRATION'S POLICIES

The new Texas legislature assembled in April 1870. It was dominated by Republicans, 11 of whom were African American. Senators Matthew Gaines and George T. Ruby led the legislative effort to stop widespread crime in the state. In particular, they aimed to stop the actions of the **Ku Klux Klan,** a secret association that threatened and murdered African Americans to prevent them from expressing their political points of view.

The Republicans also tackled an important social issue—education. Davis wanted African Americans to be treated equally by the law. The legislature created free public schools. Enrollment grew to almost 130,000 students in school during the 1872–73 school year.

To help the state recover financially, the legislature also issued **bonds**—certificates that represent money the government has borrowed—to

How did Davis want to change education?

_____

_____

help pay for railroad lines. The administration raised taxes to pay for schools, roads, and the larger central government.

What was the purpose of issuing bonds?
_____

OPPOSITION TO RECONSTRUCTION

Many Texans disliked these policies. They referred to Texans who supported the Republicans as **scalawags,** or "mean fellows." The few northerners who had come to Texas after the war were sometimes called **carpetbaggers** because some carried all they owned in bags made of carpet. Democrats opposed Davis and the Radical Republicans at every opportunity. Democrats called many of the new laws Obnoxious Acts— *obnoxious* means "very unpleasant."

THE END OF RECONSTRUCTION

In the 1873 election for governor, Governor Davis had the support of the Radical Republicans. Most white Texans supported Democrat **Richard Coke,** who won in a landslide. However, some Republicans argued that the polls had closed too early. The Texas Supreme Court ruled that the election was unconstitutional. Even so, Democrats demanded control of the government.

Eventually Davis agreed to leave. He turned the office over to Coke on January 19, 1874. This marked the end of Reconstruction in Texas. In the 1876 presidential election, each candidate claimed to have won. In the Compromise of 1877, Democrats agreed to accept the Republican Rutherford B. Hayes. In exchange for the Democrats' support, he removed federal troops from the South. Reconstruction was over.

What was unconstitutional about the 1873 election?
_____
_____

CHALLENGE ACTIVITY

Critical Thinking: Analyzing Information What brought about the end of Reconstruction in Texas?

Ku Klux Klan	scalawags	carpetbaggers	Richard Coke
bonds	Obnoxious Acts	Reconstruction	

DIRECTIONS Read each sentence and circle the term in the word pair that best completes each sentence.

1. Democrats called the laws passed by the Davis Administration (scalawags/Obnoxious Acts).

2. A secret society whose members threatened and murdered African Americans was called the (Ku Klux Klan/Reconstruction).

3. To gain more income for the state government, the Texas legislature issued (bonds/carpetbaggers).

4. Northerners who came to the South after the war were called (scalawags/carpetbaggers).

DIRECTIONS Write two adjectives or descriptive phrases that describe the term given.

5. scalawags _____

6. Richard Coke _____

7. bonds _____

8. carpetbaggers _____

Reconstruction

MAIN IDEAS
1. Texas politics changed with the Constitution of 1876 and one-party rule.
2. African Americans were denied equal rights after Reconstruction.
3. After Reconstruction, many Texas farmers became sharecroppers and tenant farmers.

Key Terms and People

Redeemers term given to many southern leaders who tried to "redeem," or restore, the South to its prewar days by limiting the size of state government and preventing political participation by African Americans

segregation the forced separation of people of different races

Jim Crow laws laws that enforced racial segregation

tenant farmers people who rent land to grow crops

sharecroppers farmers who lacked land and necessary supplies and thus promised a large part of their crop to the landowner in exchange for these items

Section Summary
THE TEXAS CONSTITUTION OF 1876

Texas voters approved a new Texas constitution in February 1876. This Constitution is still the state's basic law. Under the new constitution, the governor's term became two years rather than four. The governor's power to appoint officials was reduced, and the legislature was scheduled to meet once every two years instead of every year. The Democrats immediately began to reverse the policies of the Davis administration.

> Underline the changes that occurred under the new constitution.

SEGREGATION AND JIM CROW

African Americans' political power fell along with the influence of the Republican Party in Texas. As African Americans' political power declined, they lost many of their civil rights. After Reconstruction ended, many southern leaders tried to "redeem," or restore, the South to its prewar days. These

"**Redeemers**" limited the size of state government and cut back on political participation by African Americans. **Segregation**—the forced separation of people of different races—was written into law. **Jim Crow laws** were passed to enforce segregation. The Jim Crow system in Texas also denied African Americans equal rights, equal opportunity, and equal protection under the law.

> Underline the rights African Americans were denied under Jim Crow laws.

THE GROWTH OF TENANT FARMING

With Reconstruction over, large landowners once again returned to political power. Many Texans—particularly freedpeople—could not afford land. Many of them became **tenant farmers,** or people who rent land to grow crops. A landowner would usually receive a part of a tenant farmer's crop as payment for using the land.

Farmers who lacked land and necessary supplies, such as mules, plows, and seeds, promised a larger part of the crop to a landowner in return for these items. These farmers were called **sharecroppers.** A tenant farmer who was unable to grow enough to cover the land rental had to take out loans. These loans often had high interest rates, which made them difficult to pay back. As long as they owed money, tenant farmers and their children could not leave the land. Landowners had a great deal of control over tenant farmers and sharecroppers. By 1880 about 40 percent of all Texas farmers worked as tenant farmers.

> Why did many Texans become tenant farmers or sharecroppers?
>
> _____
>
> _____
>
> _____

CHALLENGE ACTIVITY

Critical Thinking: Compare and Contrast How were African Americans' rights affected after Reconstruction?

| Redeemers | segregation | Jim Crow laws |
| tenant farmers | sharecroppers | |

DIRECTIONS Read each sentence and fill in the blank with the term in the word pair that best completes the sentence.

1. Farmers who paid for necessary supplies with a large part of their crop were called (tenant farmers/sharecroppers).

2. Texans who wanted to restrict the political influence of African Americans were called (Redeemers/Jim Crow laws).

3. Laws that enforced (segregation/tenant farmers) were called Jim Crow laws.

4. Many Texans who could not afford to buy land became (tenant farmers/Redeemers), people who rent land to grow crops.

DIRECTIONS Write two adjectives or descriptive phrases that describe the term given.

5. Redeemers_____

6. Jim Crow laws _____

The Indian Wars

MAIN IDEAS

1. The Civil War and Reconstruction affected relations between American Indians and settlers in Texas.

2. The federal government took several steps to end American Indian raids in Texas.

Key Terms and People

commissioners representatives of a government

Treaty of the Little Arkansas October 1865 agreement between Comanche and Kiowa leaders and the federal government in which the two peoples agreed to live on a reservation in exchange for annual stipends

Satanta Kiowa chief who opposed the offer of a reservation and argued that the Panhandle belonged to the Kiowas and the Comanches

Treaty of Medicine Lodge 1867 peace treaty between the federal government and Plains Indians that offered 3 million acres of reservation land, food, clothing, and financial assistance to the Indians if they would agree to stop raiding and take up farming

Section Summary

AMERICAN INDIAN RELATIONS

During the Civil War, many men had left Texas to fight, leaving settlements open to Indian raids. When the war ended, there were not enough federal troops to protect the scattered frontier settlements from such raids. Federal **commissioners**—government representatives—met with leaders of the Comanches, Kiowas, and other southern Plains Indians in October 1865 to negotiate a peace treaty. In the **Treaty of the Little Arkansas,** Comanche and Kiowa leaders agreed to settle on a reservation that would include much of modern Oklahoma and the Texas Panhandle. The government would pay the Indians annual stipends. The reservation, however, was never created. As settlers continued to move westward, some Comanche and Kiowa Indians renewed their attacks.

> Why was the Treaty of the Little Arkansas created?
>
> _____
> _____
> _____

THE TREATY OF MEDICINE LODGE

In 1867 the federal government sent commissioners to negotiate a new peace treaty with Comanches, Kiowas, and other Plains Indians at Medicine Lodge Creek in Kansas. The commissioners offered some 3 million acres of land for a reservation in Indian Territory. In return, the Plains Indians had to stop raiding, stay on the reservation, and take up farming. Kiowa chief **Satanta** opposed the reservation policy. Other Indian leaders argued that their survival depended on moving to the reservations. Many Plains Indians agreed to the terms of the **Treaty of Medicine Lodge,** and several thousand moved to Indian Territory. Others remained on the plains.

> **What was offered to American Indians under the Treaty of Medicine Lodge?**
>
> _____
>
> _____
>
> _____

THE PEACE POLICY

In 1869 President Ulysses S. Grant established a Board of Indian Commissioners to carry out the terms of the peace treaty. The few Indians who tried farming had trouble growing food because the land set aside for them had poor soil. Government supplies failed to help. As a result, American Indians on reservations often went hungry and lacked basic supplies.

> **Why did American Indians on reservations often go hungry?**
>
> _____
>
> _____
>
> _____

CHALLENGE ACTIVITY

Critical Thinking: Compare and Contrast Write a paragraph in which you compare and contrast the Treaty of Medicine Lodge and the Treaty of the Little Arkansas.

DIRECTIONS Write two adjectives or descriptive phrases that describe the term given.

1. commissioners _____

_____

2. Treaty of the Little Arkansas _____

_____

3. Satanta _____

_____

4. Treaty of Medicine Lodge _____

_____

The Indian Wars

Section 2

MAIN IDEAS

1. The Salt Creek Raid affected military policy toward American Indians on the frontier.
2. The spread of railroad lines west and the slaughter of the buffalo greatly affected life for Plains Indians.

Key Terms and People

Salt Creek Raid an attack by Kiowas and Comanches who crossed into Texas in May of 1871 and raided a wagon train near Salt Creek, killing seven Texans

Quanah Parker Comanche leader and son of Cynthia Parker, a captured settler

Cynthia Parker a Texas settler who was captured by Comanches at 10 or 11 years of age and remained with Comanches for 25 years

buffalo guns powerful rifles that had telescopes; used to kill buffalo from a distance

Section Summary

THE SALT CREEK RAID

In 1871 the U.S. Army sent General William Tecumseh Sherman to investigate conditions in Texas. Sherman doubted that American Indians posed a serious threat in Texas. In May some 100 Kiowas and Comanches led by Big Tree, Satank, and Satanta attacked a wagon train near Salt Creek, killing seven men. A survivor of this **Salt Creek Raid** reported the raid to Sherman.

When the raiders came to the Indian Territory reservation for food supplies, Satanta admitted that he had participated in the attack. When Sherman learned of Satanta's statements, he had Big Tree, Satank, and Satanta arrested. Satank was later killed while trying to escape. Big Tree and Satanta were sentenced to death. Texas governor Edmund J. Davis worried that executing the men would only make matters worse. He changed the sentence to life in prison. Big Tree and Satanta were released from prison under condition of good behavior in 1873.

What happened during the Salt Creek Raid?
_____
_____
_____

Guided Reading Workbook

MACKENZIE'S RAIDS

Colonel Ranald S. Mackenzie led a series of attacks against Plains Indians who refused to live on the reservation. Mackenzie and his troops, called Mackenzie's Raiders, achieved great fame fighting on the Texas frontier. In late 1871, Mackenzie's troops fought a minor battle against a Comanche group led by **Quanah Parker.** Parker was the son of **Cynthia Parker,** a captured settler, and a Comanche Indian named Peta Nocona. After a series of battles, Mackenzie forced the Comanche to move to the reservation.

> Describe the impact that Mackenzie's leadership had on the Texas frontier.
> _____
> _____

THE SLAUGHTER OF THE BUFFALO

For generations, the Plains Indians had depended on the buffalo. As American railroad companies built lines across the Great Plains, non-Indian hunters killed hundreds of buffalo to feed the rail crews. The buffalo hide industry began in 1871. Buffalo hunters swarmed onto the plains to make their fortune. Most buffalo hunters would set up powerful rifles known as **buffalo guns.** These guns had telescopes, allowing hunters to hunt from a distance. Under the Medicine Lodge Treaty, buffalo hunters were not allowed onto American Indian hunting grounds south of Kansas. The army was supposed to patrol the Kansas-Indian Territory border but failed to do so. Many military officials believed the extermination, or complete destruction, of the buffalo herds would force Plains Indians onto reservations. Between 1872 and 1874, hunters killed an estimated 4.3 million buffalo.

> Why were buffalo guns used?
> _____
> _____

CHALLENGE ACTIVITY

Critical Thinking: Cause and Effect How did the railroad and buffalo hunters affect the Plains Indians' way of life?

Guided Reading Workbook

Salt Creek Raid	Quanah Parker	Cynthia Parker
buffalo guns		

DIRECTIONS Read each sentence and circle the term in the word pair that best completes each sentence.

1. (Quanah Parker/Cynthia Parker) was captured by Comanches at around age 10.

2. (Quanah Parker/Cynthia Parker) was a Comanche leader.

3. (Salt Creek Raid/Buffalo guns) killed buffalo from a distance.

4. Seven Texans traveling on a wagon train were killed in the (Salt Creek Raid/buffalo guns).

DIRECTIONS Use the words from the word bank to write a summary of what you have learned in the section.

_____

_____

_____

_____

_____

_____

_____

_____

_____

_____

MAIN IDEAS
1. The attack on Adobe Walls led to war between the Plains Indians and the U.S. government.
2. The Battle of Palo Duro Canyon marked the end of the era of American Indian control over the Texas Plains.

Key Terms

Battle of Adobe Walls 1874 battle led by Plains Indian leaders to drive out the buffalo hunters by attacking the trading post at Adobe Walls in the Texas Panhandle

Battle of Palo Duro Canyon 1874 battle led by Colonel Mackenzie to attack Comanches, Kiowas, and Cheyennes who were camping in Palo Duro Canyon

Section Summary

THE BATTLE OF ADOBE WALLS

On June 27, 1874, some 700 Indians attacked the trading post of Adobe Walls in the Texas Panhandle, hoping to drive out the buffalo hunters. Twenty-eight men and one woman were at the trading post, but they had powerful buffalo guns which could shoot long distances. Despite repeated attacks, the hunters held their ground at the **Battle of Adobe Walls.**

> Who won the Battle of Adobe Walls? How did they win?
>
> _____
> _____
> _____

THE BATTLE OF PALO DURO CANYON

In August 1874 the army began a major offensive known as the Red River War. Some 3,000 troops headed toward the Indian villages along the upper Red River. They were joined by the Frontier Battalion of the Texas Rangers. Colonel Nelson Miles led 750 soldiers into Texas from Fort Dodge in Kansas. These soldiers fought against some 600 Cheyennes, who finally escaped in late August. Major William Price defeated a band of Indians near Sweetwater Creek in the Panhandle. Meanwhile, Colonel John Davidson and Lieutenant

Colonel George Buell commanded two military forces that destroyed many American Indian villages. This forced hundreds of Indians, mainly women and children, onto reservations, where supplies were already short.

Many Comanches, Kiowas and a few Cheyennes were camping in Palo Duro Canyon, which had provided shelter to Indian families for centuries. Just before dawn on September 28, 1874, Colonel Mackenzie and about 500 troops worked their way into the canyon and attacked the Indians. The **Battle of Palo Duro Canyon** took a terrible toll on the Comanches. In their escape, the Comanches left behind most of their supplies—including more than 1,400 horses. Lacking clothing and horses, the Indians would not survive the winter in the Panhandle. They had no choice but to move to the reservations.

Why did the Indians go to Palo Duro Canyon?
_____
_____

CHALLENGE ACTIVITY

Critical Thinking: Cause and Effect List the effects that the Battle of Adobe Walls and the Battle of Palo Duro Canyon had on the lives of the Plains Indians.

Guided Reading Workbook

| Battle of Adobe Walls | Battle of Palo Duro Canyon |

DIRECTIONS On the line provided before each statement, write **T** if a statement is true and **F** if a statement is false. If the statement is false, write a corrected statement on the line after the false statement.

_____ 1. During the <u>Battle of Palo Duro Canyon,</u> Comanches left behind a few of their supplies but fled the canyon with more than 1,400 horses.

_____

_____ 2. During the <u>Battle of Adobe Walls,</u> American Indians were victorious because they used powerful rifles known as buffalo guns.

_____

_____ 3. After the <u>Battle of Palo Duro Canyon,</u> American Indians had no other choice but to move to the reservations.

_____

_____ 4. The <u>Battle of Adobe Walls</u> took place in the winter of 1874.

_____

Guided Reading Workbook

The Indian Wars

Section 4

 MAIN IDEAS
1. The Indian raids stopped when the Mexican army joined the United States on the chase.
2. The American Indian population had decreased greatly by the 1880s.

Key Terms and People

Victorio Apache chief who led Apache families to Mexico and began raids into Texas from Mexico

buffalo soldiers a name given by American Indians to African-American troops stationed along the border of Texas

Henry O. Flipper the first black graduate of the U.S. Military Academy at West Point

Section Summary
FIGHTING ON THE RIO GRANDE

The Apache chief **Victorio** led many Apache families to Mexico after they were ordered to move to a barren reservation in Arizona. They began raids into Texas from Mexico. The U.S. army ordered more troops to the area. Most of the 2,500 U.S. troops stationed along the border served in the 9th and 10th Cavalries as well as in the 24th and 25th Infantry Regiments. Although white officers commanded these regiments, all the troops were African American. They were called **"buffalo soldiers"** by American Indians. **Henry O. Flipper,** the first black graduate of the U.S. Military Academy, took part in a campaign against the Apache. The raids were not stopped until the Mexican army became active in the chase.

> **How were the Apache raids into Texas stopped?**
> _____
> _____
> _____

RESERVATION LIFE

When Texas Indians moved onto the reservations, their efforts to farm and ranch often failed. They usually received poor land, and they had little experience raising crops using the techniques taught

Guided Reading Workbook

by reservation agents. When government officials did not supply food, Indians often faced starvation. In 1883, the federal government banned many American Indian religious practices, including the Sun Dance. Indians often had to hold celebrations and ceremonies in secret. Indians preserved many of their customs, myths, and styles of dress, despite officials' efforts to eliminate these traditions.

Quanah Parker, who had surrendered and moved to the reservation in 1875, worked to better relations between the federal government and American Indians. Parker continued to try to improve the lives of the Comanches until his death in 1911. The Dawes General Allotment Act of 1887 divided up reservation lands in Oklahoma and promised Indians U.S. citizenship. This division of lands dissolved some of the unity within Texas Indian tribes. In addition, many Indians did not receive enough land to support themselves.

After dividing the reservations, the government sold the remaining lands. As a result, Indians lost an enormous amount of land. The act also failed to grant Indians full citizenship as promised. All American Indians were not granted citizenship until 1924.

The difficulties of reservation life, military attacks, and the slaughter of the buffalo took a terrible toll on Texas Indians. By the 1880s their population had been greatly reduced. Most had either been killed or moved out of the state. Settlers quickly moved onto lands that Texas Indians had called home for hundreds of years.

> Underline the reasons that American Indians often faced starvation.

> List 3 ways the Texas Indians were affected by the U.S. government?
> _____
> _____
> _____

CHALLENGE ACTIVITY

Critical Thinking: Drawing Inferences Imagine you are an American Indian forced to live on a reservation. Write a journal entry describing your new life on the reservation.

Guided Reading Workbook

| Victorio | buffalo soldiers | Henry O. Flipper |

DIRECTIONS Use all of the words in the word bank to write a summary of the section you've just read.

_____

_____

_____

_____

_____

_____

_____

_____

_____

_____

_____

_____

_____

_____

_____

_____

_____

_____

The Cattle Kingdom

 MAIN IDEAS
1. The Texas cattle industry grew from the ranchos established by the Spanish in the1700s.
2. The longhorn was uniquely suited for the hot, dry Texas weather.
3. The Civil War increased demand for Texas cattle.

Key Terms

brands identification marks made with hot metal on cattle

cattle drives herding groups of cattle to market for sale

rustlers cattle thieves

longhorn a new breed of cattle developed as Spanish breeds mixed with English cattle

Texas fever a strain of cattle disease to which the longhorn were resistant

Section Summary
SPANISH BEGINNINGS

By the early 1700s the Spanish were moving cattle herds north into Texas to support the missions that they had established in the Rio Grande and San Antonio River valleys. To identify who owned which cattle, the Spanish government began ordering cattle owners to put **brands**, or identification marks made with hot metal, on their cattle. Over time, ranching in Texas shifted from missions to private owners. Tejano ranchers staged the first **cattle drives** in Texas, herding groups of cattle south of the Rio Grande to Spanish military outposts. As U.S. settlers arrived in the early 1800s, ranching spread to other areas. The Texas cattle industry slowly expanded in the 1840s. Herding stock to sell outside of Texas, however, was a difficult and often dangerous process. Cattle **rustlers**, or thieves, threatened the herds.

> How did cattle owners identify their cattle?
>
> _____
> _____
> _____

THE TEXAS LONGOHORNS

During the mid-1800s, the **longhorn** appeared in
Texas. This new breed of cattle developed as
Spanish breeds mixed with English cattle brought
by U.S. settlers. Longhorns thrived on Texas native
grasses, could survive on little water, and could
endure both hot and cold weather. Longhorns were
resistant to the cattle disease commonly called
Texas fever. The cattle protected themselves from
predators with their long horns. When the Civil War
broke out, the demand for Texas beef increased
rapidly. By 1863, however, the Union army had
blocked trade from Confederate states, including
Texas. The herds in Texas increased, and by the end
of the Civil War some 5 million cattle roamed the
state.

> **List three things that made the longhorn suitable for Texas.**
>
> _____
>
> _____
>
> _____

CHALLENGE ACTIVITY
Critical Thinking: Evaluating What changes
made cattle ranching possible after the Civil War?

brands	cattle drives	rustlers
longhorn	Texas fever	

DIRECTIONS Use each of the words in the word bank to write a summary of what you learned from this section.

_____

_____

_____

_____

_____

_____

_____

_____

_____

_____

_____

_____

_____

_____

_____

_____

_____

_____

_____

_____

_____

The Cattle Kingdom

 MAIN IDEAS

1. The growing market for beef was profitable for many Texas ranchers.
2. Some of the most well-traveled trails included the Sedalia, Chisholm, Western, and Goodnight-Loving trails.
3. Life on the trail was difficult and often dangerous.

Key Terms and People

stockyards huge holding pens for cattle

open range unfenced land in Texas

Sedalia Trail cattle trail sometimes known as the Kansas Trail or Shawnee Trail

Chisholm Trail cattle trail leading North from San Antonio to Abilene, Kansas

Western Trail cattle trail which ran west of settled territory

Charles Goodnight one of the original Texas ranchers who was the first to recognize the potential of the eastern markets and and who pioneered the Goodnight-Loving Trail

remuda the Spanish word for "remount," used to describe a herd of horses from which cowboys choose to ride in relays

wrangler a professional horse handler

Section Summary

THE CATTLE DRIVES

The Northeast had a great demand for beef after the Civil War. In Texas, however, the supply of cattle was greater than the demand. As a result, cattle that sold for $3 or $6 a head in Texas sold for much more in Kansas or in New York. After the war, **stockyards**, or huge holding pens, and packing houses were opening in Chicago, St. Louis, and Kansas City. These plants prepared beef for shipment to cities in the North and East. Texas ranchers started driving their cattle north, letting their herds graze on the grass of the **open range**, or unfenced land. Early cattle drives used the **Sedalia Trail**. However, Kansas and Missouri passed laws to stop these cattle drives.

> **What was the purpose of the cattle trails?**
>
> _____
> _____
> _____

THE CHISHOLM AND WESTERN TRAILS

Texas cowboys were soon herding longhorns over the **Chisholm Trail** to a cattle market in Abilene, Kansas. This trail was named after Jesse Chisholm, a fur trader. In 1874 the **Western Trail** was forged across the open range to the west of settled territory. By 1879 it was the primary route for Texas cattle being moved north. In 1866 Charles Goodnight and Oliver Loving combined their herds and set out for Fort Sumner, New Mexico. Their route became known as the **Goodnight-Loving Trail**.

LIFE ON THE TRAIL

Some ranchers drove their own cattle, but most hired a drover, or cattle drive operator. A typical cattle drive had 8 to 12 cowboys to care for 2,000 to 3,000 cattle. Each cowboy used several horses in relays of two or three, so that a fresh mount was always available. The herd of these animals was known as the **remuda**, the Spanish word for "remount." A **wrangler** cared for the crew's horses. Two experienced cowboys called point men guided the herd, while other cowboys rode on the sides of the herd. Drag men traveled behind the herd. On trail drives, cowboys faced hot sunshine, bad weather, low water supplies, and prairie fires.

What was the remuda?
_____
_____
_____

CHALLENGE ACTIVITY

Critical Thinking: Mapping Locate the four trails on a map. List the Texas cities that currently lie on the routes.

stockyards	open range	Sedalia Trail
Chisholm Trail	Western Trail	Charles Goodnight
remuda	wrangler	

DIRECTIONS Use each of the words in the word bank to write a summary of what you learned from this section.

_____

_____

_____

_____

_____

_____

_____

_____

_____

_____

_____

_____

_____

_____

_____

_____

_____

_____

The Cattle Kingdom

Section 3

MAIN IDEAS

1. Ranching was a major industry in both South Texas and in the Panhandle.

2. Cowboys and ranchers had to fill many roles on a ranch.

3. Western novels and shows helped spread the myths of a carefree cowboy life.

Key Terms and People

Cattle Kingdom nickname for the cattle ranches that arose on the open range from Texas to Canada during the 1800s

King Ranch one of the most important ranches in the state, established in the 1850s

windmills used by the ranchers to power pumps to bring water to the ranches

JA Ranch one of the first ranches in the Panhandle, established in the mid-1870s

XIT Ranch a ranch established in 1885 when the state gave land to the Capitol Freehold Land and Investment Company

Section Summary

RANCHING IN SOUTH TEXAS

During the 1800s the cattle ranches that arose on the open range from Texas to Canada became known as the **Cattle Kingdom**. Richard King and Gideon Lewis established the **King Ranch** in Nueces County in the early 1850s. King died in 1885, leaving his wife to run the ranch. Henrietta King and her son-in-law, Robert Kleberg, built the King Ranch into a thriving operation.

What was the Cattle Kingdom?
_____
_____
_____

RANCHES IN THE PANHANDLE

As Plains Indians were removed from West Texas, the Panhandle was opened up for ranching. Ranchers adapted to the environment by using **windmills** to help pump water from the Ogallala Aquifer, which lay beneath the region. One of the first ranches established in the Panhandle was the **JA Ranch**, set up by Charles Goodnight and John Adair. The **XIT Ranch** was established in 1885

What were windmills used for?
_____
_____
_____

when the state gave the land to the Capitol Freehold
Land and Investment Company. In return, the
company's investors agreed to construct a new state
capitol building. The new capitol, finished in 1888,
is still the seat of Texas government.

RANCHERS AND COWBOYS

Ranches in Texas were located far from towns.
Ranchers had to rely on themselves to solve the
many challenges they faced. They could never have
succeeded without cowboys. Cowboys completed
daily tasks on the ranches. Texas cowboys wore
clothes to suit the environment—hats to keep off the
sun and rain, and chaps to protect them from thorny
bushes. Over time, cowboys became an important
part of American popular culture. The realities of
cowboy life were far different from the myths.
Cowboys faced many dangers and earned low
salaries.

> List two items of traditional
> cowboy clothing.
>
> _____
>
> _____
>
> _____

CHALLENGE ACTIVITY

Critical Thinking: Comparing and Contrasting How
did real life on a ranch differ from that in stories
and myths?

DIRECTIONS On the line provided before each statement, write **T** if a statement is true and **F** if a statement is false. If the statement is false, write a corrected statement on the line after the false statement.

_____ 1. The <u>King Ranch</u> was one of the first ranches in the Panhandle.

_____

_____ 2. In the 1800s, many ranches were built in the region that stretched from Texas north to Canada; this became known as the <u>Cattle Kingdom</u>.

_____

_____ 3. The <u>XIT Ranch</u> was established in 1885 by Charles Goodnight and John Adair.

_____

_____ 4. Ranchers used <u>windmills</u> to power pumps to bring water from underground.

_____

The Cattle Kingdom

Section 4

MAIN IDEAS

1. The use of barbed wire let to the closing of the open range and to range wars.

2. Overgrazing and heavy use of ranch land helped to contribute to the decline of the Cattle Kingdom.

Key Terms and People

Joseph F. Glidden farmer in De Kalb, Illinois, who developed barbed wire in 1873

barbed wire a type of wire fencing designed with sharp points, or barbs, at intervals along its length

range wars conflict involving ranchers and farmers over control of the open range

Section Summary

FENCING THE OPEN RANGE

West Texas farmers wanted to fence their land to protect their crops from stray cattle. **Joseph J. Glidden** developed **barbed wire** in 1873. By the end of the 1880s, there were barbed wire fences in nearly every Texas county.

THE RANGE WARS

Widespread fencing led to conflict. Ranchers complained that fencing cut their cattle off from water. **Range wars** broke out during an 1883 drought, when cattle began to die of thirst. Ranchers cut farmers' fences to get access to water. In 1884 the legislature passed a law making fence cutting illegal. Cattle ranchers were also angry with sheep ranchers because sheep ate the grass all the way down to the root, making it useless for cattle.

> **What caused range wars?**
> _____
> _____
> _____

THE LEGACY OF THE OPEN RANGE

Toward the end of the 1880s, the open range began to disappear thanks to fencing. In addition, severe winters in the 1880s caused the deaths of thousands of open-range cattle. Many ranches went out of business. Many ranchers had expanded too quickly. Years of heavy use had stripped the grass and damaged the soil itself. Some cattle operators sold their land to farmers. The damage to ranches limited job opportunities for cowboys. In addition, the extension of railroad lines to Texas eventually ended the need for long cattle drives. Newly invented refrigerator cars could move processed beef to eastern cities. Despite the decline of the cattle era, the industry created an important legacy in Texas.

How did the railroad affect the cattle industry in Texas?

_____

_____

_____

CHALLENGE ACTIVITY

Critical Thinking: Summarizing What were the main factors that contributed to the end of the open range?

DIRECTIONS Write two or three sentences to describe each phrase or name given.

1. Joseph F. Glidden _____

_____

_____

2. barbed wire _____

_____

_____

3. range wars _____

_____

_____

Railroads and Farming

 MAIN IDEAS

1. Rail travel was faster and more reliable than other forms of transportation in Texas.

2. Railroads brought trade and businesses to many towns.

3. The expansion of railroads led to the development of the Texas frontier.

Key Terms

transcontinental railroad a railroad that runs across a continent

junctions the meeting places of two or more rail lines

Section Summary

NEW RAILROAD LINES

The economic development of Texas had been slowed by its transportation problems. Railroads promised cheap, fast, and reliable transportation. In 1870 Texas railroad construction continued to lag behind the rest of the country, which had almost 53,000 miles of track. The United States even had a **transcontinental railroad**—one that runs across a continent. Many cities issued bonds to help pay for rail construction. A bond is a certificate that represents money owed by the government to private citizens. Between 1850 and 1876, Texas cities and counties issued about $2.4 million in railroad bonds. The Constitution of 1876 banned these local bonds but allowed the legislature to pass a general land grant law. Texas eventually gave more than 32 million acres of land to more than 40 railroad companies.

> **Why were railroads important for the Texas economy?**
>
> _____
>
> _____
>
> _____

> **What was the first transcontinental route through Texas?**
>
> _____
>
> _____
>
> _____

THE RAILROAD BOOM

Grants and other forms of government aid helped create a Texas railroad boom. During the boom, railroad companies began a race west. In December 1881 the Texas and Pacific Railway (T&P) met the Southern Pacific line in Sierra Blanca, some 90 miles east of El Paso. This was the first transcontinental route through Texas. Railroad companies also encouraged trade between Texas and Mexico by running lines to the Mexican border.

THE EFFECTS OF THE RAIL BOOM

The arrival of railroads greatly affected Texas. New cities were born, new areas were settled, and Texas became more connected to the rest of the country. Cities grew rapidly at **junctions**, or the meeting places of two or more lines. The economic boom in railroad towns attracted new residents. Towns that were bypassed by new rail lines often experienced drops in population and economic activity.

> **List three ways railroads affected Texas.**
> _____
> _____
> _____

FARMERS MOVE WEST

Railroads played a major role in opening up the Texas frontier to farming. As railroad companies built tracks through West Texas, settlers followed these lines and purchased land near railroad stops. People began flocking to the frontier to find inexpensive land.

CHALLENGE ACTIVITY

Critical Thinking: Mapping Locate the route of the first transcontinental railroad through Texas on a map and list the major cities along the route.

Guided Reading Workbook

DIRECTIONS Write a summary of what you learned from this section
about the development of the railroad and its effect on Texas.

_____

_____

_____

_____

_____

_____

_____

_____

_____

_____

_____

_____

_____

_____

_____

_____

_____

_____

_____

_____

_____

_____

Railroads and Farming

Section 2

 MAIN IDEAS

1. New farming technology helped Texans adapt to life on the frontier.
2. The commercial cotton-farming boom had both positive and negative effects for Texans.

Key Terms and People

dry farming a type of farming practiced in dry areas that uses various techniques to keep moisture in the soil

threshers machines that separate grain or seeds from plants

commercial farming the large-scale growing of crops to sell for profit

Dora Nunn Robert Texan farmer who struggled to survive the lengthy drought in the 1880s

Boll weevil a type of beetle that infests cotton fields

Section Summary

NEW FARMING TECHNOLOGY

Farmers soon learned that certain crops such as wheat and other grains grew well in the dry climate of West Texas. Many farmers practiced **dry farming** techniques such as terracing to keep moisture in the soil. John Deere's deep steel plow—widely used by 1845— helped West Texas farmers break through the hard soil. During the 1880s a few farmers, following the lead of ranchers, began to use windmills to pump water from aquifers for crop irrigation. Texans also began to use new mechanical farm tools. **Threshers**—machines that separate grain or seeds from plants—made harvesting crops faster and easier. In the late 1800s a few Texas farmers even began to use steam-powered threshers and tractors.

> **How did threshers improve farming?**
> _____
> _____
> _____

COMMERCIAL FARMING

New machinery, the increase in the number of farms, and the availability of railroads to ship

products all encouraged agricultural growth in
Texas. The increase in the state's agricultural
production resulted in a boom in **commercial
farming** during the late 1800s. Commercial farming
is the large-scale growing of crops to sell for profit.
In 1880 Texas farmers produced about $57 million
worth of cotton. Texas had just a few textile mills in
the late 1800s, so much of this cotton was shipped
out of state. The development of cottonseed oil,
used in cooking products, cosmetics, and roofing
material, further spurred cotton production. In East
Texas, the value of Texas agricultural goods rose
from more than $10 million to almost $40 million
during the late 1800s. West Texas experienced an
even more dramatic shift, increasing from $574,000
to more than $8 million during that same period.

> List three things that led to the increase in agricultural production.
>
> _____
> _____
> _____

FARMING TROUBLES

As farmers grew more crops, supply began to
exceed demand, and prices fell. This is the
economic law of supply and demand. Railroads had
integrated Texas with the national and international
markets for cotton. Therefore, the price of a bale of
cotton in Texas was determined by the quantity of
cotton produced in all parts of the world. The drop
in prices hit farmers hard. The **boll weevil**, a type of
beetle that destroys cotton, quickly spread
throughout Texas. Farm organizations and scientists
tried to encourage farmers to diversify and grow a
variety of crops. However, even with the falling
prices, farmers still made more money on cotton
than on other crops.

> Underline three things that led to farming troubles.

CHALLENGE ACTIVITY

Critical Thinking: Analyzing information What
were the main factors that led to the rise of
commercial farming in Texas? What factors led to
the eventual bust?

| dry farming | commercial farming | boll weevil |
| threshers | Dora Nunn Roberts | |

DIRECTIONS On the line provided before each statement, write **T** if a statement is true and **F** if a statement is false. If the statement is false, write a corrected statement on the line after the false statement.

_____ 1. <u>Dry farming</u> techniques helped Texans adapt to growing crops in the western climate.

_____

_____ 2. <u>Commercial farming</u> led to many Texas farmers growing only cotton.

_____

_____ 3. The <u>boll weevil</u> infested cotton in only certain parts of Texas.

_____

_____ 4. Farmers used <u>threshers</u> to break through the hard soil.

_____

_____ 5. <u>Dora Nunn Roberts'</u> deep steel plow was widely used in 1845.

_____

Railroads and Farming

MAIN IDEAS

1. In the late 1800s, lumber, flour milling, and cottonseed oil were major industries in Texas.

2. Labor unions in Texas had some success, but public support decreased greatly by the end of the century.

Key Terms

labor unions organizations that supported the interests of workers

Knights of Labor organization set up to support skilled and unskilled workers of almost every trade, including large numbers of farmers

strike protest in which workers refuse to do their jobs until a company meets their demands

Section Summary

LEADING INDUSTRIES

The most important Texas industries continued to be the ones that helped turn farm goods into products. Flour milling was the state's leading industry after agriculture.

By the 1890s lumber had overtaken flour milling in value. Between 1870 and 1900 the production of lumber in Texas increased more than eight times to more than $16 million. The growth of railroads created a greater demand for lumber. Railroads used timber for rail ties and bridges and for fuel. Railroads also provided cheap transportation for timber products, which were used for building in the treeless frontier of West Texas and in other parts of the United States.

Meatpacking was another leading Texas industry. The Texas mining industry developed in the 1880s, when railroad locomotives began to use coal instead of wood as fuel.

> **Why did the growth of railroads create a demand for lumber?**
>
> _____
>
> _____
>
> _____

INDUSTRIAL WORKERS

In 1900 less than 2 percent of the population worked in manufacturing. Wages and hours for industrial workers varied from job to job. Some workers joined **labor unions**—organizations that formed to support the interest of workers. Unions pushed for improvements in the hours, wages, and working conditions of laborers. In 1882 the first national labor union arrived in Texas. The **Knights of Labor** organized to support skilled and unskilled workers of almost every trade, including farmers. In Texas, the Knights organized railroad workers. The union led a successful **strike** in 1885 against Jay Gould's Wabash Railroad. Another railroad strike, known as the Great Southwest Strike of 1886, led to violence in Fort Worth. Labor unrest continued until the state militia and the Texas Rangers restored order. Many Texans were upset by the violence, while others believed that strikes and other labor actions threatened the production and transportation of goods. As a result, support for unions decreased in Texas.

> Underline a reason why workers joined labor unions.

CHALLENGE ACTIVITY

Critical Thinking: Supporting a Point of View
Imagine that you are an industrial worker in Texas in the late 1800s. Write a letter to a friend in the North describing why you support the labor union.

Guided Reading Workbook

DIRECTIONS Write a summary of why labor unions grew in Texas
and what led to their decline.

_____

_____

_____

_____

_____

_____

_____

_____

_____

_____

_____

_____

_____

_____

_____

_____

_____

_____

_____

_____

_____

The Oil Boom

MAIN IDEAS
1. The Texas oil industry began with the discovery of a major oil field in Corsicana.
2. The Spindletop strike marked the beginning of the oil boom in Texas.

Key Terms and People

petroleum a thick, dark fossil fuel commonly called oil

fossil fuel a fuel formed underground from plant or animal remains

derricks towers that support oil-drilling equipment

refinery a factory where crude oil is made pure

Patillo Higgins a brick-factory owner who believed oil would be found at Spindletop Hill

Anthony F. Lucas an engineer who drilled to find oil at Spindletop Hill in 1901

Spindletop strike marked the beginning of the Texas oil boom and the age of oil in Texas

boom-and-bust cycle a cycle of alternating periods of growth and depression in an industry or economy

Section Summary
THE SEARCH FOR OIL

The demand for oil rose dramatically after scientists developed kerosene in the mid-1800s. Kerosene was a new form of fuel for lighting that could be made from coal or **petroleum.** Commonly called oil, petroleum is a dark, thick, liquid **fossil fuel.** A fossil fuel is a fuel formed underground from plant or animal remains.

In Texas, a Civil War veteran named Lyne T. Barret drilled for oil outside Nacogdoches in 1866. His oil well was soon producing 10 barrels of oil a day. However, Barret could not raise the money necessary to continue drilling and had to shut the well down. Texas produced only 48 barrels of oil in 1889, compared to 35 million barrels produced in the rest of the United States.

> **Why did the demand for oil rise in the mid-1800s?**
> _____
> _____
> _____

In 1894, drillers searching for water in Corsicana struck oil. The Corsicana landscape was soon dotted with **derricks**, or towers that support oil-drilling equipment. To process the oil, business leaders constructed a refinery. A **refinery** is a factory in which crude oil is refined, or made pure, and then made into various products.

THE SPINDLETOP STRIKE

Pattillo Higgins, a brick-factory owner, believed that oil would be found under a salt dome at a place called Spindletop Hill, or Big Hill, near Beaumont. Salt domes are underground formations that often trap oil and natural gases. In 1899 Higgins hired an engineer named **Anthony F. Lucas,** who was an expert on salt domes. Lucas agreed that oil was probably beneath the Spindletop dome. He struck oil on January 10, 1901. The **Spindletop strike** marked the beginning of the Texas oil boom. Hundreds of oil companies formed to drill new wells.

> Underline the definition of a salt dome.

BOOM AND BUST AFTER SPINDLETOP

In 1902, nearly 20 percent of the oil produced in the United States came from Spindletop. With large quantities of oil being produced, the supply of oil soon outpaced the demand. Oil prices dropped dramatically, and the rush of companies drilling at Spindletop soon drained its oil reserves. These changes in price were part of a **boom-and-bust cycle**, or alternating periods of growth and depression, in an industry or economy. The boom and bust at Spindletop was the first such cycle the Texas oil industry would experience.

> Why did oil prices drop?
> _____

CHALLENGE ACTIVITY

Critical Thinking: Identifying Cause and Effect
Identify the events that led to the drop in oil prices.

Guided Reading Workbook

petroleum	derricks	boom-and-bust cycle	Spindletop strike
fossil fuel	refinery	Patillo Higgins	Anthony F. Lucas

DIRECTIONS Read each sentence and circle the term from the word pair that best completes each sentence.

1. (Petroleum/Fossil fuel) is the general term for a fuel made from plant or animal remains.

2. (Patillo Higgins/Anthony F. Lucas) hired an engineer to drill for oil at Spindletop Hill.

3. The (boom-and-bust cycle /Spindletop strike) occurred in 1901.

4. Drillers used (a refinery/derricks) to support oil-drilling equipment.

DIRECTIONS Write two adjectives or descriptive phrases that describe each term given.

5. petroleum _____

6. refinery _____

7. boom-and-bust cycle _____

8. derricks _____

The Oil Boom

MAIN IDEAS
1. After Spindletop, oil fields quickly sprung up in many regions of Texas.
2. New business ideas such as horizontal and vertical integration changed the oil industry.

Key Terms

wildcatters independent oil operators who searched for new fields

natural gas a gas that can be used a fuel

vertical integration owning the business involved in each step of a manufacturing process

horizontal integration owning many businesses in a particular field

Section Summary

WILDCATTERS AND NEW OIL FIELDS

Some of the new Texas companies were owned by **wildcatters**—independent oil operators who searched for new fields. Wildcatters found a large oil field in the Gulf Coast Plain. However, many Gulf Coast oil fields faced a drop in oil production when they were over pumped, as Spindletop had been. Soon oil fields were found in North Texas, the Panhandle, the Permian Basin, South and Central Texas, and in East Texas. Panhandle oil fields produced some 39 million barrels of oil in a single year. An oil strike deep in the heart of East Texas gave the oil industry its greatest surprise, as geologists claimed there was very little oil there. In fact, the East Texas oil field turned out to be one of the largest in the world.

> List in order the regions in which oil was found in Texas.
>
> _____
> _____
> _____
> _____
> _____
> _____

OIL BUSINESS IS BIG BUSINESS

Texas oil fields produced more than just oil. **Natural gas**—a gas that can be used as a fuel—was also abundant. However, there was no way to get it to market safely in the early years of the oil industry. As a result, gas coming out of oil wells was allowed to burn.

Then in the 1890s, scientists developed a leak-proof pipeline that could safely move natural gas about 100 miles. Further advances in pipeline technology during the 1920s and 1930s expanded the distance that gas could be shipped. This new pipeline technology opened the market for Texas natural gas. Some Texas oil companies began to use a business strategy called **vertical integration**—owning the businesses involved in each step of a manufacturing process. Most large companies also practiced **horizontal integration**— owning many businesses in a particular manufacturing field. The larger oil corporations would run many refineries, sharing supplies and resources to make their businesses more efficient.

> **What invention made it possible to move natural gas?**
>
> _____
>
> _____
>
> _____

CHALLENGE ACTIVITY

Critical Thinking: Making Inferences Imagine you are a wildcatter searching for oil in North Texas in 1902. Write a diary entry describing a day in your life.

| wildcatters | natural gas | horizontal integration | vertical integration |

DIRECTIONS Write a summary of what you have learned about the
growth of the oil industry using all the key terms.

_____

_____

_____

_____

_____

_____

_____

_____

_____

_____

_____

_____

_____

_____

_____

_____

_____

_____

MAIN IDEAS
1. The oil boom caused Texas to grow rapidly.
2. New technologies fueled the growth of the oil industry.
3. The oil industry affected the politics, economy, and social life of Texas.

Key Terms

boomtown fast growing towns that grew during economic booms

internal combustion engine any engine which generates power by the burning of gasoline, oil, or other fuel with air inside the engine

Texas Railroad Commission an agency originally created to regulate railroads; authority to enforce laws concerning the petroleum industry

Permanent University Fund land set aside by the Texas Legislature in 1876, the sale or use of which would generate funds for Texas universities

philanthropy the giving of money or gifts

Section Summary

BOOMTOWNS

The spectacular fortunes made in the oil business drew thousands of people to the Texas oil fields and nearby towns. Called **boomtowns** because they grew during economic booms, they were busy places where everyone was trying to make money. People were more concerned with drilling for oil than city planning, and these towns were crowded and rough, making them dangerous places to live.

> Underline a reason why boomtowns were crowded and rough.

AUTOMOBILE AND PETROCHEMICAL INDUSTRIES

Because oil was cheaper than coal, it quickly replaced coal as the fuel for steam engines that ran ships and railroad locomotives. The use of automobiles with **internal combustion engines** was also increasing. These engines used gasoline, an oil by-product, for power. As Americans bought more cars and drove longer distances, the demand for gasoline grew. The growth in popularity of the

> How did the growing popularity of the automobile help the oil industry?
>
> _____
> _____
> _____

automobile guaranteed the Texas oil industry millions of customers. In addition, scientists continued to develop new uses for petroleum. Petrochemicals, products made from oil and gas, became an important part of the Texas economy.

THE EFFECTS OF THE OIL BOOM

The oil boom attracted many young farmworkers to jobs in the oil fields. The oil boom also affected Texas politics and the environment. State officials began to pass restrictions designed to control parts of the oil industry. In 1917 the legislature gave the **Texas Railroad Commission**—an agency originally created to regulate railroads—the authority to enforce laws concerning the petroleum industry.

> **What role was Texas Railroad Commission given in 1917?**
> _____
> _____
> _____

The state government also began collecting taxes on oil production in 1905. This money helped fund the state government and education programs. In 1876 the Texas legislature had set aside one million acres of land in West Texas for the **Permanent University Fund**. Texas universities received money from the sale or use of this land. However, many people considered the land worthless until the Santa Rita No.1 oil well struck oil in 1923.

Texas also benefited from oil producers' **philanthropy**— the giving of money or gifts. Many of the wildcatters who became wealthy gave generous gifts to public institutions that influenced life in Texas.

CHALLENGE ACTIVITY
Critical Thinking: Comparing and Contrasting
What were the positive effects of the oil boom for Texas and what were the negative effects? Did the positive outweigh the negative?

| boomtowns | philanthropy | Permanent University Fund |
| internal combustion engines | Texas Railroad Commission | |

DIRECTIONS On the line provided before each statement, write **T** if a statement is true and **F** if a statement is false. If the statement is false, write a corrected statement on the line after the false statement.

_____ 1. <u>Boomtowns</u> took time to set up and were peaceful and well-planned.

_____

_____ 2. <u>Internal combustion engines</u> used petroleum and increased the demand for Texan oil.

_____

_____ 3. Texas benefitted from oil producers' <u>philanthropy</u>.

_____

_____ 4. <u>The Texas Railroad Commission</u> was granted the authority to enforce laws concerning the petroleum industry in 1902.

_____

_____ 5. The land received by the <u>Permanent University Fund</u> was worthless.

_____

Texas in the Age of Reform

MAIN IDEAS
1. Texas farmers faced serious economic challenges in the late 1800s as crop prices fell and farmers' debts grew.
2. The Grange and the Southern Farmers' Alliance worked for economic reforms to improve the lives of farmers.
3. Dissatisfaction with the Democratic Party led some farmers to help form the Populist Party in 1891.

Key Terms and People

Grange an organization of farmers established in the 1860s to address their economic and social concerns

cooperative stores businesses owned by and operated for the benefits of the organization's members

Southern Farmers' Alliance an alliance formed in 1877 by former Grange and other farmers in Texas

pooling combining efforts to prevent competition between companies

Populist Party political party formed in 1891 to reduce the influence of big business on government

Populists members of the Populist party

platform statement of political goals

Section Summary

THE GRANGE

Many Texas farmers faced serious hardships in the late 1800s as the supply of crops outpaced the demand. Farmers also faced foreign competition, high interest rates, and droughts. In the late 1860s farmers established the Patrons of Husbandry— commonly called the **Grange**— to address these problems. The Grange formed **cooperative stores**. These were businesses owned by and operated for Grange members. The Grange also tried to lower railroad rates that farmers had to pay. After pressure from the Grange to change these unfair practices, laws were passed to regulate the railroads.

> Underline the hardships farmers faced.

> What did the Grange form?
> _____

However, these new laws proved difficult to
enforce.

THE SOUTHERN FARMERS' ALLIANCE

In 1877 former Grange members and other farmers
formed the National Farmers' Alliance and
Industrial Union, or **Southern Farmers' Alliance**.
Alliance members wanted to prevent railroad
companies from **pooling**—the combining of efforts
to prevent competition between companies. In 1889
Texan Charles W. Macune, the president of the
Alliance, proposed that farmers store their crops in
U.S. government warehouses until prices increased.
The government would give low-interest loans
based on the value of those crops. Farmers could
repay the loans after selling their crops at higher
prices. This subtreasury plan, which would be
financed by newly printed currency, had much
support within the Alliance.

> What would finance
> warehouses under the
> proposed subtreasury
> plan?
>
> _____

THE POPULISTS

Southern farmers had traditionally voted for
Democratic Party candidates. However, the
Democrats' failure to back the subtreasury plan
prompted Alliance members to form the People's
Party—commonly called the **Populist Party**—in
1891. Its members were known as **Populists**. The
Populist **platform**, or statement of political goals, was
taken from the Southern Farmers' Alliance. In 1896
both the Populists and the Democrats nominated
William Jennings Bryan for president. Bryan ran as a
Democrat but lost, despite winning Texas and many
other states. The Populist Party faded as members
argued about policy issues. Democrats also weakened
the party by adopting some Populist programs.

> Why did the Populist Party
> fade?
>
> _____
> _____

CHALLENGE ACTIVITY

Critical Thinking: Sequencing Make a time line
with important dates and events from this section.

Grange	Southern Farmers' Alliance	pooling	platform
cooperative stores	Populist Party	Populists	

DIRECTIONS Use the words from the word bank to write a summary of what you have learned from the section.

_____

_____

_____

_____

_____

_____

_____

_____

_____

_____

_____

_____

_____

_____

_____

_____

_____

_____

Texas in the Age of Reform

MAIN IDEAS
1. Big businesses in Texas used trusts and monopolies to increase their power and wealth, and citizens demanded change.
2. Texas political leaders such as Lawrence Ross, James Hogg, and James Ferguson worked to reform unfair business practices.

Key Terms and People

trusts legal arrangements in which one board of trustees controls a number of companies

monopoly sole economic control of a field of business

Lawrence Sullivan "Sul" Ross a Democrat who became governor of Texas in 1887

James Stephen Hogg Texas attorney general who sought antitrust reforms and was elected governor in 1890

Hogg Laws laws regulating business; put forward by Governor James Hogg

James E. Feguson an influential member of the Texas Democratic party who worked for reforms for tenant farmers

Section Summary

REGULATING BIG BUSINESS

By the late 1800s, some businesses in Texas had formed **trusts**. These were legal arrangements in which one board of trustees controlled a number of companies. A **monopoly**— sole economic control of a field of business—could be more easily created by using a trust. A monopoly eliminates competition, allowing one corporation to control prices.

> How does a monopoly control prices?
> _____
> _____

GOVERNOR SUL ROSS

One Texas leader who contributed to new reforms was **Lawrence Sullivan "Sul" Ross**, a Democrat who became a popular governor in 1887. Major legal reform relating to land use, property value, and public school funding took place under his leadership. During Ross's governorship, Texas experienced a boom in industrial and agricultural growth. His reforms were so successful

> List three areas in which legal reform took place under Ross.
> _____
> _____
> _____

Guided Reading Workbook

that he became the only governor in Texas history to call a special session of the legislature to decide what to do with a treasury surplus.

HOGG AS GOVERNOR

Some people wanted government policies that would regulate these corporations. **James Stephen Hogg**, who was elected attorney general of Texas in 1886, believed in reform. In 1887 the federal government created the Interstate Commerce Commission. This agency regulated railroads. Hogg helped write antitrust legislation that further regulated railroads. The Antitrust Act of 1889 regulated monopolies and trusts.

Hogg was elected governor in 1890. His administration pushed for a number of laws regulating business, which became known as **Hogg Laws**. At Hogg's urging the Texas Railroad Commission was created. Governor Charles Culberson also pursued reform. Thomas M. Campbell helped enact reform laws during his terms as governor from 1907 to 1911. These laws included railroad regulation, antitrust laws, and pure food and drug laws.

> **What did the Antitrust Act of 1889 regulate?**
> _____
> _____

FARMER JIM

James E. Ferguson gained the support of poor citizens, particularly tenant farmers, by working for reform. Because of his support of Texas farmers, Ferguson was nicknamed Farmer Jim. Important reforms were passed during Ferguson's first term. As governor, Ferguson developed enemies who accused him of misusing state funds. He was impeached in 1917. Lieutenant Governor William P. Hobby became the new governor.

> **Underline the reason why James E. Ferguson had the nickname Farmer Jim.**

CHALLENGE ACTIVITY

Critical Thinking: Sequencing Make a time line with important dates and events during the Age of Reform.

Guided Reading Workbook

| trusts | monopoly | James E. Ferguson |
| Lawrence Sullivan "Sul" Ross | James Stephen Hogg | Hogg Laws |

DIRECTIONS On the line provided before each statement, write **T** if a statement is true and **F** if a statement is false. If the statement is false, write a corrected statement on the line after the false statement.

_____ 1. In the late 1800s, businesses began to form <u>trusts</u> to control a number of companies.

_____

_____ 2. <u>Governor Ross</u> called a special session to decide what to do with the treasury deficit.

_____

_____ 3. <u>James Stephen Hogg</u> was elected governor in 1886.

_____

_____ 4. <u>Hogg Laws</u> aimed to regulate the railroads.

_____

_____ 5. A <u>monopoly</u> could be made easier by establishing a trust.

_____

DIRECTIONS Write two adjectives or descriptive phrases that describe each term given.

6. Hogg Laws _____

7. monopoly _____

8. trusts _____

Texas in the Age of Reform

MAIN IDEAS
1. Beginning in the early 1900s, the progressive movement worked to reform and improve society.
2. Progressive reforms focused on areas such as working conditions, health and safety, and education.

Key Terms

progressives an organization of farmers established in the 1860s

Seventeenth Amendment allowed voters to vote directly for U.S. senators

Galveston Hurricane of 1900 a major natural disaster in Galveston in September 1900

commission plan a new form of local government, established in Galveston

Section Summary

GOVERNMENT REFORM

In the early 1900s reformers known as **progressives** worked to improve society. Progressive means "forward-looking" or "relating to progress." The passage of the **Seventeenth Amendment** to the U.S. Constitution in 1913 allowed American voters—rather than the state legislatures—to vote directly for U.S. senators.

The progressives also wanted to make local government more efficient. A major natural disaster in Galveston in September 1900 spurred this reform effort. After the **Galveston Hurricane of 1900**, a new form of local government called the **commission plan** was established. The commission plan became a major reform of the progressive movement, and it was soon adopted by other cities.

> What was formed after the Galveston Hurricane of 1900?
>
> _____

WORKPLACE AND HEALTH REFORM

Progressives also wanted to improve conditions for Texas workers and fought for higher wages, better conditions, and a shorter working week for factory workers. They also opposed child labor. Texas

passed its first child labor law in 1903, and this was
followed by further stricter regulations.
Progressives also backed food and drug regulation.
Progressive candidate Thomas M. Campbell was
elected in 1906, and passed laws to regulate the
food and drug industry.

List three causes the progressives fought for.
_____
_____
_____

EDUCATION REFORM

Many progressives, particularly women, also tried
to improve Texas schools. In the late 1800s and
early 1900s the state established schools to train
teachers. The legislature also passed laws to
improve public schools. These reforms changed the
lives of many Texans. More women gained access
to education in the late 1800s than ever before. But
African American and Mexican American students
generally did not benefit from Progressive Era
changes in education. The fight to make public
schools serve all Texans was just beginning.

CHALLENGE ACTIVITY

Critical Thinking: Analyzing How did the
progressive movement change Texas? What were
the major areas of change and what were the areas
that did not change?

Seventeenth Amendment	progressives
Galveston Hurricane of 1900	commission plan

DIRECTIONS Read each sentence and circle the term from the word pair that best completes each sentence.

1. The (Seventeenth Amendment/Galveston Hurricane of 1900) led to a new form of local government being established.

2. The (progressive/commission plan) movement was an effort to reform society.

3. The (Seventeenth Amendment/Galveston Hurricane of 1900) allowed Americans to directly vote for U.S. senators.

4. The (Seventeenth Amendment /commission plan) established a new form of local government in Galveston.

Texas in the Age of Reform

MAIN IDEAS
1. Progressives in Texas and other states worked to ban the sale of alcohol.
2. Suffrage, or the right to vote, was a major goal for women in the progressive movement.

Key Terms and People

temperance movement a social reform effort that encouraged people to drink less—or no—alcohol

prohibition a ban on the manufacture, distribution, and sale of alcohol

Eighteenth Amendment a constitutional amendment ratified in 1919 bringing in national prohibition

Annie Webb Blanton the first woman to win election to a Texas state office

Nineteenth Amendment a constitutional amendment ratified in 1919 granting women the right to vote

Jovita Idar political activist in Texas who organized people to support women's rights as well as rights for Mexican Americans

poll tax a tax on voting

Section Summary

THE TEMPERANCE MOVEMENT

The **temperance movement** was a social reform effort that encouraged people to drink less alcohol. Support for **prohibition**—the banning of the manufacture, distribution, and sale of alcohol—increased during the late 1800s and early 1900s. The **Eighteenth Amendment** won the support of enough state legislatures to be ratified in 1919. As a result, the manufacture and sale of alcohol became illegal throughout the nation in 1920.

> What did the temperance movement encourage people to do?
> _____
> _____

THE SUFFRAGE MOVEMENT

In 1918 **Annie Webb Blanton** became the first woman to win election to a Texas state office. She served as the state's superintendent of public instruction. Eleanor Brackenridge and **Jane**

McCallum were other important suffrage leaders in Texas. In 1919 the **Nineteenth Amendment** was ratified, granting women suffrage. In 1920 women across the nation were able to vote.

List three important suffrage leaders in Texas.
_____
_____
_____

LIMITS OF REFORM

African American and Mexican American women also fought for reforms. Christia Adair, an African American, worked for women's suffrage and equal rights. In South Texas, **Jovita Idar** organized people to support women's rights as well as rights for Mexican Americans. In 1902 Texas began to require a **poll tax**, a tax on voting. As a result, poor Texans, many of whom were African American and Mexican American, could not afford to vote. African Americans in Texas were denied the benefits of reform in other areas as well. Many years would go by before laws were passed to protect the rights of African Americans in Texas.

What was the result of the poll tax?
_____
_____

CHALLENGE ACTIVITY
Critical Thinking: Analyzing Information

Imagine that you live in Texas in the late 1800s or early 1900s. Create a flyer or poster outlining what type of reform you would like to see the Texas legislature put into law. Be sure to list reasons why the legislature should pass the law.

temperance movement	Eighteenth Amendment	Jane McCallum	Jovita Idar
prohibition	Annie Webb Blanton	Nineteenth Amendment	poll tax

DIRECTIONS Use the words from the word bank to write a summary
of what you have learned from the section.

_____

_____

_____

_____

_____

_____

_____

_____

_____

_____

_____

_____

_____

_____

_____

_____

_____

_____

_____

Texans at Home and Abroad

MAIN IDEAS
1. New farm technology changed life for many rural Texans in the early 1900s.
2. Industry spurred population growth in Texas cities.
3. Job opportunities drew many immigrants to Texas.

Key Terms and People

Houston Ship Channel waterway that connected Houston and the Gulf of Mexico; it gave ships access to Houston

Federal Reserve System system of government banks that distribute money to other banks and help regulate the banking industry

Carrie Marcus Neiman cofounder of the clothing store Neiman Marcus

Section Summary

LIFE IN RURAL TEXAS

Life on Texas farms required hard work and offered few luxuries. Farm production increased as new tractors and other machines made farming more efficient. The resulting surplus of agricultural products led to a drop in the prices of farm goods. With prices falling, it became hard for many farmers to pay their debts. The struggles of farm life led many rural families to move to cities for new opportunities.

> **What caused farmers and their families to move to cities?**
> _____
> _____
> _____

INDUSTRY AND THE GROWTH OF CITIES

Urbanization, or growth of cities, was also tied to the development of industry. The cattle, oil, railroad, and textile industries—among others—created jobs that attracted people to cities. City growth was concentrated in eastern Texas, which had ports and markets for farm goods. In 1914 the Buffalo Bayou, a waterway between Houston and the Gulf of Mexico, was deepened and widened to allow larger ships to travel on it. The new **Houston Ship Channel** gave the city a direct link to the Gulf. The

> **What industries contributed to the growth of Texas cities?**
> _____
> _____
> _____

jobs created by the channel attracted many rural Texans, including African Americans, to Houston.

In 1914 the federal government built a district bank of the **Federal Reserve System** in Dallas. This brought finance-related businesses to Dallas. The city was one of the largest cotton markets in the world. The cotton trade made some Dallas residents quite wealthy. By 1907, in fact, Dallas had enough successful shoppers to support specialty stores such as Neiman Marcus. Founded by siblings Herbert Marcus and **Carrie Marcus Neiman,** the store specialized in high-quality ready-to-wear clothing for women.

MIGRATION AND CITY GROWTH

The booming oil industry, the expansion of commercial farming, and industrial jobs attracted many people to Texas. The majority of immigrants came from Mexico. Many of these immigrants lived in Mexican American communities and traveled to farms when labor was needed. The German American population in Texas also grew. Many hoped to start their own farms in the rolling farmland of the Hill Country. Other European newcomers included Czechs, Irish, Italians, and Poles. Many of these groups settled in Central Texas and took up farming. Galveston was the main port of entry for immigrants from Europe.

> **Where did many immigrants from Europe enter Texas?**
>
> _____
>
> _____
>
> _____

CHALLENGE ACTIVITY

Critical Thinking: Evaluating Write a journal entry as a farmer living in rural Texas in the early 1900s. Describe how life on the farm is changing.

Houston Ship Channel	Federal Reserve System	Carrie Marcus Neiman

DIRECTIONS Read each sentence below and fill in the blank with the word that best completes each sentence.

1. _____ cofounded a famous clothing store in Dallas.

2. The _____ provided water access for ships from the Gulf of Mexico into Houston.

3. The federal government built a district bank of the _____ in Dallas.

DIRECTIONS Write two adjectives or descriptive phrases that describe each term given.

4. Houston Ship Channel _____

5. Federal Reserve System _____

6. Carrie Marcus Neiman _____

Texans at Home and Abroad

MAIN IDEAS
1. New technologies affected life in Texas cities during the early 1900s.
2. Automobile traffic and housing shortages were some of the problems faced by Texans living in urban areas.
3. Texans enjoyed new forms of leisure, entertainment, and art in the early 1900s.

Key Terms and People

suburbs residential neighborhoods built outside of a central city

Adina Emilia De Zavala a Texan who worked hard to keep the state's historic buildings from being torn down

Texas Highway Department formed in 1917 to help build and maintain highways

Texas Department of Health formed in 1903 to help prevent the spread of disease

Texas Water Commission formed in 1913 to help cities and counties manage water resources.

ragtime form of music popular during the early 1900s

Scott Joplin music pioneer from Texarkana who helped develop ragtime

O. Henry pen name of William Sydney Porter, a writer famous for his short stories about Texas cowboys

Elisabet Ney a Texas sculptor who specialized in statues of early Texas heroes

Section Summary

URBAN TECHNOLOGY

New technologies made city life different from country life. By 1906 more than 100,000 Texans had telephones. Electricity came into use more slowly in Texas than the telephone. Electricity did, however, play a role in the development of a new form of public transportation—electric streetcars. The streetcars led, in turn, to the growth of the first Texas **suburbs**, or residential neighborhoods built outside of a central city. In cities, Texans began to construct taller buildings to make room for new industries and the growing population. As new buildings rose, some Texans like **Adina Emilia De Zavala** worked to keep historic buildings from being torn down.

> What types of technology made city life different from country life in the early 1900s?
>
> _____
> _____
> _____

Guided Reading Workbook

URBAN PROBLEMS AND REFORM

Many Texas communities had to find solutions to problems created by growth and new technology. Cars were considered dangerous. In addition, rapid growth made it difficult for cities to provide services such as electricity, garbage collection, sewers, police, health care, and fire protection.

In 1917 the state government formed the Texas Highway Department to help build and maintain highways. In 1903 the agency that became the Texas Department of Health was formed to help prevent the spread of disease. The Texas Water Commission was formed to help manage water resources. To help battle the threat of fires, city governments began replacing volunteers with full-time firefighters. After experiencing several fires, the town of Big Spring purchased the first fire truck in Texas in 1909.

> **What is a problem that was a result of growth and new technology in the early 1900s?**
>
> _____
>
> _____
>
> _____

SPORTS, LEISURE, AND THE ARTS

During the early 1900s, Texans found new ways to cope with the fast pace of city life and the hard work of rural life. Texans loved sports. Children and adults alike enjoyed the circus. Concert halls often featured **ragtime**, a new form of popular music. One of the best-known ragtime musicians was **Scott Joplin** of Texarkana. The first movies in Texas were shown in cities during the early 1900s. William Sydney Porter, known as **O. Henry**, became famous for short stories about Texas cowboys. Texas artists also portrayed the state's past. Sculptor **Elisabet Ney** specialized in statues of early Texas heroes. Texas citizens paid for the construction of libraries and museums in cities across the state.

> **List three ways that Texans escaped the fast pace of city life.**
>
> _____
>
> _____
>
> _____

CHALLENGE ACTIVITY

Critical Thinking: Analyze Write a paragraph describing an urban problem in Texas in the early 1900s and explain how the problem was solved.

DIRECTIONS On the line provided before each statement, write **T** if the statement is true and **F** if the statement is false. If the statement is false, write a corrected statement on the line after the false statement.

_____ 1. The <u>Texas Department of Health</u> was formed to stop the spread of diseases.

_____

_____ 2. <u>Suburbs</u> are neighborhoods located in the center of the city.

_____

_____ 3. <u>Ragtime</u> was made popular by Elisabet Ney.

_____

_____ 4. The <u>Texas Highway Department</u> was formed to help create traffic laws.

_____

_____ 5. <u>Adina Emilia De Zavala</u> fought to tear down historic buildings, but had little success.

_____

_____ 6. <u>Elisabet Ney</u> was an artist known for her paintings of Texas cowboys.

_____

_____ 7. American music pioneer, <u>Scott Joplin</u>, helped create ragtime music.

_____

_____ 8. The <u>Texas Water Commission</u> was created to manage water resources for cities and counties.

_____

Texans at Home and Abroad

MAIN IDEAS

1. Texas served as a military training ground during the Spanish-American War.

2. The Mexican Revolution and raids along the Texas-Mexico border led to conflicts in South Texas.

3. World War I had great social and economic effects on Texas.

Key Terms and People

Theodore Roosevelt future president who served as a lieutenant colonel of the 1st U.S. Volunteer Cavalry

Rough Riders nickname of 1st U.S. Volunteer Cavalry; the first U.S. troops to land in Cuba that helped defeat Spain

Battle of San Juan Hill a battle of the Spanish-American War fought in Cuba

Francisco "Pancho" Villa a rebel and leader of the Mexican Revolution

refugees people forced to leave their homeland due to war or persecution

John J. "Black Jack" Pershing U.S. general sent to capture Villa

Plan de San Diego a document that called for Mexican Americans to take control of South Texas and other territories Mexico had lost in the U.S.-Mexican War

neutral not aligned with either side in a conflict

Section Summary

THE SPANISH-AMERICAN WAR

In 1895, Cubans revolted against Spain. When the U.S. battleship *Maine* exploded in Havana Harbor in 1898, some Americans blamed Spain. The United States soon declared war on Spain. Many Texans volunteered to fight. When Lieutenant Colonel **Theodore Roosevelt** came to Texas to recruit troops, many joined his 1st U.S. Volunteer Cavalry. This outfit, known as the **Rough Riders,** trained in San Antonio. They were the first U.S. troops to land in Cuba. They became famous for helping to defeat Spanish troops in the **Battle of San Juan Hill.**

> Why did the United States declare war on Spain?
>
> _____
>
> _____

THE MEXICAN REVOLUTION

In Mexico, rebels overthrew President Porfirio Díaz. Democratic reformer Francisco Madero worked with rebels such as **Francisco "Pancho" Villa** to attack Mexican forces. Madero became president but was assassinated. Various forces continued to fight for control of Mexico. Many Mexicans became **refugees**—people forced to leave their homeland—during this time. Thousands of refugees came to Texas.

> **Why did thousands of Mexicans move to Texas?**
> _____
> _____

BORDER TROUBLES

Pancho Villa's forces began raids on the U.S.-Mexico border. U.S. general **John J. "Black Jack" Pershing** pursued Villa's forces without success. Clashes broke out in South Texas with Mexican American families who had lived on the land for generations. Some Mexican Americans formed the **Plan de San Diego,** which urged Mexican Americans to take control of South Texas and other territories Mexico had lost in the U.S.-Mexican War.

TEXANS AND WORLD WAR I

When World War I erupted in Europe in 1914 it was difficult for the United States to remain **neutral**, or not aligned with either side in a conflict. In 1915, Americans were killed when German submarines sank the British ship *Lusitania*. Americans were also angered when Germany promised to help Mexico regain territory it lost to the United States—including Texas. The United States declared war on Germany in 1917. The Texas economy expanded during the war.

CHALLENGE ACTIVITY

Critical Thinking: Sequencing Make a time line from 1895–1918 that tells about important dates and events from this section.

DIRECTIONS Look at each set of four terms. On the line provided, write the letter of the term that does not relate to the others.

_____ 1. a. Plan de San Diego
b. Francisco "Pancho" Villa
c. Germany
d. John J. "Black Jack" Pershing

_____ 2. a. Francisco "Pancho" Villa
b. Rough Riders
c. refugees
d. Mexico

_____ 3. a. Spain
b. *Lusitania*
c. Battle of San Juan Hill
d. Theodore Roosevelt

_____ 4. a. Germany
b. *Maine*
c. World War I
d. neutral

DIRECTIONS Choose five of the words from the word bank. On the lines below, use these words to write a summary of what you have learned in this section.

Theodore Roosevelt	Battle of San Juan Hill	refugees	Plan de San Diego
Rough Riders	Francisco "Pancho" Villa	John J. "Black Jack" Pershing	neutral

_____

_____

_____

_____

_____

_____

_____

_____

_____

_____

_____

MAIN IDEAS

1. Demobilization following World War I slowed the Texas economy and caused labor unrest.
2. Texas made some progress toward protecting Texans' civil rights in the post-World War I era.
3. Miriam A. "Ma" Ferguson was both a popular and a controversial governor.

Key Terms

demobilization moving from a wartime to a peacetime economy

Miriam A. "Ma" Ferguson first female governor of Texas

National Association for the Advancement of Colored People civil rights organization that provided a way for African Americans to be politically active

primary election an election that narrows the field of candidates before the general election

white primary what primary elections were called due to methods used to stop African Americans from voting

League of United Latin American Citizens a civil rights organization put in order by Mexican Americans

Section Summary

DEMOBILIZING AND LABOR UNREST

During World War I, farms and factories had increased production to supply the military. Cities offered high paying jobs, which attracted many rural Texans. When the war ended, the United States began the process of **demobilization**. Returning soldiers were given jobs, often resulting in the displacement of other workers. Competition for jobs increased. Many were laid off or had their wages cut, so millions of American workers went on strike. Two years later, railroad strikes prompted Governor Pat Neff to declare martial law.

Discrimination and racial tension also increased. African Americans who had served in World War I demanded equal rights. These demands sparked angry reactions from white Texans and led to a

> **What caused a problem in the job market after World War I ended?**
>
> _____
>
> _____
>
> _____

deadly riot in Houston and the execution of African American soldiers. Violence increased with the formation of a new Ku Klux Klan. The Klan became a powerful political force in Texas.

THE FERGUSON ADMINISTRATION

In 1924, **Miriam A. "Ma" Ferguson** was elected governor of Texas. She was married to a former Texas governor and promised Texans "two governors for the price of one." Because the Fergusons were popular, they became known as Ma and Pa. Critics accused them of giving government contracts to friends instead of to the lowest bidder and of discontinuing education efforts started by the previous administration. Dan Moody, who questioned many actions of the Fergusons, defeated Miriam Ferguson in the 1926 race for governor.

> **Write three adjectives describing "Ma" Ferguson.**
> _____
> _____
> _____

EARLY CIVIL RIGHTS EFFORTS

Many Texans were becoming politically active and joined civil rights organizations. The **National Association for the Advancement of Colored People** opened chapters in Texas, but was weakened because of violent opposition. Texas had used several methods to stop African Americans from voting. One law barred black Texans from voting in the Democratic **primary election**. When a black doctor was unable to vote in this **white primary**, he filed a lawsuit against the state of Texas. The U.S. Supreme Court eliminated the law only to have the Texas legislature continue the exclusion of black voters. Mexican Americans also faced discrimination and struggled for equal rights. To fight for their rights, the **League of United Latin American Citizens** was organized.

> **Why was the Democratic primary election known as the white primary?**
> _____
> _____
> _____

CHALLENGE ACTIVITY

Critical Thinking: Compare and Contrast Create a visual representation comparing the civil rights of white, Mexican, and black Texans.

| demobilization | primary election | white primary |
| League of United Latin American Citizens | Miriam A. "Ma" Ferguson | National Association for the Advancement of Colored People |

DIRECTIONS On the line provided before each statement, write **T** if a statement is true and **F** if a statement is false. If the statement is false, write the corrected statement on the line after the false statement.

_____ 1. The <u>primary election</u> in 1923 excluded African American women from voting.

_____

_____ 2. To become politically active, many Texans joined government organizations such as the <u>National Association for the Advancement of Colored People</u>.

_____

_____ 3. After World War I, <u>demobilization</u> caused labor unrest.

_____

_____ 4. <u>Miriam A. "Ma" Ferguson</u> was neither popular nor controversial.

_____

_____ 5. A <u>white primary</u> was the result of a law that barred black Texans from voting.

_____

_____ 6. The <u>League of United Latin American Citizens</u> was organized before there was evidence of discrimination against Mexican Americans.

_____

Boom and Bust

Section 2

 MAIN IDEAS

1. Oil discoveries and production fueled economic growth in Texas in the 1920s.
2. Overproduction of cotton and poor weather conditions hurt Texas farmers after the war.
3. The Jazz Age brought new forms of entertainment such as music and movies to Texans.

Key Terms

C.M. "Dad" Joiner an oilman who struck oil in East Texas opening an extensive and highly productive oil field, considered the "father" of that field

Howard Hughes Sr. a Texan who developed an advanced drill bit for oil, made wealthy due to oil discoveries

blues a musical form with lyrics that often reflect the difficulties people faced in life

consumer goods items intended for personal use

Section Summary

ECONOMIC GROWTH

The economy grew as more Texans found jobs. Industries that processed farm and ranch products continued to be important. However, the discovery of oil fueled more growth. One of the biggest oil discoveries in Texas history was made by a wildcatter named **C. M. "Dad" Joiner**. His oil discovery opened one of the largest oil fields in the world. In 1933 this East Texas field produced more than 20 percent of U.S. oil. Other new fields were discovered as the oil boom continued. These oil discoveries made fortunes for a number of Texans, including **Howard Hughes Sr.**

> What new industry developed that created a boom in the Texas economy?
>
> _____
>
> _____
>
> _____

HARD TIMES FOR FARMERS

Despite industrial growth, most Texans still worked in agriculture. New irrigation methods made it possible to grow cotton and wheat in dry areas such as the Panhandle. Because the land was flat, this area

Guided Reading Workbook

was well suited for the use of large farm machines.
West Texas cotton production and Panhandle
ranches boomed with irrigation and mechanization.

As farming increased, ranchers moved their herds
and developed important ranching regions in the
south and east. Many of these areas had poor soil
for farming. But one region in South Texas was
well suited for growing citrus fruit, and orchards
were developed there.

The supply of cotton was soon larger than the
demand for it and prices fell. The development of
other types of synthetic fabrics had hurt the demand
for cotton. As costs for machinery and land
increased, prosperity for farmers did not last.

> **Why did the demand for cotton decrease?**
> _____
> _____
> _____

THE JAZZ AGE IN TEXAS

Many Texans enjoyed the social changes of the
1920s. African Americans created jazz music,
which developed from the **blues** and became
associated with the excitement of the decade.
Activities such as dancing the foxtrot and attending
sporting events became common. The development
of the radio changed entertainment. Texans also
enjoyed going to movies, especially westerns.

Consumer goods made household tasks easier.
Cars were becoming very popular. The automobile
industry's growth boosted demand for Texas oil
products. Texans became less dependent on railroads
for transportation due to a big road-building program.

Some worried that changes during the Jazz Age
could threaten traditional family values. Many
Texans supported prohibition because they were
worried people were drinking too much alcohol.

> **Write three adjectives to describe The Jazz Age.**
> 1. _____
> 2. _____
> 3. _____

CHALLENGE ACTIVITY

Critical Thinking: Mapping Create a map labeling
all of the Texas cities and towns mentioned in this
chapter. Include a map key to indicate the type of
industry found in each city or region.

C.M. "Dad" Joiner	Howard Hughes Sr.
consumer goods	blues

DIRECTIONS Write a summary of what you learned in this section about the economic and cultural changes in Texas.

_____

_____

_____

_____

_____

_____

_____

_____

_____

_____

_____

_____

_____

_____

_____

_____

_____

_____

_____

Boom and Bust

MAIN IDEAS

1. The Great Depression was a time of great hardship for Texans.
2. The Texas oil industry suffered during the depression.
3. Many Texas farmers were forced to abandon their farms in the Dust Bowl.

Key Terms and People

stocks shares of ownership in a company, sold to raise money

Great Depression the global economic slowdown in the 1930s that caused unemployment, a need for public assistance, and loss of home ownership for many families

Ross Sterling Texas governor during the early 1930s who opposed government aid for unemployment relief and supported limited government aid to businesses

soup kitchens set up by churches and private organizations to feed families and give out food

breadlines set up by churches and private organizations to feed families and give out food

scrip paper notes issued by local governments as a promise to pay at a later date

proration the proportionate division of oil production that was enforced to avoid overproduction

Dust Bowl an area in the southern Great Plains where drought and dust ruined crops, cattle died, ranchers struggled financially, and farmers needed crop loans to buy necessities

Section Summary

AN ECONOMIC CRISIS

During the 1920s the price of **stocks** rose. Many Americans bought stocks hoping to sell them at a profit. People began taking out loans to buy stock and then were unable to repay the loans when the value of the stock went down. Then in October 1929, a panic spread at the New York Stock Exchange. People rushed to sell their stocks, causing a stock market crash. People who had invested their savings were left with nothing. This resulted in the **Great Depression**. Some 300,000 Texans were left unemployed.

Explain why people bought stocks in the 1920s?
_____
_____
_____

THE DEPRESSION IN TEXAS

Most Texas farmers could at least feed their own families and the oil industry continued to provide jobs, but many others found themselves in need of help. Charitable organizations set up **soup kitchens** and **breadlines** to give out food to help the needy. Texans grew frightened and angry as the depression deepened. Jobs were cut, often affecting African Americans and Mexican Americans. **Scrip**, rather than money, was issued for some salaries. Such measures did little to help the Texas economy. President Herbert Hoover and Governor **Ross Sterling** opposed government relief programs. They believed that once business recovered, new jobs would be created.

> What did the president and Governor Sterling have in common?
> _____
> _____
> _____

A CRISIS IN THE OIL INDUSTRY

As the depression deepened, the Texas oil industry faced a crisis. The East Texas oil discovery had led to overproduction, and the price of oil had dropped. In 1931 Sterling sent in the National Guard to enforce **proration**, allowing each well to produce a certain amount of oil each day. Oil producers argued for their property rights, which caused the legislature to grant more authority to the Railroad Commission.

THE DUST BOWL AND FARMERS

The depression also hit farmers hard. Ranching and farming were changing the environment. Cattle grazing had already damaged the grasses that held the soil in place. Winds lifted the dry soil into the air, creating huge clouds of dust. Parts of the Great Plains were called the **Dust Bowl**. Drought and dust ruined crops, and thousands of cattle died.

> Underline the causes of the Dust Bowl.

CHALLENGE ACTIVITY

Critical Thinking: Comprehension Create a word web linking important terms and significant events from this chapter.

DIRECTIONS On the line provided before each statement, write **T** if a statement is true and **F** if a statement is false. If the statement is false, write the corrected statement on the line after the false statement.

_____ 1. To provide aid to needy families, charitable organizations' stocks were sold.

_____

_____ 2. During the Great Depression most Texans were able provide food for their family.

_____

_____ 3. Many government programs to aid unemployment were created and supported by Governor Ross Sterling.

_____

_____ 4. Wealthy families opened their homes to provide soup kitchens for needy Texans.

_____

_____ 5. Breadlines were set up to give out food, providing assistance to Texans.

_____

_____ 6. Local governments issued scrip to save money.

_____

_____ 7. Proration supported the property rights of the oil industry.

_____

_____ 8. The Dust Bowl was caused by human factors.

_____

Boom and Bust

MAIN IDEAS

1. Many Texans served in government leadership positions and supported New Deal programs.
2. New Deal programs created jobs and provided financial aid to many Texans during the Great Depression.
3. Though life in the depression era was difficult Texans enjoyed cultural activities and celebrated a centennial.

Key Terms and People

New Deal a variety of measures introduced by President Roosevelt to fight the depression which provided hope to Americans

Social Security a government program to provide economic security for the future

John Nance Garner vice president from Texas who played a key role in New Deal efforts

Sam Rayburn long-term U.S. representative from Texas who supported most New Deal programs

James V Allred Texas governor who brought New Deal money to Texas

J. Frank Dobie popular writer whose stories and folktales captured life in Texas

centennial 100th birthday of Texas since independence

Section Summary
THE NEW DEAL

President Franklin D. Roosevelt asked Congress to pass a variety of measures—called the **New Deal**— to fight the depression. New Deal programs created jobs by funding public works—government-sponsored building projects for public use. People worked for New Deal agencies such as the Public Works Administration and the Works Progress Administration. Workers constructed schools, dams, parks, and roads.

Roosevelt also wanted to provide Americans with economic security for the future. In 1935 Congress created the **Social Security** system. This program provided payments to retired citizens and benefits

> **How did the New Deal create jobs?**
> _____
> _____

for unemployed workers. The Social Security system collected the money it needed for its payments from employers and from workers.

Some Texans served under Roosevelt and helped with his New Deal efforts. **John Nance Garner** of Uvalde served as vice president. Lyndon Johnson of Johnson City served as state director of the National Youth Administration. In the U.S. Congress **Sam Rayburn** of Bonham served as Speaker of the House.

> **How was the Social Security system funded?**
> _____

NEW DEAL PROGRAMS IN TEXAS

Several New Deal agencies assisted Texans during the Great Depression. The Civilian Conservation Corps created jobs for 100,000 Texans. As a result of these jobs, Texans had money to spend on goods and services, thereby helping the state's small businesses.

> **Underline the purpose of the Civilian Conservation Corps.**

TEXAS POLITICS DURING THE NEW DEAL

Miriam Ferguson, who had been elected governor again in 1932, supported New Deal policies. She chose not to run for office in 1934, opening the way for Texas attorney general **James V Allred** to win election as governor. In 1938 W. Lee "Pappy" O'Daniel won the governor's race.

LIFE AND CULTURE DURING THE DEPRESSION

Life during the depression was difficult. Music provided a welcome distraction. Blues, conjunto, and western swing were among the types of music to come out of Texas during this time. Texans also read the author **J. Frank Dobie**, whose works captured many aspects of Texas life. Another bright spot came in 1936 when Texas celebrated its **centennial**, or 100th birthday. The state staged a world's fair in Dallas to mark the occasion.

> **How did Texas celebrate its centennial?**
> _____
> _____

CHALLENGE ACTIVITY

Critical Thinking: Analyzing Information How did the New Deal benefit Texans?

| New Deal | Social Security | John Nance Garner | Sam Rayburn |
| James V. Allred | J. Frank Dobie | centennial | |

DIRECTIONS Use all the words from the word bank to write a summary about what you learned in this chapter.

_____

_____

_____

_____

_____

_____

_____

_____

_____

_____

_____

_____

_____

_____

_____

_____

_____

_____

_____

World War II and the Cold War

 MAIN IDEAS

1. Millions of Texas served in World War II.

2. Texans and Texas industries supported the war effort.

3. Forces from Texas helped bring about Allied victory.

Key Terms and People

Dorie Miller the first African American sailor to receive the Navy Cross

Chester W. Nimitz Texan admiral who commanded the U.S. fleet in the Pacific in World War II

Oveta Culp Hobby leader of the Women's Auxiliary Army Corps (WAAC)

Audie Murphy the most decorated soldier of World War II

victory gardens small vegetable gardens planted by farmers to grow extra food during World War II

Section Summary

TEXANS IN THE WAR

When German forces invaded Poland on September 1, 1939, Great Britain and France declared war on Germany. World War II had begun. In Asia, Japan invaded China. Then on December 7, 1941, Japan launched a surprise attack on the U.S. naval base at Pearl Harbor, Hawaii. **Dorie Miller,** a sailor from Texas in the U.S. Navy, witnessed the attack. The following day, the United States declared war on Japan.

> **When did the United States declare war on Japan?**
> _____

Some 750,000 Texans served in the armed forces during World War II. About 80,000 of the Texans in World War II were African Americans— including Dorie Miller, who became the first African American to receive the Navy Cross. Many Texans served as officers. Admiral **Chester W. Nimitz** of Fredericksburg commanded the U.S. fleet in the Pacific. **Audie Murphy** of Hunt County was the nation's most decorated soldier in the war. Thousands of Texas women served in noncombat

positions in the military. **Oveta Culp Hobby** of
Houston organized and commanded the Women's
Auxiliary Army Corps (WAAC). Members of the
WAAC—the first women beside nurses to ever
serve with the army—were trained mostly in
operations and management tasks.

> **How did women help in the war effort?**
> _____
> _____

THE TEXAS HOME FRONT

While many Texans fought overseas, millions more
helped the war effort from home. Many soldiers and
pilots trained in Texas. Texas businesses provided
services to military bases. The state's economy
boomed, and the Great Depression came to an end.
Some 500,000 people, including many African
Americans, moved from rural areas to cities to work
in industries.

Texans made many sacrifices for the war effort.
The government rationed, or set aside for each
family, a specific amount of items such as gasoline
and meat. Some Texans planted **victory gardens,** or
small vegetable gardens, to grow extra food.

> **Underline the definition of *rationed*.**
> _____

VICTORY FOR THE ALLIES

Texas soldiers fought in Europe, North Africa, and the
Pacific. The 90th Infantry, based in Abilene, took part
in the D-Day invasion of June 6, 1944. On that date,
Allied troops invaded France to drive out the Germans.
The war in Europe ended with Germany's surrender in
1945. The war in the Pacific continued, however. After
American planes dropped atomic bombs on the
Japanese cities Hiroshima and Nagasaki, Japan
surrendered in September 1945. Some 50 million
people died worldwide—more than half of them
civilians. 23,000 Americans from Texas died.

> **When did Japan surrender?**
> _____

CHALLENGE ACTIVITY

Critical Thinking: Analyzing Information How
did Texans contribute to the war effort? Explain in a
paragraph.

| Dorie Miller | Chester W. Nimitz | Oveta Culp Hobby |
| Audie Murphy | victory gardens | rationing |

DIRECTIONS Read each sentence and circle the term in the word pair that best completes each sentence.

1. The first African American to win the Navy Cross, (Dorie Miller/Audie Murphy) had witnessed the attack on Pearl Harbor.

2. (Oveta Culp Hobby/Dorie Miller) ran the Women's Auxiliary Army Corps in Houston.

3. The government implemented (rationing/victory gardens) to set aside a specific amount of goods for each family.

4. An admiral from Texas, (Chester W. Nimitz/Audie Miller) commanded the U.S. fleet in the Pacific.

5. Many citizens used (victory gardens/rationing) to grow extra food.

Guided Reading Workbook

World War II and the Cold War

Section 2

MAIN IDEAS
1. Government programs passed after World War II benefited Texans.
2. The postwar economic boom benefited Texas greatly.
3. In the 1950s, Texas passed education laws and won a dispute with the federal government.

Key Terms and People

Cold War term describing the tensions between the United States and the Soviet Union after World War II

aerospace related to Earth's atmosphere and the space beyond it

conservatism an approach to politics that supports gradual change and favors keeping systems and programs that have worked in the past

Texas Education Agency formerly the Texas Department of Education, an elected board that sets educational policy

GI Bill of Rights bill passed by Congress in 1944 to give veterans money to attend college, buy homes, or create businesses

Allan Shivers governor of Texas who took over when Beauford Jester died in 1949

tidelands underwater lands bordering the coast

Section Summary

THE COLD WAR AND THE ECONOMY

Soviet forces remained in Eastern Europe after World War II. Many Americans believed that Soviet leader Joseph Stalin wanted to spread communism throughout the world. The tensions between the United States and the Soviet Union became known as the **Cold War** because there was no actual fighting between them.

In 1950 Communist forces from North Korea—supported by the Soviet Union and Communist China—invaded South Korea. The United Nations sent troops, consisting primarily of U.S. soldiers, to aid South Korea in a conflict that became known as the Korean War.

> Why were the tensions between the United States and the Soviet Union known as the Cold War?
>
> _____
>
> _____

The Korean War ended in 1953, but the Cold War continued. Still worried about the spread of communism, the United States increased its military spending. Some Texas industries boomed, including the **aerospace** industry, which manufactured airplanes and missiles for the military.

> **How was Texas affected by the Cold War?**
> _____
> _____

POSTWAR POLITICS

Within Texas, politics were changing with a rise in conservatism. **Conservatism** is an approach to politics that supports gradual, rather than rapid, change. Conservatives support lower taxes, limited government regulation of business, and strong national defense.

Texas Governor Beauford Jester made education a priority. He signed laws that funded teachers' salaries. He created the state Department of Education—now called the **Texas Education Agency**—which sets and reviews standards for schools and teachers. It also reviews and approves textbooks. In 1944 Congress passed the **GI Bill of Rights.** Under this law, veterans could receive money to attend college. The GI Bill also provided veterans loans to buy homes or create businesses.

> **What is the purpose of the GI Bill of Rights?**
> _____

THE TIDELANDS DISPUTE

Allan Shivers became governor in 1949. He defended the state's ownership of **tidelands**— underwater lands bordering the coast. When oil was discovered in the tidelands, the federal government claimed the land. In 1960, the U.S. Supreme Court ruled that Texas had a right to some 2.4 million acres of tidelands. Revenue from oil drilling in the tidelands goes to the Permanent School Fund.

CHALLENGE ACTIVITY

Critical Thinking: Analyzing Information What changes occurred in Texas politics after World War II?

DIRECTIONS For each term or name below, write a sentence defining the term or person and its significance in Texas history.

1. Cold War _____

_____

2. aerospace _____

_____

3. conservatism _____

_____

4. Texas Education Agency _____

_____

5. GI Bill of Rights _____

_____

6. Allan Shivers _____

_____

7. tidelands _____

_____

MAIN IDEAS
1. The growth of industries and the creation of jobs led to urbanization in Texas.
2. American culture changed in the 1950s as people moved to suburbs and new art forms developed.

Key Terms and People

commute to travel back and forth, as for a job when one lives in one place and works in another

Robert Rauschenberg well-known Texas artist

Katherine Anne Porter popular Texas author who wrote about Texas

Buddy Holly early rock 'n' roll musician from Lubbock, Texas

Horton Foote award-winning screenwriter and playwright from Texas

Babe Didrikson Zaharias Olympic champion, founding member of the Ladies Professional Golf Association (LPGA), and native of Port Arthur, Texas

Section Summary

URBAN GROWTH

By 1950 some 7.7 million people lived in Texas, a 20 percent increase from 1940. In 1960 the state's population reached some 9.6 million. As the population grew, Texans experienced urbanization.

Industries that had grown during World War II continued to draw people to cities. Aircraft manufacturers, electronics firms, oil refineries, and ship manufacturers all needed workers. With the growing population of cities, more people found jobs in service industries such as health care, banking, construction, plumbing, and retail sales. The growth of industries also changed the look of Texas cities. Quiet towns were rapidly turning into major cities, with skyscrapers that towered over the surrounding landscape.

> **List some examples of service industry jobs.**
>
> _____
>
> _____
>
> _____

TRANSPORTATION

The popularity of the automobile helped the process of urbanization. To handle all the new cars, Texans built thousands of miles of new roads. Congress authorized an interstate highway system in 1956. Texas air transportation also expanded. Dallas became a stopover for many coast-to-coast flights.

How did transportation in Texas change?
_____

1950s CULTURE

Urbanization and the popularity of cars led to the growth of suburbs. Texans living in the suburbs chose to **commute** to their jobs. They lived in one area but drove elsewhere to work.

Wages for many Texans increased, even as their work hours declined. With more leisure time, they went to concerts, theater productions, and movies. **Robert Rauschenberg** was a well-known Texan artist. Texas writers such as **Katherine Anne Porter** published works about Texas.

Texans also enjoyed a new form of communication and entertainment—television. Television soon became a feature in nearly every Texas home. Texan **Horton Foote**, who became an award-winning screenwriter and playwright, got his start writing for television.

Television allowed Texans to see a new kind of music called rock'n'roll. Popular with teenagers, rock'n'roll had roots in African-American blues music. Texans **Buddy Holly** and Roy Orbison were popular rock'n'roll artists.

Texans were also big sports players and watchers. **Babe Didrickson Zacharias,** a native of Port Arthur, was a founding member of the Ladies Professional Golf Association (LPGA).

What new forms of entertainment did Texans enjoy in the 1950s?
_____
_____
_____

CHALLENGE ACTIVITY

Critical Thinking: Analyzing Information

Imagine you are growing up in 1950s Texas. Write a letter describing to a friend what you do for fun.

commute	Robert Rauschenberg	Katherine Anne Porter
Buddy Holly	Horton Foote	Babe Didrikson Zaharias

DIRECTIONS Read each sentence and circle the word from the pair
that best completes each sentence.

1. One popular early performer of rock 'n' roll music was (Buddy Holly/Robert
   Rauschenberg).

2. (Babe Didrikson Zaharias/Katherine Anne Porter) was a Texan writer famous for
   writing about Texas.

3. Formerly a television writer, Texan (Robert Rauschenberg/Horton Foote) became
   an award-winning playwright.

4. A founding member of the Ladies Professional Golf Association was (Babe
   Didrikson Zaharias/Katherine Anne Porter).

DIRECTIONS Write two adjectives or descriptive phrases that describe
each term given.

5. commute _____

6. Horton Foote _____

World War II and the Cold War

Section 4

MAIN IDEAS
1. Through legal action and peaceful demonstrations, African Americans in Texas gained many civil rights.
2. Hispanic Texans also took steps to secure civil rights.
3. Women worked for equality in the 1950s.

Key Terms and People

Lulu Belle Madison White former head of the Houston chapter of the NACCP

desegragate to stop the practice of separating people by race

nonviolent resistance the use of peaceful means to achieve a goal

James L. Farmer Jr. cofounder of the Congress of Racial Equality (CORE)

Hector P. García U.S. Army surgeon who founded the American GI Forum

American GI Forum organization formed to protect the rights of Mexican Americans and to help veterans with education and health care

Heman Sweatt plaintiff in a lawsuit against the University of Texas that led to the decision by the Supreme Court that segregation was unconstitutional

Benjy Brooks first female pediatric surgeon in Texas

Section Summary

AFRICAN AMERICAN RIGHTS

Although African Americans fought for their country during World War II, at home they faced discrimination. Organizations like the National Association for the Advancement of Colored People (NAACP) tried to stop discrimination. One of the major figures in the fight for equal rights was **Lulu Belle Madison White.** She served as head of the Houston chapter of the NAACP and later became the organization's state director.

In 1948, Predident Truman ordered the military to **desegregate,** or stop the practice of separating people by race. He also banned racial discrimination in hiring federal employees. To call attention to their lack of rights, African Americans in Texas and other parts of the country held demonstrations and

> What was the purpose of the NAACP?
>
> _____
>
> _____

marches. They were following a policy of
nonviolent resistance, or the use of peaceful means
to achieve a goal. James L. Farmer Jr. of Marshall,
Texas was a cofounder of the Congress of Racial
Equality (CORE), formed in Chicago in 1942.

> How did African Americans call attention to their lack of rights?
>
> _____
>
> _____
>
> _____

THE AMERICAN GI FORUM

Mexican American veterans in Texas also
experienced discrimination, despite their service in
the war. In 1948 **Hector P. García,** a highly
decorated U.S. Army surgeon, founded the
American GI Forum. Its purpose was to protect
the rights Meixcan Americans and to help veterans
with education and health care.

DESEGREGATING PUBLIC SCHOOLS

African Americans still had to attend schools
separate from white students. In 1946 **Heman
Sweatt** was denied entry to the University of Texas
School of Law. In *Sweatt* v. *Painter,* the U.S.
Supreme Court ruled that segregated facilities in
professional schools were unconstitutional. In 1954,
in the case of *Brown* v. *Board of Education,* the
U.S. Supreme Court ruled that separate educational
facilities are by definition unequal.

> Underline the two lawsuits that maintained that segregation was unconstitutional.

NEW OPPORTUNITIES FOR WOMEN

Texas women also fought for recognition of their
civil rights. In the 1950s more women began
attending colleges and universities. They demanded
equal pay and supported an equal rights amendment
that was approved in 1972. **Benjy Brooks** became
the first female pediatric surgeon in Texas.

CHALLENGE ACTIVITY

Critical Thinking: Analyzing Information What
organizations struggled for civil rights, and what
were their achievements?

Lulu Belle Madison White	desegregation	nonviolent resistance	James L. Farmer Jr.
Hector P. García	American GI Forum	Heman Sweatt	Benjy Brooks

DIRECTIONS On the line provided before each statement, write **T** if the statement is true and **F** if the statement is false. If the statement is false, write a corrected statement on the line after the false statement.

_____ 1. As a leader of the NAACP, <u>James L. Farmer Jr.</u> helped fight for equal rights for African Americans.

_____

_____ 2. The policy of <u>desegregation</u> was the use of peaceful means to achieve a goal.

_____

_____ 3. <u>Hector P. García</u> founded the American GI Forum.

_____

_____ 4. After earning a degree from the University of Texas Medical Branch in Galveston, <u>Lulu Belle Madison White</u> became the first female pediatric surgeon in Texas.

_____

_____ 5. <u>Heman Sweatt's</u> lawsuit against the University of Law School led the way for the *Brown v. Board of Education* decision.

_____

Texas in Transition

MAIN IDEAS
1. Lyndon B. Johnson served in many elected positions before he became president of the United States.
2. The Great Society included programs to improve healthcare, education, and other aspects of American life.
3. The Vietnam War had significant effects in Texas.

Key Terms and People

Lyndon B. Johnson vice president from Johnson City who became president when John F. Kennedy was assassinated in Texas

Great Society a series of reforms designed to improve the lives of Americans, including efforts to eliminate poverty and racial injustice

Head Start a program designed to offer early childhood education and nutrition information to low-income students and their families

Economic Opportunity Act legislation that provided funds for job training and created community action programs

Tonkin Gulf Resolution act of Congress that gave the president the authority to order troops into combat in Vietnam

Section Summary

A TEXAN IN THE WHITE HOUSE

President John F. Kennedy was shot and killed in Dallas on November 22, 1963. Soon after, Vice President **Lyndon B. Johnson** of Texas took the presidential oath of office. Johnson was a Democrat. He had held the majority leadership position in the Senate since 1955. In this powerful position, Johnson influenced policy in a number of areas, including civil rights and space exploration.

> **When was Johnson sworn in as president?**
>
> _____

THE GREAT SOCIETY

Johnson believed that the United States should provide equal rights, education, jobs, and decent housing for all its citizens. After winning the 1964 presidential election by a landslide, he launched a

program that he called the **Great Society**. This
program was a series of reforms— including efforts
to eliminate poverty and racial injustice —designed
to improve the lives of Americans. Two major
programs created were Medicare and Medicaid.

> **List two goals of the Great society.**
> _____
> _____

Another part of Johnson's education reform plan
was the creation of the **Head Start** program in
1965. This program was designed to offer early
childhood education and nutrition information to
low-income students and their families. Head Start
is still active today.

> **Underline two types of aid offered by the Head Start program**

Another program, the **Economic Opportunity
Act**, provided funds for job training and created
community action programs. While many
Americans supported the goals of the Great Society,
some felt that too much money was being spent on
it, and that federal government had too much power
over the states.

THE VIETNAM WAR

At the same time, conflict was brewing in Vietnam.
In 1964, upon Johnson's request, Congress passed
the **Tonkin Gulf Resolution**. This gave the
president the authority to order troops into combat.
The number of U.S. troops in Vietnam quickly rose.
The booming defense industry boosted the Texas
economy. As casualties in the Vietnam War
mounted, so did opposition to the war. Some
Americans criticized Johnson's handling of the war
and demanded that he bring U.S. troops home. On
March 31, 1968, he announced that he would not
run for re-election. The war continued well into the
1970s.

> **What power did the Tonkin Gulf Resolution give the president?**
> _____

CHALLENGE ACTIVITY

Critical Thinking: Analyzing information What
were the most successful aspects of Johnson's
presidency? List reasons why you think so.

| Lyndon B. Johnson | Head Start | Tonkin Gulf Resolution |
| Great Society | Economic Opportunity Act | Nineteenth Amendment |

DIRECTIONS Use the words from the word bank to write a summary
of what you have learned in the section.

_____

_____

_____

_____

_____

_____

_____

_____

_____

_____

_____

_____

_____

_____

_____

_____

_____

_____

_____

MAIN IDEAS
1. The civil rights movement arose in the 1960s to secure equal rights for African Americans.
2. Through the efforts of politicians and activists, Hispanic Americans won many civil rights.
3. Texan women also worked to gain equal rights.

Key Terms and People

sit-ins protests that involve sitting down in a public facility and refusing to leave

Barbara Jordan elected state senator in 1966; the first African American to represent Texas in Congress

Henry B. González the first Mexican American elected to the Texas senate

Raymond L. Telles elected major of El Paso in 1957, the first Hispanic mayor of a major American city

Chicano movement a political movement to empower Mexican Americans

La Raza Unida Party a political party formed in 1970 to highlight issues affecting Hispanic Americans

Section Summary
NONVIOLENT PROTEST

The movement for civil rights grew during the 1960s. Protesters staged boycotts and **sit-ins**—protests that involve sitting down in a public location and refusing to leave—to end segregation. President Johnson's first address to Congress called for civil rights laws. Texan James Farmer was a national leader of the civil rights movement. In 1963 Martin Luther King Jr. and hundreds of thousands of Americans joined a March on Washington in support of civil rights. Meanwhile, some 900 Texans of all races marched on the state Capitol. Soon after, Congress passed the Civil Rights Act of 1964. In 1965 Congress passed the Voting Rights Act. In Texas, African Americans began to win state offices for the first time since

> List two important civil rights acts passed in the 1960s.
>
> _____
>
> _____

Reconstruction. In 1966 **Barbara Jordan** of
Houston was elected as a state senator. Jordan was
elected to the U.S. House of Representatives in
1972, the first African American to represent Texas
in Congress.

HISPANIC AMERICAN RIGHTS

Hispanics also pushed for civil rights. In 1956
Democrat **Henry B. González** became the first
Mexican American elected to the Texas Senate in
the 1900s. In 1961 he was elected to the U.S. House
of Representatives, where he served for 37 years. In
1957 **Raymond L. Telles** was elected mayor of El
Paso—the first major American city to elect a
Hispanic American mayor. Because of new laws
and the work of civil rights organizations, large
numbers of Hispanics were registering to vote. The
demand for political change was part of a
nationwide effort known as the **Chicano
movement.** In 1970 José Angel Gutiérrez and
Mario Compeán formed **La Raza Unida Party**
(RUP), to highlight issues affecting Hispanic
Americans.

> Underline two reasons
> large numbers of Hispanic
> Americans were registering
> to vote.

THE WOMEN'S MOVEMENT

The Texas Women's Political Caucus, founded in
1971, worked to elect more women to political
office. The organizers of this group included Liz
Carpenter and Jane Wells. Women made significant
political gains on national and local levels
throughout the 1970s and 1980s.

CHALLENGE ACTIVITY

Critical Thinking: Analyzing Information What
organizations fought for civil rights, and what were
their achievements?

Guided Reading Workbook

| sit-ins | Barbara Jordan | Henry B. González |
| Raymond L. Telles | Chicano movement | La Raza Unida Party |

DIRECTIONS On the line provided before each statement, write **T** if the statement is true and **F** if the statement is false. If the statement is false, write a corrected statement on the line after the false statement.

_____ 1. Barbara Jordan was elected to the state senate in 1966.

_____

_____ 2. The first Hispanic mayor of a major American city was Henry B. González.

_____

_____ 3. The Chicano movement worked to elect more women to political office.

_____

_____ 4. Raymond L. Telles was elected mayor of San Antonio in 1957.

_____

_____ 5. La Raza Unida Party (RUP) was set up to highlight issues affecting African Americans.

_____

DIRECTIONS Write two adjectives or descriptive phrases that describe the term given.

6. sit-ins _____

Texas in Transition

 MAIN IDEAS
1. The aerospace and defense industries in Texas grew in the 1950s and 1960s.
2. The high-tech and medical industries have attracted people and businesses to Texas.

Key Terms and People

National Aeronautics and Space Administration (NASA) the agency responsible for the civilian space program and for aeronautics and aerospace research

Manned Spacecraft Center NASA's headquarters in Houston, built in 1961, now called the Johnson Space Center

Walter Cunningham lunar module pilot on the 1968 *Apollo 7* mission

Michael DeBakey Texas cardiac surgeon who performed the first arterial bypass

Denton Cooley Texas cardiac surgeon who placed the first artificial heart in a patient

Section Summary
TEXAS IN THE SPACE AGE

As a leader in aircraft and weapons production, Texas was a logical choice to become a center for the nation's developing space program. **The National Aeronautics and Space Administration (NASA) was created in 1958.** In 1961 NASA chose Houston as the headquarters for its astronauts. The **Manned Spacecraft Center** brought many jobs to the Houston area. In 1968 NASA launched the *Apollo 7* mission, the first manned flight of the Apollo program. Astronaut **Walter Cunningham** was the lunar module pilot on the flight. In 1969, NASA's *Apollo 11* mission safely landed a man on the Moon.

Later, NASA operated the space shuttle program, which continued until 2004. The defense industry grew along with the space industry. In addition, the state continued to be home to many military bases and personnel during the 1980s. The defense industry—

> What location did NASA choose as the headquarters for its astronauts in 1961?
>
> _____
> _____

both military bases and weapons production—added millions of dollars to the state's economy.

HIGH TECH INDUSTRIES

Texas rapidly became a leader in other high-tech industries as well. Texas companies manufactured a variety of electronic devices. Developments in communications, radar, and other technologies led to even greater growth in the industry. The Texas high-tech industry began to design and manufacture semiconductors and microchips to meet the national and international demand for computers.

> Underline two products manufactured by the high-tech industry in Texas.

MEDICAL TECHNOLOGY

Texas doctors such as **Michael DeBakey** and **Denton Cooley** helped revolutionize the treatment of heart disease. In 1964 DeBakey performed the first arterial bypass operation to repair a damaged heart. In 1968 Cooly placed the first artificial heart in a patient. As a center for medical research, Texas has attracted patients seeking quality health care from all over the world. Medical technologies that were developed in the state have been used throughout the world. Many medical technology companies have moved to Texas.

> How did medical technology help the Texas economy?
> _____
> _____

The booming Texas high-tech and medical technology industries also affected the cities in which they were based. The population of these cities grew rapidly. Museums and other attractions were established. People moved to Texas in increasing numbers to take advantage of not only the jobs in these industries but also the quality of life that a growing economy helped provide.

CHALLENGE ACTIVITY

Critical Thinking: Analyzing Information What achievements came out of the high-tech and medical industries in Texas?

Guided Reading Workbook

Manned Spacecraft Center	Walter Cunningham	Denton Cooley
	Michael DeBakey	National Aeronautics and Space Administration

DIRECTIONS Use the words from the word bank to write a summary of what you have learned in the section.

_____

_____

_____

_____

_____

_____

_____

_____

_____

_____

_____

_____

_____

_____

_____

_____

_____

_____

Texts in Transition

MAIN IDEAS

1. Population increases led to rapid growth for Texas cities and many industries in the 1970s.

2. An international increase in oil prices led to a boom in the Texas oil industry.

3. Texas politics changed in the1970s as women, members of minority groups, and Republicans won elections.

Key Terms and People

John Tower the first Republican elected to the U.S. Senate from Texas since Reconstruction

scandal an action or event regarded as morally or legally wrong and causing general public outrage

William Clements the first Republican elected Texas governor since Reconstruction

Section Summary

THE SUNBELT AND URBAN GROWTH

Between 1940 and 1980, the population of the Sunbelt—the South and the Southwest—grew by more than 110 percent. By 1980 about one third of the U.S. population lived in this region. Much of this growth took place in Texas.

NEW JOBS AND CITY LIFE

During this time, the Texas economy entered a cycle of growth. Many people moved to Texas to work for oil and gas companies. These workers usually settled in cities, adding to a workforce that attracted more national and international businesses to the state. This in turn brought even more people to Texas. As Texas cities grew, so did the need to provide services to residents. This sparked job creation in industries such as restaurants, utilities, construction, and banks. New freeway systems were built to allow Texans to commute from suburbs into cities. Public transportation systems such as buses helped people travel throughout the growing urban areas.

> List two methods of transportation that helped people travel in urban areas.
>
> _____
>
> _____

THE OIL BOOM AND BUST

The oil business boomed in the 1970s. With rising oil and gas prices, profits for oil companies grew. This boom came to a halt in 1982 when oil prices dropped. More than 200,000 jobs were lost in Houston alone. The oil bust also hurt other businesses in Texas.

POLITICS IN THE 1970S

Texas government changed along with the population and the economy With the success of the civil rights movements of the 1960s, Texans of all backgrounds became involved in state government. During the 1970s the strength of the Republican Party grew in the state. Ever since the end of World War II, the Republican Party had been supporting more conservative viewpoints. In 1961 **John Tower** became the first Republican from Texas elected to the U.S. Senate since Reconstruction.

Democrat Dolph Briscoe won the governor's race in 1972 amid demands for reform. In 1971 several officials were convicted of taking bribes in what became known as the Sharpstown stock-fraud **scandal.** As a result, the next legislature passed several reforms. A Republican, **William Clements,** won the governor's race in 1978. Texas had not had a Republican governor since 1874.

> What were two successes for the Republican Party in Texas politics in the 1970s?
> _____
> _____

CHALLENGE ACTIVITY

Critical Thinking: Analyzing Information What led to the rise of the Republican party in the 1970s? List reasons why you think the Republican Party gained support.

DIRECTIONS Write a summary of what you have learned in this section.

_____

_____

_____

_____

_____

_____

_____

_____

_____

_____

_____

_____

_____

_____

_____

_____

_____

_____

_____

_____

_____

Name _____ Class _____ Date _____

Contemporary Texas

Section 1

 MAIN IDEAS
1. Republicans, women, and members of minority groups won state offices in the 1970s and 1980s.
2. The Texas oil industry crashed in the 1980s.

Key Terms and People

two-party system political system in which two major parties compete to gain political office

Ann Richards Democrat elected state treasurer and, later, governor

Kay Bailey Hutchison first female Republican elected to state office, first as state treasurer and, later, as senator

Raul A. Gonzalez Jr. Texas Supreme Court judge and first Hispanic Texan to hold a major state office

budget surplus money remaining after all expenses have been paid, created when income exceeds expenses

savings and loans associations banks originally established to help people buy homes

Section Summary
POLITICAL CHANGE IN TEXAS

The election of Bill Clements as governor in 1978 marked a turning point in state politics. For the first time since Reconstruction, the Republican Party had gained enough support to challenge the Democrats' control of Texas. The **two-party system**—a political system in which two parties of comparable strength compete for political office—was reemerging in Texas.

Many Texans had turned to the Republican Party because of its reputation as the party of business. Clements, for example, pledged to lower taxes and reduce government regulation of business. Clements won a second term as governor in 1986.

Women and minority groups were also becoming more prominent in state politics. In 1982, **Ann**

> In what way did Clements's election mark a turning point in state politics?
>
> _____
> _____

Richards, a Democrat, was elected state treasurer, the first woman elected to a statewide office since 1932. A few years later Republican **Kay Bailey Hutchison** won the same office. In 1993, she became the state's first female U.S. senator. **Raul A. Gonzalez Jr.** became the first Hispanic Texan to hold a major state office—he was appointed to the state Supreme Court in 1984.

BOOM AND BUST IN THE 1980s

The oil industry boom continued into the early 1980s. Money from oil poured into the state, creating a **budget surplus**—the state's income exceeded its expenses. The state used the extra money to fund education and public works. Many oil workers invested in real estate.

> What was the result of the state's budget surplus?
>
> _____
>
> _____

In the mid-1980s, however, the price of oil dropped, and many workers in the oil industry lost their jobs. Real estate prices fell and banks were hit by defaulted loans. Between 1985 and 1992, some 470 Texas banks went out of business. Even harder hit were **savings and loans associations,** or S&Ls, which had been created to loan people money to buy homes. Many S&Ls had issued risky loans that could no longer be repaid. Hundreds of S&Ls failed nationwide. The Texas and national economies fell into a recession.

> Underline the purpose of a savings and loans association.

CHALLENGE ACTIVITY

Critical Thinking: Summarizing What contributed to economic problems in Texas in the 1980s?

Guided Reading Workbook

two-party system	Ann Richards	Kay Bailey Hutchison
Raul A. Gonzalez Jr.	budget surplus	savings and loans associations

DIRECTIONS Answer each question below.

1. What is a two-party system and what explained its reemergence in Texas in 1978?

_____

_____

2. How did women become more prominent in state politics in the 1980s?

_____

_____

3. Who was Raul A. Gonzalez Jr.?

_____

_____

4. What caused the budget surplus in the early 1980s?

_____

_____

5. What caused the failure of S&Ls in the 1980s?

_____

_____

Name _____ Class _____ Date _____

Contemporary Texas

MAIN IDEAS
1. Texans George H.W. Bush and George W. Bush both served as president of the United States.
2. Texas governors during the 1990s and 2000s focused on economic and social issues.
3. During George W. Bush's presidency, the United States launched the War on Terror.

Key Terms and People

George H. W. Bush former Texas oil executive who served as president of the United States from 1989 to 1993

James A. Baker III secretary of state under George H. W. Bush

George W. Bush son of George H. W. Bush, governor of Texas, and president of the United States from 2001 to 2009

bipartisanship cooperation between political parties to achieve goals

Bob Bullock Democratic lieutenant governor of Texas from 1991 to 1999

Rick Perry Republican governor of Texas from 2000 to 2015

terrorism the use of fear or terror to advance political goals

Section Summary

PRESIDENT GEORGE H. W. BUSH

George H. W. Bush, a former Texas oil executive, became president in 1988. He brought several several Texans into his administration. One was Houston lawyer **James A. Baker III,** who was named secretary of state.

On August 2, 1990, Iraq invaded its neighbor, Kuwait, threatening much of the world's oil supply. In 1991 an international coalition launched Operation Desert Storm to push Iraq out of Kuwait. Many Americans approved of the way that Bush handled the war, but a downturn in the economy damaged his popularity. In 1992, Bush lost the presidential election to Democrat Bill Clinton, who went on to serve two terms.

> **What was the aim of Operation Desert Storm?**
> _____
> _____

STATE POLITICS SINCE 1990

In 1994 George H. W. Bush's son, **George W. Bush,** became Texas governor. Bush encouraged **bipartisanship,** or cooperation between parties. He developed a strong working relationship with Democrat **Bob Bullock,** who was lieutenant governor from 1991 to 1999. Bush won reelection but soon ran for president. Republican Lieutenant Governor **Rick Perry** then became the new governor of Texas in 2000 when Bush won the presidential election. Perry decided not to pursue reelection in 2014.

THE DIVERSIFYING TEXAS ECONOMY

During the 1990s, Texans worked to diversify the state's economy. Texans turned to manufacturing, retail trade, sales, tourism, and medical technology. The growth of communication technologies and the birth of the Internet also spurred the economy.

> Underline the industries in Texas that spurred the economy.

GEORGE W. BUSH AS PRESIDENT

On September 11, 2001, the United States was victim to shocking acts of **terrorism**—violent acts by a person or small group to advance political goals. U.S. officials determined that al Qaeda, an Islamic terrorist group based in Afghanistan, was responsible for the attacks. The Taliban, an extreme Islamic group, ruled Afghanistan. The United States attacked Afghanistan and drove the Taliban from power.

Later, President Bush argued that Saddam Hussein, dictator of Iraq, posed an imminent threat to U.S. security. In March 2003, the United States and its allies launched an attack on Iraq. The government collapsed, and Hussein was eventually captured and executed. After Bush left office in 2008, policies he had begun in Iraq and Afghanistan continued.

> What is the name of the group that ruled Afghanistan?
> _____

CHALLENGE ACTIVITY

Critical Thinking: Analyzing Information How did terrorism affect the presidencies of both Bushes?

Guided Reading Workbook

| George H. W. Bush | James A. Baker III | George W. Bush | bipartisanship |
| Bob Bullock | Rick Perry | terrorism | the Taliban |

DIRECTIONS Read each sentence and fill in the blank with the word
from the pair that best completes each sentence.

1. Under George H. W. Bush, _____ (James A. Baker III/Bob
   Bullock) served as secretary of state.

2. The biggest issue faced by George W. Bush during his presidency was
   _____ (terrorism/bipartisanship).

3. After George W. Bush was elected president, _____ (Rick
   Perry/Bob Bullock) became governor of Texas.

4. One example of bipartisanship under George W. Bush's governorship was his
   partnership with _____ (James A. Baker III/Bob Bullock).

DIRECTIONS Write a few words about the events that occurred during
each person's presidency.

5. George H. W. Bush _____

   _____

6. George W. Bush _____

   _____

MAIN IDEAS
1. Migration from within the United States and immigration from other countries have led to population growth in Texas.
2. Water shortages are a problem in Texas today.

Key Terms

illegal immigrants people who moved to a country without following the proper legal procedures

deportation the forced removal of people from a country or region

infrastructure public works such as roads and water systems

desalinization the process of removing salt from seawater to make it fresh to drink

Section Summary
A GROWING POPULATION

Texas has the second-highest population of any state. Between 1980 and 2010, the Texas population grew from 14 million to about 25 million. About half of this increase is from births, and the other half is the result of people moving to Texas.

About 85 percent of Texans live in cities. Three Texas cities—Houston, San Antonio, and Dallas—have populations of more than 1 million each.

According to 2011 estimates, more than 5 million people living in Texas were born in other states. People move to Texas for a variety of reasons. The oil and gas and high-tech industries in Texas have expanded, creating jobs. The cost of living in Texas is lower than in some parts of the country. The absence of a state income tax appeals to people.

In 2011, about 4 million people in Texas had been born in other countries. Most foreign-born immigrants come for work. Other immigrants come for school or to live with family already in the state.

In 2009 the U.S. Department of Homeland Security estimated that about 1.8 million **illegal immigrants** lived in Texas. Illegal immigrants do

> **What are the ways by which Texas's population increased between 1980 and 2010?**
> _____

> **What are some reasons people have moved to Texas from other states?**
> _____
> _____

not follow legal procedures for moving to the United States. The issue of illegal immigration is a source of debate for Texas leaders. Some want all illegal immigrants to be returned to their home countries—a process called **deportation.** Others want to create programs that will help illegal immigrants become U.S. citizens.

Underline the definition of *deportation*.

EFFECTS OF POPULATION GROWTH

As the Texas population has grown, so has the strain on government resources, including a need for improved **infrastructure**—public works such as roads, bridges, electrical grids, and water systems. State and local governments have built new roads to improve traffic congestion. There has also been an increase in the demand for education and health care. School districts have struggled to pay for more teachers and staff. Likewise, more hospitals had to be built in Texas.

List three effects of population growth in Texas.   1._____   2._____   3._____

WATER SHORTAGES

Increasing population has also strained water resources. The strain is due in large part to increased water usage, including use from increased industrial activity. In addition, drought has contributed to the state's water shortage. Texans are seeking new sources of water for home and industrial use. One possibility is to use water from the Gulf of Mexico. This water would need to undergo **desalinization,** a process that removes salt from seawater, before it could be used for drinking or irrigating crops.

CHALLENGE ACTIVITY

Critical Thinking: Analyzing Information How has an increased population affected Texas?

Name _____ Class _____ Date _____

Section 3, *continued*

| illegal immigrants | deportation | infrastructure |
| desalinization | | |

DIRECTIONS On the line provided before each statement, write **T** if the statement is true and **F** if the statement is false. If the statement is false, write a corrected statement on the line after the false statement.

_____ 1. Illegal immigrants follow legal procedures to enter the United States.

_____

_____ 2. Deportation is the process of returning immigrants to their home countries.

_____

_____ 3. Roads and bridges are examples of infrastructure that is strained by population growth in Texas.

_____

_____ 4. The process of adding salt to seawater is called desalinization.

_____

Contemporary Texas

MAIN IDEAS

1. The Texas population grew and became more diverse in the 1990s.
2. Ethnic groups in Texas celebrate their heritage.
3. Texas musicians, writers, and artists have reflected the state's diversity.

Key Terms and People

Cinco de Mayo holiday celebrating Mexican victory of May 5, 1862

Larry McMurtry Pulitzer Prize-winning Texas writer

John Graves a well-known writer who has written about Texas and the land's effect on people's lives

Sandra Cisneros Texas author whose work focuses on the lives of Mexican American families

Diane Gonzales Bertrand Texas author of books for children about the lives of Mexican American families

John Biggers visual artist whose work portrays African American experiences

Amado Peña Jr. visual artist whose work captures the Southwest

Wilie Nelson country music performer who works in and around Austin

Section Summary

A LAND OF MANY CULTURES

As the population of Texas has grown, its diversity has increased. The 2010 census results reflect this diversity.

- More than 45% of Texans identified themselves as non-Hispanic white.
- More than 37% identified as Hispanic.
- About 12% identified as African American.
- 3.8% identified as Asian.
- Less than 1% identified as American Inidan.
- Nearly 3% reported belonging to more than one race.

The various groups who live in Texas have maintained elements of their traditional cultures. For example, each year on May 5, Mexican

> **What group is the majority in Texas according to the 2010 census?**
>
> _____

Americans celebrate **Cinco de Mayo.** It was on May 5, 1862 that a Mexican army defeated an invading French force at the Battle of Puebla.

TEXANS IN ART AND LITERATURE

Texas writers and artists have provided the world with glimpses of the state in their work. Pulitzer-Prize winning author **Larry McMurtry** has written several novels about life in Texas. **John Graves** has written about the effect of the land of Texas on people's lives. Other Texas writers focus on the people of Texas. For example, **Sandra Cisneros** and **Diane Gonzales Bertrand** have received national attention for their works, which focus on the lives of Mexican American families in America. Ciseneros writes for adults, while Bertrand writes for children.

Texans have also excelled in the visual arts. **John Biggers** has produced works of art that portray African American experiences. **Amado Peña Jr.** has captured the Southwest through his depictions of American Indian life.

> How are the works of Sandra Cisneros and Diane Gonzales similar?
> _____
> _____

MUSIC, POPULAR CULTURE, AND SPORTS

Texas music reflects the state's diversity. Texans have written and performed blues, country, folk, jazz, rap, rock, Tejano, and classical music. In 1970s a group of Texas musicians including **Willie Nelson,** Waylon Jennings, and Jerry Jeff Walker developed a new type of music called progressive country.

Among the most popular forms of entertainment in Texa today is sports. The state is home to many professional sports teams in football, men's and women's basketball, baseball, soccer, and hockey.

CHALLENGE ACTIVITY

Critical Thinking: Researching Write a brief report on one artist or writer mentioned in this section.

Name _____ Class _____ Date _____

Section 4, *continued*

DIRECTIONS Write a brief description of each term or person listed below.

1. Cinco de Mayo _____

_____

2. Larry McMurtry _____

_____

3. John Graves _____

_____

4. Sandra Cisneros _____

_____

5. Diane Gonzales Bertrand _____

_____

6. John Biggers _____

_____

7. Amado Peña Jr. _____

_____

8. Willie Nelson _____

_____

Guided Reading Workbook

Contemporary Texas

MAIN IDEAS

1. Several challenges face Texas as it moves to the future.
2. Texans have taken steps to protect the environment.

Key Terms and People

biomass plant and animal material used to generate energy

wind farms groups of wind turbines in one area used to create energy

globalization the interdependence of the nations of the world that has been created as goods, ideas, and people move across the globe

Texas Commission on Environmental Quality an organization formed to balance the increased costs businesses must bear to protect the environment with efforts to safeguard the state's air and water

Foreign-Trade Zones areas in which export regulations are reduced to promote trade

Section Summary
NEW SOURCES OF ENERGY

Historically, Texas has gotten most of its energy through the burning of fossil fuels, such as coal, oil, and natural gas. However, the world's oil and gas deposits are not limitless. Texans—and the rest of the world—will need to rely on other sources of energy.

One potential source of energy is nuclear power. As of 2013, two nuclear plants operated in Texas, producing nearly 10% of the state's electricity. Supporters of nuclear power point out that it causes less pollution than burning fossil fuels. Opponents, however, fear that accidents or disposal of hazardous wastes could release radiation.

Many Texans are also looking to renewable energy sources, those that do not depend on limited resources like oil, gas, or nuclear material. For example, some new power plants generate energy from **biomass**—plant material and animal waste—

> **What are the arguments for and against nuclear power?**
>
> _____
> _____
> _____

rather than fossil fuels. Others harness the power of rivers to generate hydroelectricity. Many businesses and individuals use solar panels to turn the sun's energy into electricity.

The most successful new form of energy in Texas today is wind power. **Wind farms** use the wind to move turbines that generate electricity. Texas now produces more wind power than any other state.

PROTECTING THE ENVIRONMENT

As the Texas population has grown, so has demand on water and other natural resources. In some parts of the state, air and water pollution have become an issue. To help stop pollution, the state created the **Texas Commission on Environmental Quality,** an organization that tries to balance the increased cost businesses must bear to protect the environment with efforts to safeguard the state's air and water. It tracks air and water quality and enforces state and federal regulations regarding the environment.

> **What is the purpose of the Texas Commission on Environmental Quality?**
> _____
> _____
> _____

GLOBALIZATION

Nations have become increasingly interdependent as goods, ideas, and people moved all across the globe. This process of **globalization** has boosted the state's economy as Texas businesses have gained greater access to global markets. Many nations have offices in Texas to improve trade with the state. Texas also maintains several **Foreign Trade Zones**—areas in which export regulations are reduced to promote trade.

CHALLENGE ACTIVITY

Critical Thinking: Analyzing Information In a paragraph, describe some of the challenges Texas faces in today's society.

biomass	wind farms	globalization
Texas Commission on Environmental Quality		Foreign-Trade Zones

DIRECTIONS Read each sentence and circle the term in the word pair that best completes each sentence.

1. An increasing interdependence of nations is a result of (globalization/Foreign-Trade Zones).

2. One way to limit the use of fossil fuels is the installation and use of (Foreign-Trade Zones/wind farms.)

3. In order to help stop pollution, an organization called (Foreign-Trade Zones/Texas Commission on Environmental Quality) was created to track air and water quality and enforce environmental regulations.

DIRECTIONS Write two adjectives or descriptive phrases that describe the term given.

4. biomass _____

5. Foreign-Trade Zone _____

MAIN IDEAS
1. Ideas from the U.S. Constitution have influenced the Texas Constitution.
2. The Texas Constitution is based on several key principles intended to protect the rights of citizens.
3. The Texas Constitution includes a bill of rights to protect people's freedoms.

Key Terms

federalism a division of authority between two levels of government

republicanism a system in which voters elect officials to represent them in the government

limited government a government with specific limits on its power

separation of powers division of power among different government branches

checks and balances government arrangement under which each branch has ways to check, or restrain, the other two

veto rejection

amendments additions and changes to a constitution

Section Summary
BASIC PRINCIPLES OF GOVERNMENT

The Texas Constitution is the basis of the state's government and laws. It reflects several principles found in the U.S. Constitution: popular sovereignty, republicanism, limited government, separation of powers, checks and balances, federalism, and protection of individual rights. Popular sovereignty means that all political power comes from the people. The U.S. Constitution grants certain authority to state governments. This division of authority between two levels of government is called **federalism. Republicanism**, a system in which voters elect officials to represent them in the government, is central to the Texas Constitution. These officials are then responsible to voters. The Texas Constitution limits government power. This is **limited government**.

> **What principles from the U.S. Constitution are reflected in the Texas Constitution?**
>
> _____
>
> _____

BALANCING GOVERNMENTAL POWER

The **separation of powers** divides power among government branches. The legislative branch makes the laws. The executive branch carries out the laws. The judicial branch, or court system, interprets laws. The Texas Constitution includes a system of **checks and balances** to keep any one branch from having too much power. For example, the governor can reject a law proposed by the legislature. This rejection is called a **veto**. In turn, the legislature can override, or reverse, the governor's veto. The judicial branch can check the legislature if it thinks a new law violates the Constitution.

> **What divides power among branches of government?**
> _____
> _____

THE TEXAS BILL OF RIGHTS

The Texas Constitution provides a bill of rights—an outline of the individual rights that a government protects.

The Texas Bill of Rights was modeled after the U.S. Bill of Rights, and lists many of the same rights and freedoms. The freedoms of speech and of the press protect Texans' right to express their ideas and opinions. The freedom of worship protects Texans' right to practice any religion they choose. The bill of rights also protects the rights of crime victims and the rights of people accused of crimes.

> **What is the Texas Bill of Rights?**
> _____
> _____

CHANGING THE CONSTITUTION

Like the U.S. Constitution, the Texas Constitution is a flexible document. It can be changed to reflect the changing needs of the people. Additions and changes to a constitution are called **amendments**. The Texas Constitution restricts government powers. The state often must ask permission of the voters to take on new activities.

CHALLENGE ACTIVITY

Critical Thinking: Classify Describe the duties of each branch of government. Then draw a visual to explain all three branches.

DIRECTIONS On the line provided before each statement, write **T** if the statement is true and **F** if the statement is false. If the statement is false, rewrite the statement on the line after it to make it true.

_____ 1. When a governor accepts a proposed law, the law is called a <u>veto</u>.

_____

_____ 2. A <u>limited government</u> has an unlimited amount of power.

_____

_____ 3. <u>Republicanism</u> is a system in which voters elect officials to represent them in government.

_____

_____ 4. The way in which the powers of the branches of government are divided is called the <u>separation of powers</u>.

_____

_____ 5. <u>Federalism</u> is a division of authority between two constitutions.

_____

_____ 6. An arrangement under which each branch has ways to check, or restrain, the other branches is called a system of <u>checks and balances</u>.

_____

_____ 7. Rejections to the Texas Constitution are <u>amendments</u>.

_____

Texas Government

MAIN IDEAS
1. The Texas legislature makes the state's laws.
2. The lawmaking process is long and complex.

Key Terms

bicameral having two legislative houses

sessions periods in which the legislature meets

bill potential law

conference committee a committee in legislature that includes members of both houses, who work to revise bills to satisfy both houses of the legislature

Section Summary

THE TWO HOUSES

The legislative branch makes the state's laws. Like the U.S. Congress, the Texas legislature is **bicameral**, or made up of two houses: the House of Representatives and the Senate. The House has 150 members. The Senate has 31 members. The leader of the House of Representatives is the Speaker of the House. The lieutenant governor leads the Senate.

LEGISLATIVE DUTIES AND POWER

Among the duties of the legislature is to make laws and propose amendments to the Texas Constitution. Members of either house can propose new laws. Laws that raise money must originate in the House, however. The Texas legislature works during periods called **sessions**. Sessions are held in odd-numbered years.

> What does the legislative branch do?
> _____
> _____

HOW A BILL BECOMES A LAW

Lawmaking is a complex process. The leaders of each house influence which **bills**, or proposed laws,

Guided Reading Workbook

get considered. Legislators in either house can create a bill. The house leader assigns bills to committees to study. Committees discuss which bills to recommend to the entire house.

After discussion, the committee approves or rejects the bill. If approved, the entire house debates it. If approved by the house, the entire process repeats in the other house. The other house can reject the bill— in which case it dies—or approve the bill and send it to the governor.

Frequently, though, the second house approves a revised version of the bill. In such cases, the two houses form a **conference committee.** This committee revises the bill so it will satisfy both houses. After the committee is finished, both houses vote again on the bill.

The governor can deal with a bill in three ways. He or she can sign the bill into law. If the governor ignores the bill, it automatically becomes law after 10 days. The governor can also veto the bill. A vetoed bill returns to the legislature. If two-thirds of the members of each house vote to override a veto, the bill becomes law.

| Who can propose a bill? |
| _____ |

| Underline the ways in which the governor can deal with a bill. |

CHALLENGE ACTIVITY
Critical Thinking: Summarize Write a paragraph explaining how a bill becomes a law.

bicameral	sessions	bill	conference committee

DIRECTIONS On the lines below, use the words in the word bank to write a summary of what you have learned in the section.

_____

_____

_____

_____

_____

_____

_____

_____

_____

_____

_____

_____

_____

_____

_____

_____

_____

_____

Texas Government

MAIN IDEAS

1. The powers and duties of the governor of Texas are outlined in the state constitution.

2. In addition to the governor, several other officials and agencies are part of the executive branch.

Key Terms

line-item veto power held by a government executive that allows for the veto of specific lines, or parts, of budget bills

pardon power held by a government executive to free people convicted of crimes

Section Summary

THE GOVERNOR

The governor of Texas is the head of the state's executive branch, described in Article IV of the Texas Constitution. The executive branch enforces the laws passed by the legislature. It also manages and conducts the daily business of the state. The executive branch includes several elected officials. These officials keep state affairs running smoothly. Other than the secretary of state, all of them are elected by the people. The secretary of state is appointed by the governor. The Texas Constitution outlines the qualifications to serve as governor. The governor's salary is set by the Texas legislature. He or she lives in the Governor's Mansion in Austin, built by the state in 1856. The state provides the governor with a staff, transportation, and money for job-related expenses.

> How is the secretary of state chosen?
>
> _____
>
> _____

THE POWERS AND DUTIES OF THE GOVERNOR

The governor cannot make laws; however, he or she can make recommendations for new laws to the legislature. Bills must be sent to the governor for approval. The governor can veto a law if he or she opposes it. The governor also has the power of the **line-item veto.** It allows him or her to delete specific lines, or parts, of budget bills. The governor oversees many of the state's agencies, boards, and commissions, and appoints officials to these agencies.

The governor also appoints judges when positions in the judicial system need to be filled. On the recommendation of the Board of Pardons and Paroles, the governor can issue a **pardon**, or forgiveness, to a person convicted of crimes. In addition, the governor serves as commander in chief of the state's military and represents Texas at state functions. He or she is responsible for declaring a site a disaster area after natural disasters.

Despite the governor's many responsibilities, he or she does not have as much power as the Texas legislature. For example, the legislature, rather than the governor, is responsible for officially determining the state's budget.

> Underline the governor's responsibilities as the head of the executive branch.

EXECUTIVE OFFICIALS AND AGENCIES

One of the most important officials in the executive branch is the lieutenant governor. The lieutenant governor serves as the leader of the Texas Senate. He or she also chairs the powerful Legislative Budget Board. The lieutenant governor serves as acting governor when the governor is out of Texas. He or she also takes over if the governor leaves office for any reason. Other officials in the executive branch are the attorney general, and the comptroller of public accounts, as well as the officials of some 200 agencies, boards, and commissions. These departments enforce state laws and provide Texans with various services to help keep the state running smoothly.

> What is the lieutenant governor's role?
> _____
> _____
> _____

CHALLENGE ACTIVITY

Critical Thinking: Making Inferences Write an advertisement for the position of Texas governor. Include a description of the duties, and identify some skills that the candidate must have to be a successful governor.

DIRECTIONS On the line provided before each statement, write **T** if
the statement is true and **F** if the statement is false. If the statement is
false, rewrite the statement on the line after it to make it true.

_____ 1. The line-item veto allows the governor to make laws as the head of the
executive branch.

_____

_____ 2. The Texas Board of Pardons and Paroles can revoke a pardon by the
governor.

_____

line-item veto	pardon

DIRECTIONS On the lines below, use the words in the word bank to
write a summary of what you have learned in the section.

_____

_____

_____

_____

_____

_____

_____

_____

_____

_____

MAIN IDEAS
1. The Texas judicial system includes many levels of courts.
2. Juries play important roles in the judicial system.

Key Terms and People

civil law law relating to private rights or obligations

criminal law law determining what actions are illegal within a society

trial courts courts that hear new cases and give a verdict, or ruling

appellate courts courts that review trials to determine if correct procedures were followed

judicial review courts' power to determine if a law is constitutional

petit jury a jury that decides the verdict in a trial

grand jury a jury that decides if a person accused of a felony should be indicted, or formally charged

Section Summary
JUDGES AND COURTS

The judicial branch of Texas state government includes all of the state's courts. Its main role is to interpret and apply the law in cases involving civil and criminal law. **Civil law** deals with legal disputes between individuals. Examples of civil law matters include contract disputes, divorce proceedings, and property settlements. **Criminal law** deals with people accused of committing crimes such as murder, assault, and theft. Criminal cases are brought by the government. Civil and criminal cases are tried in different types of courts.

What is the judicial branch?
_____
_____

THE STRUCTURE OF THE TEXAS COURTS

Cases that go to trial in Texas are heard in **trial courts.** These courts hear new cases and give a verdict, or ruling, in each. Texas has three levels of trial courts: municipal courts, county courts, and district courts. Each level has a specific jurisdiction, or authority to hear certain types of cases.

After a case is heard in trial court, the losing party may appeal the case to the next level of court. These courts are called appellate courts. They review trials to determine whether correct procedures were followed. Based on its review of a case, an appellate court may order a new trial or overturn a verdict.

The Supreme Court and the Court of Criminal Appeals are the state's highest courts. They mainly review the rulings of the courts of appeals. The Supreme Court reviews only civil cases. The Court of Criminal Appeals reviews criminal cases and all cases involving the death penalty. Both high courts also have the power to judge the constitutionality of a law, a power called **judicial review**. Laws that the courts consider unconstitutional cannot be enforced. This gives the judicial branch the ability to check the power of the state legislature and keep it from passing unfair laws.

THE JURY SYSTEM

Judges are not the only people involved in the judicial system. Juries are groups of six or twelve citizens who hear trial cases and make decisions. Under the Texas Bill of Rights, all Texans have the right to a trial by jury. Serving on juries is part of every Texan's civic responsibility. Texas courts use two very different types of juries. A **petit jury** decides the verdict in a civil or criminal trial. A **grand jury** decides whether a person accused of a felony should be indicted, or formally charged with a crime.

Who decides the outcome of a trial?

_____

_____

CHALLENGE ACTIVITY

Critical Thinking: Compare and Contrast Create a Venn diagram to compare and contrast civil law and criminal law.

DIRECTIONS Look at each set of three vocabulary terms. On the line provided, write the letter of the term that does not relate to the other terms in the set.

_____ 1. a. divorce disputes   b. civil law   c. theft

_____ 2. a. assault   b. property settlements c. criminal law

DIRECTIONS Write two adjectives or descriptive phrases that describe the term given.

3. petit jury _____

4. trial courts _____

5. grand jury _____

6. judicial review _____

7. appellate courts _____

Texas Government

 MAIN IDEAS
1. The Texas budget includes revenue from taxes, fees, and others sources.
2. Public education is funded and governed at both state and local levels.

Key Terms

Legislative Budget Board the agency made up of nine senior legislators and the lieutenant governor that prepares budget requests and prepares appropriation bills

appropriation bill a bill that sets the amount of money to be spent by a government

sales tax a tax added to the price of may goods and services at the time of purchase

Section Summary

THE STATE BUDGET

The Texas state government requires billions of dollars to function. The state budget specifies how this money will be distributed. Texas uses a biennial, or two-year, budget. Preparing this budget is the responsibility of two state agencies. One is the Office of Budget, Planning, and Policy, which is part of the executive branch. The other is the **Legislative Budget Board,** which is made up of nine senior legislators and the lieutenant governor. The two boards send out instructions and goals to all state agencies. The agencies then send funding requests back to the boards.

After receiving all requests, the Legislative Budget Board prepares an **appropriation bill**—a bill dealing with the spending of public money. Both houses of the Legislature must approve the bill before it gets sent to the state comptroller. This official determines whether the state will receive enough revenue, or income, to cover expenses. Once the budget bill is approved, it goes to the governor to be signed.

> **What does *biennial* mean?**
> _____
> _____

> **What does the state comptroller do?**
> _____
> _____

REVENUE AND SPENDING

The Texas state government gets the revenue it
needs from several sources. The largest source is
federal grants. Another major source of state
income is taxes. More than half of this tax income
comes from sales taxes. A **sales tax** is added to the
price paid for many goods and services at the time
of purchase. Other taxes include taxes on
corporations, oil production, gasoline, and motor
vehicle sales.

Texas also gains revenue from fees for licenses
and services. In addition, the state gets money from
fines charged to people who break state laws. State
funds are used to build highways, pay state
employees, and provide public services.

> List some ways the Texas
> state government obtains
> revenue.
>
> _____
>
> _____
>
> _____
>
> _____

TEXAS PUBLIC EDUCATION

The Texas Constitution requires the legislature to
maintain a free public school system. The state
provides money through the Permanent School
Fund, which receives money from state taxes and
investments. Local governments raise money for
schools through property taxes and bond issues. The
federal government also provides funds from
federal taxes, such as income tax.

The Texas legislature passes laws governing
public schools, including the subjects they teach.
The Texas Board of Education sets education policy
and reviews textbooks for use in schools. The Texas
Education Agency reviews standards for learning
materials, schools, and teacher certification.

Locally, schools are governed by more than
1,000 independent school districts. Boards of
trustees or school boards govern each district.

> Underline three sources of
> funding for public
> education in Texas.

CHALLENGE ACTIVITY

Critical Thinking: Analyzing Information How
are public schools funded in Texas?

DIRECTIONS Answer each question below on the lines provided.

1. List the steps the Legislative Budget Board follows in order to approve a new budget.

_____

_____

_____

2. What happens to an appropriation bill after it is prepared?

_____

_____

_____

3. What is a sales tax and why is it important for the Texas government?

_____

_____

_____

Local Government and Citizenship

MAIN IDEAS
1. Local governments in Texas include county and municipal governments and special districts.
2. Local governments raise money with bonds and taxes.

Key Terms

precinct county subdivisions

commissioners' court panel of elected commissioners that governs a county in Texas

home-rule charters charters that allow citizens of Texas muncipalities to choose among the three forms of municipal government

general-law cities small towns and villages that operate under the general laws of the state

special districts a district formed for a particular purpose, often handling services that other local governments do not provide

Section Summary

COUNTY GOVERNMENTS

Texas has 254 counties, each with its own government. Each county is divided into four **precincts**, or county subdivisions. Voters in each precinct elect a county commissioner. Voters countywide elect a county judge. These five elected officials serve four-year terms and make up the **commissioners' court** that governs the county. The county judge directs the commissioners' meetings, in which they prepare the county budget and address local issues. Other officials also serve at the county level. These include the county clerk, treasurer, sheriff, and tax assessor-collector.

> Underline the officials who serve at the county level.

MUNICIPAL GOVERNMENTS AND SPECIAL DISTRICTS

More than 85 percent of Texans live in urban areas run by municipal governments. There are several types of municipal governments. In a mayor-council government, voters elect a mayor and a city council to directly run the government. Many cities have a council-manager government in which voters elect members of a city council. The city council hires a city manager who manages the city under the council The commission plan, also known as the Galveston Plan, was developed in 1901. No cities today operate under this plan.

The two types of municipalities in Texas are home-rule cities and general-law cities. **Home-rule charters** allow citizens in home-rule cities to choose among the three forms of municipal government. **General-law cities** operate under the general laws of the state. **Special districts**— particularly school districts—are the most numerous form of local government in the state. Special districts provide services that other local governments do not. Examples include hospital districts and transportation districts. The people in charge of special districts may be either appointed or elected.

List the two types of municipalities in Texas.
_____
_____

CHALLENGE ACTIVITY

Critical Thinking: Summarizing List and describe the types of local governments and how they are run.

Guided Reading Workbook

commissioners' court	home-rule charters	special districts
precinct	general-law cities	

DIRECTIONS Read each sentence below and fill in the blank with the word that best completes each sentence.

1. _____ allow citizens to choose among the three forms of municipal government.

2. _____ are the most numerous form of local government in the state.

3. _____ operate under the general laws of the state.

DIRECTIONS Write two adjectives or descriptive phrases that describe each term given.

4. precinct _____

5. commissioners' court _____

Local Government and Citizenship

Section 2

 MAIN IDEAS

1. The freedoms of speech, the press, and assembly are all crucial to a successful democracy.
2. The Texas Bill of Rights extends protections to Texans accused of committing crimes.
3. The Bill of Rights outlines several additional rights that cannot be taken from Texans.

Key Terms

slander a false statement made on purpose that damages another's reputation

libel intentionally false written statements

due process the legal process that governments must follow before taking away a person's property or punishing a person

bail money that a defendant promises to pay to the court as a guarantee to appear at the proper time

eminent domain a government's power to claim privately owned land for public use

Section Summary

BASIC RIGHTS AND FREEDOMS

The Texas Bill of Rights protects the individual liberties of Texans. Its placement at the front of the Texas Constitution emphasizes its importance. It states that all political power stems from the people and that Texans have equal rights under the law. The Bill of Rights also protects Texans' freedom of worship and the freedoms of speech and of the press. **Slander**—a false statement made on purpose that damages another's reputation—is not protected. **Libel**, an intentionally false written statement, is not protected either.

> Underline the two types of speech not protected by the Bill of Rights.

PROTECTION OF THE ACCUSED

The Texas Constitution includes protection for people accused of wrongdoing. The government has to take certain legal actions before it can seize a person's property or punish a person. This is known as **due process**. The Texas Constitution also gives defendants in criminal cases some protections. Texas courts cannot set unreasonably high **bail**, or money the defendant promises to pay the court in exchange for release from jail.

> **Whom does due process protect?**
> _____

OTHER RIGHTS

Texans benefit from other protections as well under the Texas Bill of Rights. Some rights deal with property. For example, the Constitution gives the government the right of **eminent domain**—the ability to take land from private individuals for public use in some cases. However, the Bill of Rights ensures that the property owner must be paid for the property. The Bill of Rights also protects the right of Texans to keep and bear arms.

In addition, the Texas Bill of Rights guarantees that the state will not fall under military rule. A Texas citizen cannot be banished from the state for committing a crime. Under the Texas Bill of Rights, the national government has authority in Texas only as long as the right of the state to govern itself is maintained. These protections help ensure the freedom of all Texans from the abuse of government.

> **When does the national government not have authority in Texas?**
> _____
> _____

CHALLENGE ACTIVITY

Critical Thinking: Summarizing What are some of the rights guaranteed to Texans under the Bill of Rights ?

slander	due process	eminent domain
libel	bail	

DIRECTIONS On the line provided before each statement, write **T** if the statement is true and **F** if the statement is false. If the statement is false, rewrite the statement on the line after it to make it true.

_____ 1. <u>Slander</u> is protected as free speech under the Texas Bill of Rights.

_____

_____ 2. <u>Libel</u> is a false statement made on purpose that damages another's reputation and is protected by the Bill of Rights.

_____

_____ 3. <u>Due process</u> is the requirement of the government to take certain legal actions before it can seize a person's property or punish them.

_____

_____ 4. The Bill of Rights protects property owners in cases of <u>eminent domain</u>, ensuring that they are paid for any property taken for public use.

_____

Guided Reading Workbook

Local Government and Citizenship

MAIN IDEAS
1. Citizens in Texas have many responsibilities.
2. Texans take part in several types of elections.

Key Terms

runoff election an election to determine a winner in a contest in which no candidate received a majority of the vote

general elections elections held to decide who wins a particular state or local office

special election elections in which voters cast their ballots to fill a vacant office or approve a government change such as a constitutional amendment or local bond issue

referendum election in which voters directly decide a legislative issue

Section Summary

CIVIC RESPONSIBILITIES AND PARTICIPATION

Citizens have rights and responsibilities. U.S. citizens have the right to vote in elections and to run for government office. By voting, citizens can voice their approval or disapproval of the leaders' positions.

Texans also have civic responsibilities. Some responsibilities are required, such as obeying the law and paying taxes. The government needs taxes to pay for important public services.

Public service is another responsibility of citizenship. Serving in the military is one form of public service; so is volunteering in projects that help the community.

> Underline two civic responsibilities.

ELECTIONS

To vote, a Texan must be a U.S. citizen and at least 18 years old. Voters must also have lived in Texas for at least 30 days before the election. Political parties hold primary elections at all levels of

> List three types of elections.
>
> _____
>
> _____
>
> _____

government to decide who will represent the party
in later elections. If no one receives more than 50
percent of the vote, the top two vote getters compete
in a **runoff election**.

General elections decide who wins a particular
state or local office. The voters may also be asked
to decide certain issues, such as constitutional
amendments. A vacancy might occur in an office
before the next general election is held. When this
happens, voters return to the polls for a **special
election** held to fill the vacancy.

In a representative democracy like Texas, elected
officials represent the people. Texas also has direct
democracy—voters decide issues directly rather
than going through their representatives. Direct
democracy takes several forms in Texas. For
example, a **referendum** allows voters to decide on
issues such as constitutional amendments. A
referendum can also be used to repeal, or do away
with, laws. Another form of direct government
participation in Texas is the recall. A recall is an
election that gives voters the chance to remove a
local official from office.

When is a special election held?
_____
_____

Underline the definition of a recall.

CHALLENGE ACTIVITY
Critical Thinking: Evaluating List some civic
responsibilities and describe their importance.

DIRECTIONS Write a summary of what you have learned in the
section.

_____

_____

_____

_____

_____

_____

_____

_____

_____

_____

_____

_____

_____

_____

_____

_____

_____

_____

_____

_____

_____

Local Government and Citizenship

MAIN IDEAS
1. Political parties nominate candidates and help shape policy in Texas.
2. Interest groups can influence officials' points of view.

Key Terms

interest groups groups united by a common interest that try to affect government policy

lobby to try to persuade legislators about an issue

political action committees (PACs) groups that raise and spend money for a candidate elections

Section Summary
POLITICAL PARTIES

Political parties are one way for citizens to participate in democracy. Political parties try to shape governmental policy by nominating candidates and working to get them elected. Political parties elect or appoint delegates to attend their party's convention, where they decide the party's platform, or stated goals. The candidates a party nominates for office generally support the party's platform.

> Underline the purpose of political parties.

The two major political parties in Texas—and in the United States—are the Democratic Party and the Republican Party. The Democratic Party—the older of the two parties— traditionally supported slavery. The Republican Party was founded to oppose slavery. For much of Texas history, the Republican Party was seen as liberal, while the Democratic Party was seen as conservative. Today, however, those roles are reversed. Although third parties have sometimes influenced Texas politics, they have not greatly affected the state in recent years.

INTEREST GROUPS

Many Texans take part in the political process by forming or joining **interest groups**. These groups try to affect decisions made by those in government. They **lobby**, or try to persuade public officials, to support the group's goals. Interest groups hire lobbyists to meet with public officials. Many interest groups direct their lobbying efforts at the state's legislators.

Fund-raising is also an important part of the political process. **Political action committees** (PACs) raise and spend money for candidates. Campaign money pays for advertisements on radio, television, and in newspapers. Texas sets no limit on how much money a PAC can accept or spend. But PACs must report information about their contributors and how the money is spent.

> What is the purpose of political action committees (PACs)?
>
> _____
>
> _____

CHALLENGE ACTIVITY

Critical Thinking: Comparing and Contrasting

Read more about the Democratic and Republican parties and make a comparison chart of the two parties. Include such things as policies, famous governors or presidents, and areas in which the party is strong.

Name _____ Class _____ Date _____

Section 4, *continued*

| interest groups | lobby | political action committees |

DIRECTIONS Use the vocabulary words to write a summary of what you have learned in this section.

_____
_____
_____
_____
_____
_____
_____
_____
_____
_____
_____
_____
_____
_____
_____
_____
_____

The Texas Economy

MAIN IDEAS
1. The free enterprise system allows people to run businesses with little government interference.
2. Market forces like supply, demand, and competition drive business decisions.
3. The government plays several roles in the economy.

Key Terms

free enterprise economic system in which businesses operate with little interference from government

profit the money that a business has left after it pays expenses

supply the amount of a good or service that is available for purchase

demand the amount of a good or service that people are willing to buy

competition economic rivalry between companies selling similar products

Section Summary

THE OPPORTUNITY FOR SUCCESS

Free enterprise is an economic system in which business can be conducted with limited direction or interference from the government. The free enterprise system offers Texas business owners the opportunity to become successful and make profits. **Profit** is the money that a business has left after it pays its expenses. In a free enterprise system, profits belong to the owners of the business. The opportunity to create wealth through profits is what inspires most new business owners and investors. However, by starting a business, an individual also opens himself or herself to the possibility of failure. The state government encourages the creation of businesses in Texas.

> **What is the free enterprise system? Explain.**
> _____
> _____

THE ROLE OF THE MARKET

The American free enterprise system is a system in which people are free to buy and sell whatever goods they wish. Companies must figure out how to make products that appeal to customers. Companies use pricing to attract customers. Pricing is governed by two economic principles called *supply* and *demand.* **Supply** refers to how much of a given product businesses are willing to produce. In general, businesses will produce more products when they can sell them at higher prices. They will produce fewer products when prices are low. **Demand** refers to how much of a product buyers are willing to purchase. The demand for a product is usually higher when prices are low and tends to drop as prices rise. Supply and demand work together to determine prices. Another factor that affects pricing is **competition,** the rivalry between companies selling similar products. If two companies produce goods of equal quality but price them differently, more customers will be drawn to the company with lower prices. Competition can also push a company to improve its products or develop new ones in order to lure customers.

> **What is one factor that affects pricing?**
>
> _____
>
> _____

GOVERNMENT REGULATION

The goverment passes and enforces laws that ensure businesses are run fairly and safely. For example, the government requires factories to meet basic standards for worker safety and food sellers to meet certain standards for quality. Those that do not follow government regulations can be fined or shut down. The government has also passed laws that prohibit employers from paying their workers less than a minimum amount. The government also works to protect competition in the marketplace by stopping practices that would limit or prevent competition. Similarly, the government protects the ideas of the people who create products through patents and copyrights.

> **What happens if a business owner does not follow government regulations?**
>
> _____
>
> _____

CHALLENGE ACTIVITY

Critical Thinking: Analyze Explain supply and demand. Then give an example for each.

Guided Reading Workbook

DIRECTIONS On the line provided before each statement, write **T** if a statement is true and **F** if a statement is false. If the statement is false, write a corrected statement on the line after the false statement.

_____ 1. <u>Profit</u> is what money remains after expenses have been paid.

_____

_____ 2. <u>Competition</u> is economic rivalry between two companies selling the same or similar products.

_____

_____ 3. <u>Demand</u> is the amount of product a business is willing to make.

_____

_____ 4. In <u>free enterprise</u> systems, business owners must always get direction from the government to make business decisions.

_____

_____ 5. <u>Supply</u> is the amount of product customers are willing to buy.

_____

Guided Reading Workbook

Section 2

MAIN IDEAS
1. Farming and ranching have been major economic activities in Texas since the state's earliest days.
2. Oil and gas dominated the Texas economy in the twentieth century.
3. New industries have developed and expanded in Texas since World War II.

Key Terms and People

agribusiness the large-scale farming and processing of crops

feedlots large area of enclosed land on which animals are kept and fed to be made ready for market

information technology the development, maintenance, and use of computer hardware and software

semiconductors materials that conduct some electricity but not as much as most metals do, necessary for modern electronics

Michael Dell founder of Dell Inc.

dot-coms online companies

Section Summary
AGRICULTURE

Agribusiness, or large-scale farming and processing of crops, brings about $36 billion dollars to Texas each year. Like farming, ranching has long been a major industry in Texas. Texas produces more beef and wool than any other state. Modern ranching has changed since the 1800s. Instead of living and eating off of grassland, most cattle are raised in commercial **feedlots.** A feedlot is a large area of enclosed land on which animals are kept and fed to make ready for market.

OIL AND GAS INDUSTRY

As oil production was expanding, natural gas was also increasing. Gas was first discovered as a by-product of oil drilling. The oil and gas industry is a

How was natural gas discovered in Texas?
_____
_____
_____

major part of the Texas economy. Texas produces more oil and natural gas than any other state.

AVIATION AND AEROSPACE INDUSTRIES

In 1939 the state's first airplane-manufacturing center opened near Houston. By the 1960s, Fort Worth became a leading aviation and aerospace center. Texas is still a major center for aircraft manufacturing.

MEDICAL INDUSTRY

Research and technological developments have led to the growth of a major medical industry in Texas. Many Texas hospitals have reputations as excellent care centers. Texas is also home to several medical equipment manufacturers and pharmaceutical companies.

> List 3 medical businesses that make Texas a leader in medicine.
> _____
> _____
> _____

COMPUTER AND INFORMATION TECHNOLOGY INDUSTRY

Information technology (IT) is the development, maintenance, and use of computer hardware and software. It is one of the fastest-growing segments of the Texas economy. In the 1950s and 1960s, Texas Instruments of Dallas developed devices that used **semiconductors,** or materials that conduct some electricity but not as much as most metals do. Semiconductors are vital to computer electronics. In the 1980s, companies began building computers. In 1985 **Michael Dell** started Dell Computer Corporation—now Dell Inc. By the 2000s it had become one of the largest computer companies. In the late 1990s, Texans founded online companies, often referred to as **dot-coms**.

> Explain the role of semiconductors in modern electronics.
> _____

CHALLENGE ACTIVITY

Critical Thinking: Draw Conclusions Explain how life has changed for ranchers and cattle compared to ranching in the 1800s.

| agribusiness | feedlots | information technology |
| dot-coms | Michael Dell | semiconductors |

DIRECTIONS Use the words in the word bank to write a summary of
what you have learned in the section.

_____

_____

_____

_____

DIRECTIONS Write two adjectives or descriptive phrases that describe
the term given.

Michael Dell _____

dot-coms _____

The Texas Economy

MAIN IDEAS
1. Texas trades more goods with Mexico than with any other country.
2. Products are shipped to and received from countries around the world.
3. Events in other parts of the world can affect the Texas economy.

Key Terms

North American Free Trade Agreement agreement between the United States, Mexico, and Canada that eliminated many trade barriers

maquiladoras Mexican factories near the U.S.–Mexico border that assemble products using parts imported from the United States

embargo the banning of trade with a country

Section Summary
TRADE WITH MEXICO

Texas has long been the main entry point for Mexican products being brought to the United States. These products include machinery, vehicles, oil, and agricultural products. It is also the main transit point for goods being sent to Mexico, including machinery, oil, plastic goods, and agricultural products.

Although trade with Mexico has existed for many years, the Texas economy received a big boost in 1994 when the **North American Free Trade Agreement** (NAFTA) went into effect. This agreement eliminated many trade barriers. As a result of NAFTA, trade between Texas and Mexico more than doubled.

Most products shipped between Texas and Mexico travel on trucks. This overland trade profited border towns such as Eagle Pass, Laredo, Brownsville, and El Paso. Increased border trade also created challenges. As cities along the border grew, many could not build infrastructure fast enough to keep pace with the growth. Hundreds of **maquiladoras,** or factories, have been built in Mexico, near the Texas border. These factories have

> Why do you think Texas is the main entry point for Mexican goods?
> _____
> _____
> _____

> Underline the names of some border towns.

provided jobs, but air and water pollution have increased in the border region.

TRADE WITH OTHER COUNTRIES

Products from Texas are shipped all around the world. In return, Texas receives imports from nearly every region of the globe. As technology and transportation improve, international trade increases. Among the top products exported from Texas are refined oil and other petroleum products, chemicals, machine parts, aircraft, and computers.

Not counting Mexico, the countries from which Texas imported the most goods in 2012 were China, Saudi Arabia, Venezuela, and Canada. Each of these countries sent more than $10 billion worth of products to Texas. By far the most valuable product imported to Texas is crude oil. Other imports include cellular phones, televisions, computer parts, and passenger vehicles.

> **What is the most valuable product imported to Texas?**
> _____

GLOBAL INFLUENCE

Events that happen far from Texas can still affect the state's economy. Political disruption and turmoil in oil-producing regions of the world have led to increased business for Texas oil companies. In 1973, for example, several members of the Organization of Petroleum Exporting Countries (OPEC) declared an **embargo,** or ban, on shipments of crude oil to the United States. Faced with a national oil shortage, the United States turned to domestic sources, including Texas. Statewide oil production boomed.

> **What was the result of OPEC's embargo?**
> _____
> _____

International events can also hurt Texas industries. When a cow in the United States tested positive for mad cow disease in 2003, several nations banned imports of U.S. beef, which hurt the Texas cattle industry.

CHALLENGE ACTIVITY

Critical Thinking: Analyzing Information How can international events affect trade in Texas?

DIRECTIONS Answer each question using complete sentences.

1. What is the North American Free Trade Agreement and how did if affect trade between the United States and Mexico?

_____

_____

_____

2. What are maquiladoras and what problems have they introduced along the Texas border?

_____

_____

_____

3. How can an embargo on a product affect international trade?

_____

_____

_____